ONE TOWN, MANY VOICES

ONE TOWN, MANY VOICES

A History of Davidson, North Carolina

Jan Blodgett & Ralph B. Levering

Davidson Historical Society   Davidson, North Carolina

This book is dedicated to all residents,

named and unnamed, past and present,

who have made Davidson the community that it is.

Acknowledgments

We gratefully acknowledge the support of the following contributors to the Davidson Historical Society for the publication of this book. The collective, corporate, and private philanthropy of our members and friends enabled it to become a reality.

Corporate Gift

Wells Fargo

Academic Gift

Davidson College, Vail History Chair Funds

In-Kind Gifts

DavidsonNews.Net
Davidson College, Friends of the Arts
Mervil Paylor Design

Leadership Gifts

Bob and Jane Avinger
Carol B. Barber, in memory of Rupert T. Barber, Jr.
Bill and Sarah Boehmler
Ed and Liz Harris
Randy and Mary Mac Kincaid
Steve and Margaret Kuras
Dave and Sherry Malushizky
Dave and Elizabeth Martin
John B. and Diana Woods, in memory of Dr. James B. and Elizabeth Woods

Our sincere thanks to all the other individuals in the Davidson community and beyond who so generously contributed to this publication.

Contents

Preface

While "memory is the thread of personal identity," historian Carter Lindberg wrote recently, "history is the thread of community identity."[1] The authors hope that readers' appreciation of the Davidson community will grow as they learn more about the town that during its first 175 years has been both typical of its time and place and extraordinary. We also hope that current and future residents who read this book will want to emulate the many Davidsonians over the years who have cared deeply about the well-being of their community and have worked to make the town a better place to live.

Focusing on the town much more than on the college, this book grew out of a desire to write a more comprehensive history of Davidson than Mary Beaty was able to do in her pioneering *Davidson: A History of the Town from 1835 until 1937* (1979). While not ignoring the generally better educated, more prosperous "college" and "town" whites who largely have lived east of the railroad tracks that bisect the town, this book—more than Beaty's—also includes extensive discussion of the African-Americans and working-class "mill" whites who mainly have resided west of the tracks. These four basic groups in the town's population from the nineteenth century until roughly the early 1980s—and the often diverse viewpoints between and within each group—prompted the "many voices" of the title. Chronologically, whereas Beaty covered the first 100 years of the college/town, this book offers a detailed account of 147 years (1837–1984), plus an epilogue that brings the story up to shortly before the 175th anniversary of the college and town in 2012.

Jan Blodgett came up with the idea for the book, and researched and wrote the early drafts of chapters 1 through 5. At her invitation, Ralph Levering joined the project and researched and wrote the early drafts of chapters 6 and 7, plus the Prologue and Epilogue. Each author then read critically—and hopefully improved—the sections that the other had written. Because the authors have worked together closely and agree about how to interpret the town's history, they view the book as a unified whole.

Mary Beaty and the two current authors share important similarities. For one thing, Beaty was and Jan Blodgett is a Ph.D. professional employee at the college library, and Ralph Levering also is a college employee, having taught U.S. history there since 1986. For another, all three authors had the privilege to live and work for many years in this "one town," and wanted to give back to the community by helping to preserve and record its history. A third similarity is that the authors conducted numerous interviews to supplement the large volume of written records in the college archives. "People in town were so kind to me," Beaty commented in September 1979 about the interviewees; "everyone I asked was so helpful and interested."[2]

The current authors feel exactly the same way about the seventy-eight Davidsonians who agreed to be interviewed for this book. Their names—and the dates of the interviews—are listed in the Selected Bibliography; references to these interviews in the Endnotes are abbreviated. If more time and energy had been available, many additional residents easily could have been interviewed. All of the transcribed interviews, and the cassette tapes on which they were recorded, are available in the Davidson College archives.

The authors wish to thank everyone who has helped to make this book possible, starting with the interviewees who usually spent between one and two hours patiently answering many questions about their participation in the town's history and their memories of other residents and events. We also benefited from the numerous interviews with residents conducted over roughly the last ten years by students under the guidance of Davidson College professors Pamela Grundy and Kristi Multhaup. And we are deeply grateful for the generosity of Professor Ed Palmer, who made available a room in his home for Ralph Levering's writing during his sabbatical between June 2010 and June 2011.

We also appreciate the college's support for this project, including funds for a capable, hard-working student research assistant, Patricia Massey, in the summer of 2006, and support for the painstaking work of Tomm Lorenzin, Emily Hammock, and others who transcribed the interviews. Bill Giduz in College Communications supplied color and black and white photographs. Several of Jan Blodgett's colleagues in the library—notably Susanna Boylston, Sharon Byrd, Sara Enders, Joe Gutekanst, Hannah Rozear, and Sara Swanson—cheerfully provided invaluable research assistance. Marion Payntor, the *Charlotte Observer*'s head librarian, allowed Ralph Levering to peruse the *Observer*'s files of stories relating to Davidson. We also appreciate the seven local friends, including three professional historians, who read and commented on a preliminary draft of the manuscript: Robin Barnes, Ann Lee Bressler, Sharon Byrd, Sandy Carnegie, Susan Campbell, Dora DuBose, Earl Edmondson, Marsha Green, Richie King, and Margaret Kuras. The authors, of course, are fully responsible for this history.

In addition, we are deeply grateful to the Davidson Historical Society for giving us an opportunity to share some of our research in several talks, and especially for raising the money and providing the guidance for publishing the book. The town has a long history of people coming together to accomplish worthwhile projects; the members of the Davidson Historical Society are yet another example. We wish to acknowledge the particular work done by the DHS Book Committee: Jane Avinger, John Cunningham, Kelly Knetsche, Margaret Kuras, Cynthia Lewis, Dave Malushizky, and Ed Harris, Chair.

Finally, we wish to thank our beloved spouses, Clarence Fox and Patty Levering, for their love, support, and encouragement for more years than we would like to count. Without them, this book could not have been written.

Prologue Implementing a Community's Vision

On 7 April 1836 "a large concourse of people" gathered on the site of the Davidson College campus. They were there for a special meeting of the Presbytery of Concord, the governing body for Presbyterian congregations located west of the Yadkin River and the organization responsible for establishing the college.[1]

The day's celebration centered on the dedication of the chapel, the largest of the seven buildings constructed in 1835–36, in part with volunteer labor from local Presbyterian congregations and using (among other materials) 250,000 bricks made by slaves on a nearby plantation at a cost of $1,000. The structures "were all of brick with rock foundations and tin roofs, and were not prepossessing," historian Mary Beaty observed.[2]

The Reverend Robert Hall Morrison provided a sermon that, according to the presbytery's minutes, was "an appropriate and forcible discourse on the importance of learning generally and especially of a learned ministry to the happiness of a community and the security of a free and righteous government."[3] Morrison asserted, "At last our youth can be offered the benefits of Christian education," and added, "We as mortals take no credit and vain glory in our achievements, but turn our faces humbly towards God and render our deep-felt appreciation."[4] The service closed with a hymn selected by another prominent Presbyterian minister, the Reverend James McGee, a key figure in the vigorous but unsuccessful effort in 1820—also led by Presbyterians—to establish a state-supported college about thirty miles to the southwest.[5]

Davidson College—and the town that grew up around it—arose from

Robert Hall Morrison

the beliefs and ambitions of the Scots-Irish Presbyterians who had moved south from Pennsylvania and Virginia to central North and South Carolina in the 1700s and early 1800s and carried with them a profound respect for education.[6] By the 1830s a substantial number of Presbyterians who lived in central North Carolina and northern South Carolina had become moderately prosperous, frequently as slave-holding farmers or merchants, thus making it possible for a fund-raising campaign for the college in 1835 to obtain pledges that exceeded $30,000, a large sum for that time.

The determination of Presbyterian clergy and laity in the region to start a college located on a site somewhere between the small towns of Charlotte (1830 population: 717) and Concord to the south and southeast and Statesville and Salisbury to the north and northeast kept committee members busy finding a location, studying other schools, and designing a course of study. Their work was shaped in part by a belief that education at the University of North Carolina had become largely secular and hence "godless." They believed that religious as well as secular learning, required religious services, and strict rules of behavior were all necessary both to train ministers properly and to prevent young men from straying morally and intellectually. As Davidson religion professor Karl Plank has noted, the college's founders espoused "a philosophy of education that aimed at the formation of character and found the coupling of religion and education to be not only desirable, but necessary."[7] They also believed that character could best be formed in a rural setting away from the temptations and depravities that they associated with cities.[8]

The college's founders demonstrated, as has been shown countless times throughout human history generally and during Davidson's history especially, that individuals working together can create lasting institutions and thus help to shape communities and the broader society. In this case individual Presbyterians working together in the presbytery and in local churches—e.g., Centre Presbyterian and Bethel Presbyterian, both serving rural congregations within a few miles of the location selected for the college—implemented their vision of higher education for young men, especially for those who wished to prepare to become Presbyterian ministers.

Morrison did the most to turn this vision into reality. In early 1835, this well-educated thirty-six-year-old man was pastor of the Sugar Creek Presbyterian Church in Mecklenburg County. At a meeting of the Concord Presbytery on March 11 that year, he offered a resolution calling for "the establishment of a manual labor school"—that is, a college at which students would have to do manual labor to lower the institution's costs while pursuing their education in the classics.

After the resolution passed unanimously the next day, Morrison was appointed chair of a committee to locate a site for the college.[9] The presbytery authorized Morrison's committee to raise funds and to pay for land and the buildings to be constructed on it. Morrison himself raised more than $18,500 of the $30,900 pledged in 1835 for the founding of the college. He later remarked that "we begged the college into existence."[10]

Another key founder was William Lee Davidson II, a local planter and public servant, and a ruling elder at Bethel Presbyterian Church, who served on Morrison's committee. Davidson lived at Beaver Dam, a 785 acre plantation in northern Mecklenburg County. In addition to his plantation, Davidson owned 469 acres of undeveloped land about two miles to the west. A public road connecting Charlotte and Statesville ran through the property, and a fairly level section east of the road on the ridge dividing the watersheds of the Catawba and Yadkin rivers would make a good site for the college. On 13 May 1835, the five members of Morrison's committee, including Morrison and Davidson, traveled on horseback to examine Davidson's land.

Following dinner at Beaver Dam that evening, the committee, "after solemn and special prayer to Almighty God for the aid of his grace," agreed to pay $1,521 for the land, with the acknowledgment that the presbytery was getting a very good deal. Davidson had paid $1,790 for the 469 acres in the 1820s, and the current value, the committee believed, was "at least $2,500."[11]

On 26 August 1835 the presbytery resolved that the college would be

Beaver Dam

named for Davidson's father, General William Lee Davidson, a Revolutionary War hero who had been killed in the battle of Cowan's Ford in 1781 while encouraging Patriot troops to prevent British forces from crossing the Catawba River.[12] In addition to being a revered general on the side that virtually all Scots-Irish Presbyterians in the area supported, Davidson had been a prominent member of Centre Presbyterian Church, located only a few miles north of the land his son was selling to the presbytery.[13]

In December 1836, Morrison reluctantly consented to serve as the college's first president, as well as to be one of the college's two faculty members when classes for the initial sixty-five students began on 12 March 1837. He and his large family lived in a small, two-story brick house—located where the current, greatly expanded president's home now stands—that visitors in 1845 described as "incommodious."[14]

Despite his reluctance, Morrison accepted the presidency, he wrote, because "I know not how to get over the solicitations of my friends, and the overthrow of our institution which might result from a failure to secure officers."[15] The latter motive was almost certainly paramount. Like many who have accepted leadership positions at the college and in the town ever since, a sense of calling underlay Morrison's decision to give up his "well situated" life as a pastor and to help to implement the compelling vision he shared with many fellow Presbyterians.

1 College Begets Town, 1837–1860

In a letter to his mother in August 1839, Davidson College student James Morrow gave his first impressions of the college: "[I] am very much pleased with the college here; it is far better as to external appearance than I expected to find. . . . It appears to be an enlightened healthy and wealthy part of the country."[1] Nearly eighteen years later, in February 1857, appearances had shifted enough to prompt Murdock McLaughlin to write, "I am in hope Davidson will come out and be something yet, as much as it is run down as being a 'one horse affair.'"[2]

These observations suggest that the early years of the college—and of the town that grew up around it—were not always smooth. There was no guarantee when the first buildings appeared near the newly founded college that either the college or the town would survive their infancy. Certainly the bright hopes expressed in 1839 were not yet realized in 1857.

Imagine Davidson in the late 1830s: a dusty, or muddy, road with a store or two perched alongside and a few scattered college buildings—president's house, a couple of faculty homes, chapel, Steward's Hall, dormitories—alongside small sheds housing student blacksmith, carpenter, and cabinet shops and fields of crops. Even one of the college's strongest supporters, Jethro Rumple, class of 1850 and trustee from 1858 to 1905, did not try to disguise the rudimentary nature of the college during its early years:

> Many of the students had just come from the farm and the work shop, and the teachers were fresh from college or from the pulpit

College campus circa 1850

and country school room. The trustees were from neighboring pulpits or were rural ruling elders, utterly destitute of any experience in college affairs. These inexperienced men got together, put up a few buildings, and with the aid of catalogues from Princeton and Chapel Hill compiled a course of study and began work. It must have demanded a large amount of courage and faith in God to cheer them in the great enterprise.[3]

When students arrived for first classes in March 1837, there was no town as such; the college was the community. The entire population consisted of two faculty, their families and slaves, the college steward (business manager, in today's usage) and his slaves, students, and probably at least one shopkeeper. The title of "first family" rightly went to the Morrisons. The college's first president, Robert Hall Morrison, also served as the pastor for both students and townspeople, sharing pulpit duties with Professor Patrick Sparrow.

Mary Morrison gave birth to their seventh child shortly after their move to Davidson; Elizabeth Lee Davidson Morrison was probably the first child born in the town. Along with the children ranging from newborn to twelve years of age, the Morrison household had several slaves. Robert had inherited a slave named Mary and later bought her husband

Bagwell as well as a young woman named Sarah. Mary and Bagwell had four sons ranging in age from four to twelve in 1837. From its beginning, therefore, Davidson, like most southern towns, was racially mixed.

Initially everyone in Davidson—masters and slaves, students and local children—lived in very close proximity. This pattern shifted over time to accommodate changes in population, driven primarily but not entirely by college growth. The history of Davidson's housing patterns is both particular (neighborhoods created in response to faculty needs) and general. Increasing separation of economic classes took place during Reconstruction as former slaves moved away from the families they served.

Davidson's Defining Characteristics

Looking closely at the town's plain and practical beginning as well as its gradual development, the themes that run throughout its history and contribute to its special character become apparent. Central to the town's character are the economic and political linking of town and college, an attitude of distinctiveness and separateness from neighboring communities, the reliance on civic cooperation juxtaposed with the interrelatedness and division of social groups within the town, and an ongoing interweaving of regional traits and external, including international, influences.

The college not only offered employment for laborers during construction projects; it also created ongoing, if low-paying, work for servants, cooks, laundresses, and woodcutters. In some cases, the work was done by hired-out slaves. In other areas, residents supplemented farm income by selling wood or providing services for students and faculty.

The college also provided land for the first businesses and regulated town activities through leases that stipulated that the tenant "will not sell, barter, give or deal in any way in any ardent spirits, wine, gin, porter, ale, or any other intoxicating liquor or any other article which may be prohibited by the regulations or ordinances of said board of trustees"; and, further, "that he will not engage in or permit . . . any game of chance . . . in said premises or any usage or practice whatever . . . contrary to good morals and that he will . . . conform to the regulations which may be adopted by said board." The college punished students for transgressions more than it did townspeople, but on occasion the board did press charges against shopkeepers for selling alcohol.[4]

The concern about moral behavior required that the college and town maintain a separateness and distinction from "the allurements and noise" of more established towns such as Charlotte and Salisbury. The trustees proclaimed that the college's location was "healthy . . . agreeable and moral, and at a distance from all haunts of dissipation."[5] This claim to moral superiority, at least regarding the prohibition of alcohol, was of much greater interest to the college than to townspeople, and conflicts eventually arose over violations of lease restrictions regarding "ardent spirits." But Davidson residents soon prided themselves on being from a college town rather than a trading center or mill town.

The hiring of new faculty, the presence of visiting lecturers, and public debates by students guaranteed that the town would be exposed to new ideas. As early as 1839, Davidson students entertained residents and visitors with a debate on the question, "Ought foreign immigration into this country be restricted?", thus demonstrating that the college did not limit itself to Latin and Greek classics but also examined contemporary issues. Later topics for debate included slavery, the treatment of Indians, education for women, the war with Mexico, and the Missouri Compromise. Contemporary accounts show that, in 1844, the speakers arguing that slavery was a moral evil won their debate, and that, in 1856, anti-secession positions were acceptable.[6]

College Governs Town

Initially the faculty and trustees served as a surrogate town government. The standard practice in North Carolina during this period was for the governor or state legislature to appoint local officials. The city of Charlotte, for example, did not hold its first elections until 1852. So it was not unusual that, in 1851, the trustees appointed a committee to "ascertain the powers of the faculty or Trustees for the Governance of the village of Davidson College."[7]

Unfortunately, because trustee committees frequently failed to report back to the board, there is no further reference to governance issues until August 1854, when the faculty petitioned the trustees for "the power . . . of controlling the College premises so as to prevent disturbances and annoyance, either from persons not members of the College, or from [live] stock running in the campus." The board responded by granting the faculty "liberty . . . to prevent disturbances on the College premises" and by directing the faculty to employ marshals to "enforce the laws of the State and By-Laws of [the] College."[8]

The first police officers in Davidson were not marshals but a patrol formed in May 1855 with the concurrence of townspeople. Members of this patrol were to serve at least three nights a week and receive fifty cents per night for their services. Some signs of the local tensions between the races can be seen in the creation of this patrol: along with dealing with errant livestock, they were charged with dispersing "any negroes who may collect about the College on Sundays." Interestingly, this regulation suggests that slaves in the area had some personal liberties on Sundays and at night, and that areas of college property served as a gathering place. Either conditions improved or the concern flagged, for the patrols were not maintained.[9]

Shortly before his departure from the college in 1858, Professor Daniel Harvey Hill revived the idea of a patrol. He proposed that "some action be taken . . . for the general safety and to keep the peace during Commencement week." The faculty granted him authority to appoint and supervise a patrol whose compensation was increased from the fifty cents of 1855 to two dollars per day.[10] The college's commencement ceremonies lasted almost a week and attracted visitors from the surrounding community to listen to bands and speeches and to enjoy the opportunity to catch up on news, renew acquaintances, and perhaps do a little courting.

Townspeople should not be blamed if they sometimes viewed commencement with a sigh of relief. Some residents disliked the incidents of late night "mischief" that occurred in this college town as well as in many others. Students at the college were prone to serenade their neighbors, ring the college bell for hours, and engage in "shooting a boo." One such shooting in 1851 knocked glass out of the chapel and houses; in a series of powder explosions the noise could be heard "some four or five miles around the College." More seriously, in an incident in 1849 students firing pistols disturbed neighbors, "actually wounding one of them."[11]

The Battle Against "Spirituous Liquors"

In addition to concerns about disturbances, preventing access to "spirituous liquors" kept the faculty and board busy. Seeking to safeguard the reputation of moral probity of the college and town, they took this duty seriously. They were determined to set Davidson apart from the baser aspects of the area.

The fact that alcohol played an important role in the local economy complicated their efforts. The 1810 census had recorded twenty-one grist mills and sixty-two stills in the county, evidence that shipping corn liquor was considerably more profitable than shipping grain. And, as one local historian noted, "a distillery . . . was almost as much a part of a plantation as the plows and other farming implements."[12]

In the fall of 1837, President Morrison inspired students and townspeople to organize a temperance society. Its first regular meeting was 1 January 1838, with the rationale that "the day cannot be better celebrated than in promoting the glorious cause of temperance." Its membership grew to 110 in 1839, and the society with enthusiastic hyperbole reported that "[i]n few, if any, of the literary institutions of our country is the cause as popular and prevalent, as in this, our own beloved institution." The society's "beneficial effects" had been seen both at the college and "in the surrounding country."[13]

Although one student who graduated in 1860 later wrote that he "did not see or hear of a flask of intoxicating spirits" in Davidson, there is ample evidence that some students consumed alcohol in the 1840s and 1850s. In 1845, for example, two students were expelled for being intoxicated, and eleven other students were expelled after protesting the punishment of the first two.[14] That same year the board appointed a committee to investigate "certain person or persons" selling alcohol to students, and in 1848 another committee was charged with enforcing the policy against the sale of spirituous liquors to students. Yet another committee was appointed in 1854 to have the college charter amended "to forbid the sale of intoxicating liquors within three miles of the College, except for medicinal, mechanical, or sacramental purposes."[15]

Two years later, local merchant James Henderson was charged with selling alcohol to students. The attempt to sue Henderson for violating his lease apparently failed, as did another suit in 1859. The trustees' response was to urge the faculty to continue to "protect the College from the Temptations of wicked men, notwithstanding any want of success in previous attempts," and to resolve that "in the future, no sale or [five-year] lease . . . of any of the Real Estate around the College be made except by order of the Trustees." By requiring all real-estate transactions to come to the full board, the trustees hoped to regulate who lived and worked in the village.[16]

The outcome of the trustees' efforts was mixed at best. Beginning with the first leases and land sales, the need for income and services tempered the desire to regulate village residents. The wording of the leases gave the trustees some power to dictate town standards, but the ease with which the leases could be ignored and the lack of judicial support undermined the college's ability to dominate the town.

Population Growth

Between 1837 and 1850, the town of Davidson (known then as Davidson College, the town taking its name from the college) grew from a handful of households to a settled village of more than 200 residents. The college itself did not grow much in these decades. The number of faculty increased from two to four, and enrollment was usually seventy to eighty students. But the college did attract more businesses to the town. The combination of campus purchases and the trade from area farm families contributed to modest economic prosperity and growth.

The Morrison and Patrick Sparrow families lived in town only from 1837 to 1840. Additional faculty and their families followed in 1840 and 1841. Samuel Williamson, soon to be the college's second president, moved from his plantation in the Hopewell Presbyterian Church area with his wife, Jane, five children, and household slaves. They lived in town until 1854 with two additional children born to the family. Two other faculty members, Samuel Wilson and Mortimer Johnston, arrived with their families in 1841 and stayed until 1853. Both households also had slaves: the 1850 census listed Johnston as owning fourteen slaves and Wilson nine.

Relatives of faculty families moved into town as well. Patrick Sparrow's brother, Thomas, arrived with his wife, Martha, and two children. Theirs may well have been the first store in town, and they later operated one of the first boarding houses.[17] Dan and Susan Alexander, in-laws of Mortimer Johnston, came to live near their daughter, Mary. Dan served as the college steward from 1841 to 1843, with responsibility for feeding the students and also providing overnight accommodations as needed for visiting trustees and other travelers. The steward and his family lived on the second floor of Steward's Hall.[18]

While it is not possible to locate all the names of people living in or near Davidson, existing deeds, store ledgers, and post office records provide some clues. Families owning land adjacent to the college included the Armours, Sloans, Jettons, Pattersons, Catheys, and Potts. These families along with neighboring planters—e.g., the Davidsons of Beaver Dam, the Houstons of Mount Mourne, the Caldwells of Glenwood, the Torrences of Cedar Grove, the Stinsons of Woodlawn, the Johnstons of Walnut Grove and Cedar Grove, and the descendants of slaves who lived and worked on the plantations—have long maintained ties to the town. While most farmers in the area held no or only a few slaves, planters typically had at least twenty-five or thirty.[19] Local planters frequently sent their sons to the college and their daughters to nearby academies.

The 1850 census for Davidson College, conducted in August of that year, reveals that, along with the 68 students registered at that time, the town's population included 100 free white men and 86 free white women, no free blacks, and roughly 70 to 100 slaves. As was usually the case in nineteenth-century America, the town's population was relatively young: within the free white population excluding college students, there were 88 children under the age of eighteen, 73 adults between the ages of 18 and 49, and only 18 adults over age fifty.

Occupations for men listed in the census included two blacksmiths, three tailors, three carpenters, six cabinet makers and two apprentices, two clerks, one shoemaker, two physicians, two merchants, three college professors, the college steward, one school teacher, and six farmers. The college hired townspeople and slaves as servants and as day laborers repairing college buildings. Trustee minutes for 1854 refer to the rise in the cost of labor as justification for raising board fees, and the treasurer's report lists fees paid for hiring slaves and day laborers for such odd jobs as fixing locks, laying a hearth, hauling rocks for well walls and "burning fluid" for the chapel, painting Professor Hill's blackboard, and assisting the steward.

No occupations were listed in the census for any women, but student letters and other records show that area women worked in family businesses and as cooks, laundresses, housekeepers, seamstresses, and occasionally as teachers. This work was in addition to the time spent raising children, preparing or supervising the preparation of meals, cleaning, tending gardens and livestock, making and mending clothes, and caring for those who were sick or infirm. Faculty wives had the advantage of slaves for household help; slave women with families worked double duty.

The slave census lists at least 114 slaves owned by Davidson residents, with some almost certainly living outside the town. Because slaves often had a trade, more men may have been working in Davidson as blacksmiths, carpenters, shoemakers, and cabinetmakers than the census records show.[20]

During the 1850s eight new faculty families came to town, some staying only a few years but most living in the area from five to ten years. Two of the professors hailed from the North. Yale-educated E.F. Rockwell was originally from Connecticut and James Gilland came from Pennsylvania. Professor D.H. Hill, while having strong ties to South Carolina and to the college through his marriage to Robert Hall Morrison's daughter Isabella, also had attended the U.S. Military Academy at West Point and had served in the Mexican War. Along with R.D. Parker, a local physician originally from Ireland, a handful of students from other states, and visiting missionaries, these professors helped to connect Davidson with developments outside the region. While the town was not a cultural crossroads, it was less isolated from ideas and contacts than its rural location might imply.

Early Businesses

Local historian Mary Beaty uncovered the names of sixteen businesses operating between 1837 and 1860. Apart from brief credit reports filed by agents of R.G. Dun & Company, information about them is meager, but it is likely that most were mercantile businesses.[21] Given that storekeepers in the area often marked goods up 100 percent and that farm supplies sold briskly in Mecklenburg County, operating a store was a popular profession. Yet high transportation costs and the practice of buying on credit made many of these enterprises short-lived.

Town residents frequently took advantage of anyone traveling to Charlotte or Salisbury to obtain supplies that were not available in local stores. Mary Rice Lacy, the wife of college president Drury Lacy, found herself thanking her stepdaughter for sending supplies and including a new shopping list in the same letter. The letter also contained an apology: "You must excuse the haste with which we usually send for things. We have to seize such opportunities as occur."[22]

Local merchant Thomas Sparrow lowered some of the prices in his store to attract customers and then assured his profits by raising the cost of other goods. "This is the bill just as Mr. Sparrow gave it to me," college student James Morrow wrote his parents. "They sell clothes cheap but charge very high for trimming." Another student noted that the price of wood "goes up if the roads are bad."[23]

Students opened the way for new businesses in town when their vociferous complaints about the quality of food at the Steward's Hall moved the trustees to allow students to eat at local boarding houses. The trustees kept the right to limit students to only approved establishments, thereby extending college influence in town affairs for many years. Indeed, dining at boarding houses continued well into the twentieth century. The college continued to operate the Steward's Hall on a smaller scale. In 1857, Ann Brown became the college's first female employee when she was appointed "Stewardess."[24]

Local entrepreneurs and town residents also benefited from the college's need for funds. The trustees began selling lots in town in 1848 and leasing additional lots in 1857. Mary Lacy's cheerful proclamation in 1859—"We have one of your Charlotte Jews up here & I am glad of it for Withers does charge exorbitantly. . . . Now the Jews have opened a store maybe I can do more of my shopping here"—reflected the need for more stores and competition as well as identified a connection between Charlotte and Davidson.[25]

Helper Hotel in 1870s

The Helper Hotel (known later as the Carolina Inn), one of the town's earliest businesses and now one of its most recognizable buildings, began as a small store on property Lewis Dinkins acquired from the trustees in 1848. During the 1850s Leroy Springs operated a store and possibly an inn there, selling the property to Hanson P. Helper in 1855. According to the R.G. Dun & Company reports, Helper began his career in David-son as a clerk in James Henderson's store. In 1859 he was described as "a man of small means" and a year later was reported to be "worth about 2 thousand" and "a prudent man & trustworthy." Helper eventually turned the store building into a thirteen-room hotel, which became known as Helper's Hotel. His family also operated a store and the town post office on the property just south of the inn.[26]

Fifty years after his graduation, J.J. Stringfellow could still recall "Pink Helper, merchant and postmaster" and "most pleasantly" his boarding house family, Mr. and Mrs. Farrow, "familiarly called Uncle Tom and 'Aunt Tom' who were always kind in treatment and generous *at table. No boy* of the olden time can *ever* forget their famous *molasses pies!*" [italics in original].[27]

George Laurence Petrie, class of 1859, had equally fond memories of the opening of G.F. Shepard's ice cream salon in 1857. He reported to his family that the confectioner "makes very good ice cream, and sells it very cheap, he gives a tumbler full and heaped up for ten cents, he is almost too near my room being just across the street." His letter home also revealed some of the economic uncertainties of the time:

> I have just witnessed an amusing, and rather serious affair. John received some money from home this evening and went around and paid up his bills, he paid twenty dollars at the Confectionary; and just a minute ago the confectionary man came in and told John that the twenty dollar bill was counterfeit; John coolly shook his foot and pulled out another $20.00 bill and gave it to him; the amusing part was that John thought he had squared up all around, but at the same time it will be a rather serious loss to him; he says he can manage to do without it—it is well he can for he would not have time to hear from home again before commencement. The twenty dollar bill was on the bank of Charlotte, NC. My money is no doubt all good, being South Carolina money.[28]

The shops and homes clustered along a road running on the west side of campus—an area initially controlled by the college—shaped the character of Main Street for generations to come. Yet the college was not entirely responsible for defining neighborhoods or controlling growth because it owned only a portion of the land. In contemporary terms, the northern boundary of the college property ended at the college cemetery on North Main Street, the southern boundary ended just short of the intersection of South and Main streets, the eastern boundary just short of Woodland Street, and the western boundary a few blocks west of Main Street. The Potts, Jettons, Armours, and other families with land abutting the campus also were important influences on the town's eventual layout.

Maxwell Chambers' Timely Bequest

The construction of a large new college building in 1858 contributed to the economy of the town and neighboring communities. The Chambers Building was made possible by the very generous bequest of a Salisbury merchant and one-time Davidson College building committee member, Maxwell Chambers. Designed by the renowned architect Alexander J. Davie, it was an imposing structure, almost 300 feet long, and had 45-feet-high columns surrounding the entrance. The projected construction cost was $95,000, and much of that money went to area businesses and work-

Chambers Building, circa 1880

ers. Bricks for the building, like those for the earlier structures, were made locally; stones were quarried just a few miles north in Mount Mourne; and lumber was either hauled from Charlotte or cut a few miles to the south in what is now Huntersville.

Beyond the immediate economic gain, the Chambers bequest and building brought longer-term benefits. First, it brought to town the family of the contractor responsible for the building's construction, John Scofield. Although Scofield's family left Davidson after the building's completion, his widow and children returned in 1867 and became part of the town's fabric for many decades.

More important, the Chambers Building gave the college a new stature and renewed hope for growth. An infusion of positive energy was much needed at the time. A student revolt in 1854–55 put the entire town at risk. The *Chester* (S.C.) *Standard* provided the following account on 11 January 1855:

> We much regret to learn that this flourishing institution [Davidson College] was virtually . . . broken up on [January 3] by nearly . . . every student leaving it in a body. It appears that on a prior occasion some person threw a stone and struck one of the Professors with it. One of the students who is alleged was innocent was tried by the faculty on suspicion of having committed the offense and

expelled. Upon hearing this the other students all petitioned the faculty, stating that the one expelled was innocent and requesting his reinstatement. The Faculty refused to grant the petition and thereupon they all, except perhaps two or three, abandoned the college and went home.

A newly hired professor, Clement Fishburne, discovered to his surprise that "when the day came [to resume classes] there were perhaps three or five [students] reporting out of over 100 who had been there before the [Christmas] holidays. It was soon ascertained that I had nothing to do. . . . In a week after reopening the number of students increased to 10 or 12."[29]

The loss of so many students raised the possibility of shutting down the college and by extension the town, for the economic well-being of the town was still strongly linked to the college. Whether Davidson could have survived as a trading center is uncertain. Happily for both town and college, Maxwell Chambers's unexpected bequest gave the college new life. As student James McCombs explained to his brother,

> when I came here there were only five students . . . but they have been gradually increasing since that time [and] there are twenty nine here now. I do not expect there will be many more here this session but I look for a good many here next. I suppose that the old College would have broken down if it had not been for Chambers of Salisbury. He died soon after it broke up and left it between two and three hundred thousand dollars. When that report got out the students began to come back and the Trustees elected two new professors and a president and everything is going on very smoothly here now with considerable improvement.[30]

Chambers's gift thus not only allowed the construction of the main campus building that bore his name; it also made it possible for the college to stay open as enrollment slowly returned to normal. Only three seniors graduated in 1855, eight in 1856, and four in 1857. But by 1857 the enrollment had grown to 102, the highest it had been since 1842.

Main Road and Railroad

Given its combined roles of dormitory, classroom, and administrative space, Chambers Building was truly central to the college. On a more mundane scale, Davidson's main street also meant a great deal to the town. Not much more than a wide path, it served as Davidson's connection to the world. A passing comment in a letter written by William Bynum in October 1837 serves as a reminder both of Davidson's rural origins and of the beginnings of this road as a trading path from the days of the Catawba Indians. He wrote that "there [are] a great many herds going by here to the south. There was a drove of 100 very fine large ones passed here yesterday going from Virginia to Columbia."[31]

Although Davidson's main road was important, it was not well established or carefully maintained. At the time of the college's founding, it was a wagon trail cut across the meadows and fields. In 1844 the trustees appointed a committee to oversee moving the "great road" so that all college buildings would be east of it. A decade later another board committee was formed to "ascertain the views of owners of property of Davidson College as to a change in the location of the public highway passing through said place." The next year the "practicability and expediency of having the public road changed" was still under discussion. The outcome was never reported to the full board, but it is clear that, by 1856, the great road had become a plank road.[32]

A nineteenth century mode of paving, plank roads consisted of rows of eight-foot-long wooden planks placed on wide wooden rails. An improvement over the mud and dust of dirt roads, plank roads required considerable upkeep. By 1860 efforts to main the road between Statesville and Charlotte had been abandoned.

The loss of the plank road meant the return of the nickname "Red Sea," which students and townspeople disparagingly called the public road when rains turned the red Piedmont clay into a muddy morass. Offsetting this inconvenience was the long-anticipated arrival of the railroad. Across the state during the 1840s and 1850s, committees of interested citizens pushed for railroad construction, and rail lines began crossing the countryside. One such committee held a public meeting in Charlotte in March 1845 to make "exertions to have the Branch Rail Road continued from Camden to Charlotte." Believing that a railroad could help to lower shipping costs, they argued that "no enterprise that could suggest itself to the minds of our citizens . . . would have so beneficial an effect on the prosperity of Charlotte and Western North Carolina."[33]

This effort failed, but on 21 October 1852 Charlotte's railway dreams were realized as the first passenger train of the Charlotte and South Carolina Railroad rolled into town. Two years later the North Carolina State Railroad reached Charlotte, connecting it to Greensboro, Raleigh, and ports on the North Carolina coast. Not coincidentally, Charlotte's population grew rapidly during these years.

At least one trustee served on the 1845 Charlotte committee, and by the 1850s trustees were investing in railroad bonds. In 1859 students were eagerly anticipating riding the train home, and townspeople looked forward to the ease of travel and reduced shipping costs that a railroad could bring. In 1861 the Atlantic Tennessee and Ohio Railroad Company completed its line into Charlotte. The ambitious geographic scope of its name notwithstanding, the line ran primarily from Statesville to Charlotte. Whatever its limitations, this line was enough to connect Davidson, if only temporarily, to the new rail age.[34]

Patterns of Social and Religious Life

By today's standards, the daily life of Davidson townspeople in the 1840s and 1850s might seem dull—or worse, bleak and isolated. But within the context of the time, town residents had numerous outlets for civic and social activities and, given the relatively cosmopolitan mix of backgrounds, goodly access to regional and national news and debates. A town is more than roads, businesses, and a college: equally important in creating a community are social interactions and institutions. Churches and schools, health care and race relations, civic clubs and entertainments—all are essential threads in the tapestry of Davidson's history.

Patterns established in the 1840s and 1850s linger still in habits of civic activism and social divisions, and in the contrast of regional traits with local exceptionalism. In religion and race, Davidson clearly followed regional habits. Health care, education, and civic activities tended to go beyond regional to national patterns, while entertainments reflected both local influences and international contacts.

Given the role of the Presbyterian church in the founding of the college and the predominance of this denomination in the Piedmont region, it is not surprising that the first church in town was Presbyterian. Yet even in matters of religion the college, while playing a central role, never overshadowed the lives of villagers. The only church building in town was the college's chapel, but church attendance was required only of students. Townspeople could attend the college church but could also choose to spend Sunday mornings and Wednesday evenings in other pursuits. Residents were also free to attend other churches, although to do so required some travel. There were other Presbyterian churches in the surrounding area and at least one Methodist church, Mt. Zion, located a few miles south of town.[35]

The church's membership records show that only a few non-college

Original chapel building

families joined. Slaves had less choice, typically attending services along-side their masters. A few—including June, a slave of Professor Elijah F. Rockwell, and Sarah from the Houston household—joined the church as members; but overall membership remained low, with only twenty-five communing members in 1850 and twenty-seven in 1860.[36] A number of townspeople attended services without joining and participated in the days of special preaching and fast days. On 6 January 1845, for example, townspeople joined Presbyterians across the state in observing a fast day with preaching in the morning and afternoon.[37]

The church also offered an outlet for faculty wives and other local white women, who formed committees and took an active part in furnishing the church. In 1855 women not only painted the church and acquired new furnishings, but they came forward and asked to be reimbursed. A reluctant board of trustees voted to pay only any remaining amount up to forty dollars.[38]

These women's involvement in painting and furnishing the chapel provides insights into women's interest in religion and also into the relationship between the women and the college. By the 1830s women throughout the nation were assuming new roles in churches, helping to raise funds and to do good works in their communities. From this activity emerged a new pattern of forming voluntary organizations. This pattern was more prevalent in the North, but the ladies of the town, especially those from college families, happily joined together to work for changes and opportunities.[39]

By creating a space for themselves and their families as well as for students, these women helped the chapel become an important center for town and college life. Because the town did not yet have a public school or a town hall, the chapel was the town's primary gathering place. Here public lectures as well as sermons were given and local civic groups met. Here also were opportunities for education, and women assisted with Sunday schools for their children.

And here also was division, for the town followed prevailing patterns in the South and began to establish separate black congregations. By 1858, a contemporary source noted, a "Sabbath school for the black children and adults" was being taught "by a few ladies and two of the students in the [private] School House near [the] College, to whom, with other negroes who assemble, a sermon is preached in the afternoon of the Sabbath by the Chaplain."[40]

Race Relations

Overall the interactions of slaves and white villagers, a complex blend of familiarity and unease, were typical of the region. Children may have played together in their free time, but adults generally stayed apart. Or at least they were expected to. President Morrison reportedly relied heavily on the advice of a slave known as "aunt Mary," but in 1837 and 1838 students were dismissed from the college for overstepping social boundaries. In one instance students allegedly spent an evening enjoying "a general feast with Lemly's Negros"; in the other it was "keeping company with negro women."[41]

The experiences of Mary Rice Lacy provide a window on the tensions and twists of race. Lacy wrote regularly to her stepdaughter, Bess, telling of daily events. In two of the letters she refers to slaves:

[6 August 1856] Aunt Amy continues so sick. . . . She is now entirely confined to her bed taking quinine every three hours. . . . I sent out to Mrs. Read today for someone to come and take care of her, for Aunt Maria must needs make herself sick eating green watermelons and see[ing] Aunt Amy was nursed and waited on. She went to bed too, and wouldn't be at work today, if I hadn't told her the Doctor said she was well. She is a hard old case.

[2 January 1857] Your Father was saying tonight he was getting tired of making fires, feeding the cow and carrying water. We find [that]

Portion of 1860 slave census for Davidson area

living in this country we must conform to the ways of the people
and buy our own servants. I wish we could afford a nurse now, but
as your Father has to pay for William, that is not practicable. . . .
I had my mind set upon a girl belonging to the Torrence estate,
about twelve or thirteen and thinking we would get her or some
other one . . . the girl was bid up to forty nine dollars and fifty
cents [and] he let her go . . . maybe you could hear of some child
[free] that we could have bound as you have Lizzie, rather older
than she is; or maybe there might be one to hire privately from ten
to fifteen that we might get on more reasonable terms.[42]

The first letter reflected both Mary Lacy's concern for slaves and a
slave's wiliness. The Lacys were willing to provide medical care for a slave
for an extended period, and Aunt Maria was willing to use any means she
could to get rest. Mary Lacy acknowledged Aunt Maria's tricks as part of

their relationship, and referred to the older woman as one might refer to a child.

In the second letter, despite her qualms about "conforming to the ways of the people," Lacy expressed greater concern about prices than about the institution of slavery or the indenture of a child as young as ten years of age. In her social position, she wanted the assistance of servants, and if the only servants available were slaves or indentured children, then she accepted and worked within those relationships. She was not a woman of leisure. Her days were full of gardening, child care, entertaining traveling guests, and managing on limited funds. But she was privileged enough to be able to afford to hire and purchase slaves, and was willing to do so.[43]

Whites were not always in the right in their dealings with slaves. In 1853, for example, three students were suspended after an altercation in a local store. The students accosted slaves outside the store, demanding that the men remove their hats and knocking off one hat. They encountered more slaves inside the store and knocked off another hat. The owners challenged the students and a fight ensued. Upon hearing the case, the faculty suspended the students. Similarly, in 1863 two students were dismissed for "assaulting a negro woman."[44]

Yet slaves were subject to arrest and whipping with little legal recourse. In 1859 the faculty voted to ban Mrs. White's slaves from the college grounds after sunset. Mary Lacy recorded the incidents that led to the banning:

Last Sunday week when we were all at Monthly Concert, one of the students' rooms was entered through the window, his clothes hanging round the room, trunks, his money, everything in it stolen. The whole college went out on Monday to try to track the thief and they succeeded in doing so for two miles nearly, but lost it. A Negro of Mrs. White's was shipped, whose shoe exactly fitted the track with some peculiarities of half soling, pegs, etc., but he confessed nothing. Another was whipped for having a pistol.

After noting that a "wagoner" attempting to sell whiskey to students was sent to jail in Charlotte, Lacy declared that "we are much in hopes these two events will strike terror into the negroes and the whiskey sellers."[45]

By 1859 the town of Davidson was well aware of abolitionists, not only from local newspapers such as the *Western Democrat* but also from the controversy surrounding the brother of Hanson Helper after the publication of his book, *The Impending Crisis of the South*. Hinton Rowan Helper was no friend of slaves; his interest was in protecting the economic futures of free white laborers. The book was banned in North Carolina—although a copy later made its way into the college library. Yet for most Davidson families, keeping loved ones clothed, fed, and healthy took precedence over national and regional controversies. Even the most affluent families faced difficulties in acquiring goods, and affluent and poor alike feared the outbreak of fevers.

Challenges in Health Care

Frequent claims of the college and town "being in a healthful region" reflected serious concerns of the era. Davidson based its claim on its location atop a high point between two rivers. At the time there was a general understanding that low-lying areas near water were prone to diseases. Even in a college town, medical knowledge remained a mixture of fanciful beliefs and scientific knowledge. Residents were all too aware of the dangers of contagious diseases and the limitations of medical care, including among other things the absence of laws requiring certification for doctors practicing medicine in the state.[46]

The inability to treat communicable diseases brought deep sadness to many parents and other family members and friends. The first graves in the town cemetery were those of Sarah Walker Morrison, aged 3 years, and Elizabeth Lee Morrison, aged 13 months. The president's young daughters died within a day of one another in April 1838. Patrick Sparrow's family felt the next known loss with the death of his four-month-old niece, Mary, in 1842. The Thomas Sparrow family would lose two more children: a two-year-old son in 1847 and a three-year-old son in 1853.

Of the first twenty known graves, eleven were for children aged four months to seven years, and two others were for boys aged sixteen and seventeen. Although there are no records for slave deaths except for an occasional mention in letters, in the South generally more than 50 percent of slave children died before the age of five.[47]

During 1850 and 1851 a smallpox outbreak struck Charlotte and Mecklenburg County. "We have been kept worked up and frightened by [smallpox] for the last month or two," one student wrote his parents, "and have been quite uneasy from fear of its getting on the hill."[48] The college did vaccinate students, with President Samuel Williamson taking on medical duties alongside teaching and administration. Unfortunately these efforts came too late to save Williamson's son, John, who succumbed to illness in September 1850. In 1854 an outbreak of scarlet fever closed the college just before spring exams. No deaths were reported, but in 1858 Clement Fishburne lost his wife to dysentery.

Like cities, towns, and rural areas throughout the nation at the time, Davidson felt the fear and sorrow of epidemics. Sermons and other commentary on the brevity and uncertainty of human life had an experiential veracity in nineteenth-century America, including in Davidson.

Limited Opportunities in Education

Oddly enough for a college town, Davidson lacked sufficient teachers for local children. Before the 1850s the state legislature passed few laws regarding public schools—and even fewer to raise the tax money needed to support them. Elementary education thus was mostly limited to private academies and tutors. A statewide system of school districts was established in 1839, but the first state superintendent of common schools, Calvin Wiley, was not appointed until 1853. He noted that the state's school system was "obscured in darkness." By 1860, however, Wiley was able to increase the number of licensed teachers from 800 to 2,752 and funding from $150,000 to $278,000.[49] According to historian D.A. Tompkins, there were seventy-seven school districts in Mecklenburg County at the time and "salaries of teachers ranged from fifteen dollars to thirty dollars a month, and the books used included Webster's speller, North Carolina reader, Davie's arithmetic and Smith's grammar."[50]

In the town's early years, some childen would have attended the private school run by Thomas Sparrow, while others were taught their letters at home or remained unschooled. With public schools still many years in the future and private schools often short-lived, only children whose parents could afford school fees at area academies or whose parents were sufficiently educated to teach them received any schooling. Although teaching a slave to read or write was prohibited by state law, how thoroughly this legislation was enforced or whether any slave children were educated in Davidson is unknown.

Some young ladies of the town attended academies, partly to prepare for assuming maternal teaching roles when they became parents. Four of Robert Hall and Mary Graham Morrison's daughters attended Salem Female Academy, founded in 1772 by Moravians in Salem, North Carolina. Initially only a day school for girls from the community, the school began taking boarders in 1802 and added advanced work in 1844. In 1851 John Cooper reported to his friend Thomas Britton that storekeeper James Henderson's daughter had returned home from Salem looking "as blooming as a rose."[51]

Opportunities for young women's education increased in 1856, when

the Concord Presbytery established the Concord Female College in Statesville, and in 1857, when the Charlotte Female Institute opened under the
leadership of the Reverend Robert Burwell. Although these schools followed national trends by stressing the acquisition of socially acceptable
female pursuits such as learning needlework and playing musical instruments, they also taught such subjects as Latin, history, and mathematics.

Activism and Entertainments

Girls' studies did not include politics, but they could learn civic activism through their mothers. In 1855 growing concern over the shabby
condition of the college prompted a few ladies to "earnestly" petition the
trustees to "take into consideration the propriety of enclosing the College campus and a general remodeling of the College Grounds." While
acknowledging the need, the trustees were reluctant to spend any funds
at the time. The women spent their own money on the chapel, later receiving some reimbursement. It would take until 1861 to get a fence, but
the ladies' limited success was enough to launch a legacy of civic interest
and activism passed on through generations of Davidson women. While
initially only white women had sufficient time and resources to form civic
organizations, over time ethnically diverse groups formed to address issues
relating to health care, schools, and housing.

Women's gatherings not only gave them some power to improve their
surroundings, but also provided an occasional social outlet. Davidson had
little if any high society; even among the most educated and affluent citizens, social interactions were more casual and practical. While hospitality
remained important, city manners held little sway.

Comments in Mary Lacy's letters provide glimpses of the constraints
and simplicity of her social circle. There is wistfulness in her observation
that "there is less temptation here to worldliness, fashion or anything of
that sort than any place I ever saw," especially when it is followed immediately by the request to borrow her stepdaughter's furs and a report that
"I have a pretty purple silk scarf I got from New York (the exact shade of
my bonnet strings) which I can wear when I am dressed and that is not
very often." So few were the opportunities for vanity in Davidson that she
later commented that the wife of a proposed new faculty member "won't
like it here and she won't be a help to us" because she was reputed to be "a
fashionable lady and a beauty."[52]

Professors and businessmen also had few organized social outlets. As
noted earlier, a Temperance Society formed in 1837, and in 1855 the faculty

granted permission for a Masonic Lodge to use a college building for its meetings. More informal social ties were formed through the practice of single men and even young couples boarding with families.

For slaves, entertainments were even more limited, with work consuming much of their days. After completing their work, whether in fields or in households, they had to care for their families and maintain any garden plots they were allowed. Their food was generally less varied than that of the families they served, with an emphasis on cornmeal and fat pork. Until the formation of the patrols, they were able to gather some evenings on campus to share time and perhaps meals together. As noted earlier, some slaves also had time off on Sunday afternoons to attend the Sabbath School.

Preaching and temperance meetings were not the only available sources of diversion, however. A number of circuses and exhibitions came through Charlotte, and by the 1850s the college was hosting "Magick Lantern" shows and phrenology lectures. The town also held celebrations for the Fourth of July, Mecklenburg County's own patriotic holiday of May 20th honoring the Mecklenburg Declaration of Independence, and, of course, commencement. Christmas was a plain affair; in 1858 Mary Lacy planned to give her children a work box and a knife for their gifts.[53]

State and national politics brought more excitement. Student James Morrow wrote home in 1840 that "politics are raging here at this time. Everything for Harrison and Tyler, and Morehead for governor of this state. . . . The candidate for governor goes about electioneering, at all public gatherings, and even rides around with the Tax Collector for votes." The war with Mexico in the 1840s raised concerns but few volunteers from the Davidson area; even the formation of a company of light horse dragoons in Charlotte sparked only talk, not enlistments.[54]

The congressional elections in the mid-1850s stirred considerable interest as the Know-Nothing (or Whig) party had a large following in Davidson, many of whom no doubt were disappointed when their candidate lost to Democrat Burton Craige. Some of that disappointment may have been tempered by Craige's later procurement of seventy volumes of government publications, including valuable editions of the American state papers, for the college library.[55]

Conclusion

The criticism, quoted earlier, that Davidson in 1857 was a "one horse affair" is not surprising. With only a few homes and businesses scattered largely on the other side of a dirt track from the campus, it certainly could not rival Charlotte, Statesville, or Salisbury. But considering the obstacles and challenges of its first decades, Davidson's progress was, if not miraculous, certainly noteworthy. The perseverance of the Presbytery of Concord in founding and funding the college is remarkable. Once launched, both the college and the town struggled to overcome faculty turnover, student riots, epidemics, and uneven economic fortunes. In doing so, these first residents shaped the town.

From the shared work of slaves, farmers, and farm hands building the first houses to the women who helped furnish homes, dormitories, and the chapel, from the professors who gave the town distinction to the often rowdy students, patterns took hold. Life took different forms depending partly on a person's age, race, gender, and economic circumstances, but everyone's lives overlapped. The husbands of the women teaching the Sunday school for slaves formed the patrols to ban slaves from campus. Carpenters and seamstresses boarded with business owners and professors and ate meals prepared by black cooks. And within this network, the regional patterns of deference and social position held, establishing complex relationships among black and white, town and gown.

The town remained rural with its unpaved street and livestock pens; but it also hosted travelers from across the country and missionaries from around the world. While taking a keen interest in state and national politics, residents were mostly content to leave local political power in the hands of the college. The college's good fortune in receiving Maxwell Chambers's gift was also the town's. The economic boost and stability it brought happened at just the right time, for town and college were about to face their greatest challenge in the coming decade.

2 New Challenges in the 1860s and 1870s

While the most obvious challenge facing any Southern town during the 1860s and 1870s was the Civil War, the years following the war were equally important in Davidson's history. For Davidson, the years after the war brought more political, economic, and social transformations than did the war itself. Although the town suffered during the war, primarily through the absence of men to work crops and the loss of the railroad, the larger challenges came in adjusting to shifting political, economic, and social landscapes in subsequent years.

From 1860 to 1879 the town's finances and politics remained integrally linked with the college, with the faculty serving as the de facto town government. In 1869 the trustees considered securing "an act of incorporation for the better government of the village."[1]

Ten years later, the villagers took matters into their own hands, incorporating the town as "Davidson College" and thus ending an era in the town's history. The composition of the new town council assured continued college influence but also marked a new stage in the village's identity. During these years, the established pattern of civic cooperation overlapping and reinforcing social divisions deepened. And despite the deprivations of the war years, the town's belief in its distinctiveness was reinforced.

Davidson on the Eve of the War

Capturing a clear picture of Davidson in 1860 is difficult. That year's census records are hard to interpret because the information was not listed by post office, and the census taker appears not to have followed any logical pattern in covering the area. Some gaps—but not all—can be filled in with other contemporary records. Taking into account the possibility of omissions and misidentifications, the village and surrounding farm population, excluding college students, appears to have grown to slightly more than 400 people with 85 dwellings. Forty-nine of the dwellings housed 51 free families, and an additional 36 slave dwellings are listed. Of the 240 people identified as free, 21 are listed as slave owners with a total of 172 slaves. The census also identifies one free mulatto household, that of Frank Clark, a brick mason, which included the twenty-nine-year-old Frank, his wife, Eliza, six children, and another adult, Thomas Heally, a painter.[2]

The village's residents remained relatively young, with almost 85 percent of the population under age forty. In contrast to the 72 black children and the 108 white and mulatto children under the age of fifteen, only 11 adults were sixty or older. While most free citizens listed North Carolina as their place of birth, the village had some geographic diversity, with listings for Alabama, Connecticut, Indiana, Maryland, Massachusetts, Mississippi, Pennsylvania, Ireland, and Germany.

Occupations for free white males included professor, hatter, farmer, cabinet maker, laborer, minister, classics teacher, physician, tailor, stone mason, overseer, hotel proprietor, boot and shoemaker, clerk, druggist, merchant, coach maker, blacksmith, brick mason, painter, tanner, and, in the case of Archy Brown, "gentleman." For white women, occupations included housekeeper, farmer, seamstress, and hotel proprietor.

The presence of twenty laborers and two stone masons as well as the brick mason indicates that buildings were going up on campus and in town. The listings for seamstresses and housekeepers, along with those of the laborers, show that Davidson continued to be a mix of social and economic groups, from affluent merchants to students and from skilled workers to unskilled domestics. Some men had multiple jobs. E.F. Rockwell, for example, is listed as a professor, but he also owned a farm and served as a minister for local churches. The total value of personal property listed for townspeople and nearby residents was $219,180, with slightly more than half of those listed having less than $1,000 in property. At the affluent end of the spectrum, six people had property valued at more than $10,000.

Despite the college's improved prospects, business conditions remained uncertain. In order to earn more money, in the fall of 1860 boarding house owners, excepting the manager of the Steward's Hall, agreed to set their board at twelve dollars for the semester. Returning students disliked the plan. As student James Greenlee reported, "when the boys returned they would not stand it; about twenty-five clubbed together, hired a house and cook and are boarding themselves. . . . The boarding house keepers are caught in their own trap and I think they begin to rue their bargain, for boarders at $12 are almost as scarce as hens teeth."[3]

Even before this dispute, Hanson Helper sought to sell his business. In June he ran notices for his "good, large and comfortable hotel and board-inghouse . . . where all who may wish can find good accommodation." In November he announced his intention to "go to farming" and offered three lots for sale, including his hotel with "thirteen good comfortable rooms."[4] Nevertheless, both town and college, while not overly prosperous, could look south to Charlotte's booming economy and hope that, with the completion of a rail line through Davidson, better times were just ahead.

The Railroad Comes to Davidson

Davidson finally entered the railway age in the summer of 1860. That July the trustees granted a right of way to the Atlantic, Tennessee and Ohio Railroad for a track through college property and authorized up to two acres to be conveyed to the railroad for a depot. The trustees placed the track west of the plank road, just beyond the boundaries of their leased lots.[5] The location allowed the trustees to make use of property not intended for campus grounds, and it allowed faculty to limit student use of the railroad because campus regulations limited student mobility even within the town. While the college proclaimed in newspaper articles that "Davidson will be . . . in constant communication with the outer world," it did not intend that students would have easy access to the temptations of Charlotte and Statesville.[6]

Unlike Charlotte in the 1850s, Davidson did not see its population double with the arrival of railroads. Beginning in 1861, steam engines rolled into town for only three years before the tracks were disassembled and used by the Confederate government for other, more essential, lines. There simply was not enough time for the railroad to effect any significant changes in the village of Davidson.

Moving Slowly Toward Secession

As sectional differences grew more pronounced after John Brown's raid on Harper's Ferry in 1859, the Democratic party split into northern and southern factions. Reflecting the intensity of sectional feelings in the South,

Abraham Lincoln, the Republican party's antislavery candidate, was not even listed on the ballot in North Carolina and nine other southern states. While Lincoln could be expected to get the votes of most northerners who formerly had supported the Whig party, the new Constitutional Union party, whose nominees were John Bell of Tennessee and Edward Everett of Massachusetts, was likely to attract the votes of former Whigs in North Carolina and other southern states. Most North Carolina Democrats supported John Breckinridge, the pro-slavery, pro-states' rights candidate of the southern Democrats, and not Stephen Douglas, the unionist northern Democratic candidate.

In the 1860 presidential election, the Whig-leaning majority of Davidson voters supported Bell, who favored national unity and upholding the federal constitution. Henry Chambers recalled students erecting a tall flag pole on campus just south of the literary society halls and having a big Bell and Everett flag raising. In October 1860, James Greenlee reported, "there is considerable stir here now about the presidential election; nearly everybody are for Bell and Everett, even the Democrats with . . . little silver bells on their watch guards. I saw a man drive in the other day with a silver bell on his horse's head to show that he was a Bell man."[7]

A letter in the *Iredell Express* supports Greenlee's account, noting that in Davidson "there was a grand display of fireworks, etc. A bell was obtained and rung, the citizens caught the spirit, rung their bells and made every possible demonstration. . . . A large boom was then prepared and let off amidst deafening shouts for Bell and Everett." There were some Breckinridge supporters, but "their voices were all hushed by the long and loud huzzahs for the noble standard bearers of the Union, the Constitution, and the enforcement of the laws."[8]

The election results reflected how evenly North Carolina voters divided between supporting southern rights and maintaining the union: Breckinridge received 48,539 votes and Bell, 44,990. Voters in Mecklenburg County, which had a larger percentage of slaves than the state as a whole, cast 1,101 votes for Breckinridge and 826 for Bell. Douglas, a favorite of northern Democrats, received only 2,701 votes in the state and 135 votes in the county.

With Lincoln's election, the question of secession became more urgent. People across the state organized petitions, listened to speeches, and debated the best course of action. Unlike in South Carolina, secessionist fervor in the Tar Heel state was moderated by internal political divisions and a willingness to wait before acting. North Carolina would be the last state to secede from the union, finally prompted by Lincoln's call for troops to put down the rebellion launched at Fort Sumter in April 1861. While the reversal of feeling was swift and many pro-Union supporters enlisted in the Confederate army, areas of dissension remained, especially in the Piedmont and western counties.

In Davidson, popular sentiment appears to have been equally varied, with caution tempering sectional fervor. "There is nothing stirring here at the present worthy of notice," Duncan Buie wrote to a cousin in November 1860. "Disunion and secession are in the mouth of all—old and young, men and women, black and white. I am not in favor of secession until some overt act is committed. I think that the consequences of disunion would be awful. . . . It would satisfy me to see all the demagogues, fire-eaters, abolitionists and fanatics get together and fight [to] their satisfaction." His classmate James Greenlee offered similar sentiments, writing his father that "I am considerably amused at your warning me not to desert my books and become a soldier. I shall always hold myself ready at the call of my country, but shall make it a point to wait until I am *called,* and will try not to mistake the call of fanatics for that of country. . . . If South Carolina wants to withdraw, I say, let her rip."[9]

Even after fighting began at Fort Sumter in April 1861, responses on campus and in the town varied. Some students waited, reluctant to "lay down the 'toga' for the sword," while others raised a secession flag on the roof of the main campus building and headed home to enlist. Some faculty, notably W.C. Kerr, were vocally pro-Union; others were pro-Confederacy, especially V.C. Barringer, who enlisted in the Confederate army, and W.B. Lynch, who formed a local militia company.[10]

Despite the enlistments and the formation of militias, the legacy of this division and reluctance to leave the union was reflected in the treatment of North Carolina troops. Governor Zebulon Vance complained that too many Virginians were appointed as officers for North Carolina troops and that few Confederate offices went to North Carolinians because of the "loyalty of the great body of our people, because of the great reluctance with which they gave up the old Union."[11]

The War Years

War came to Mecklenburg County on 20 April 1861 when a company of Charlotte Grays seized the U.S. Mint in Charlotte. For Davidson, the war was characterized mostly in terms of gradual loss. The college's president, John Kirkpatrick, described developments in a report to the trustees:

Up to the first of April, our students appeared to be diligently pursuing their studies, and but slightly affected by the political excitement pervading the country. A few days later, two of them, . . . from . . . South Carolina, having previously enrolled their names in a company . . . formed for the military service of the state, were ordered home by their commanding officer. . . . Their leaving the college under such circumstances of course created some excitement among their [fellow students] until some ten days later, when [President Lincoln's] proclamation calling for a large army to operate against the seceded states of the South reached the college.

The excitement became intense and uncontrollable. Some made up their minds at once to enter the [Confederate] army, in compliance with calls of [southern governors]; some received orders from their parents to come home and join volunteer companies then organizing; some were called away to protect widowed mothers. . . . There were then only eleven students in regular connection with the college, six of the sophomore class and five of the freshman. [The sophomores] remained between two and three weeks longer, when they all withdrew and returned home. [The freshmen] remained at their studies about two weeks longer . . . , when they too left us. For nearly a month past we have not had a student in his place.[12]

In 1862, with an unpopular conscription bill pending in the Confederate Congress, students again left the college early to join volunteer companies.[13] Their places in local boarding houses and private homes were temporarily filled by volunteers from surrounding counties who joined Professor Lynch's company. The Confederate government compensated housekeepers, and the young men received knapsacks made from the oil cloth that had covered dining tables, the village women working together once again to provide for others. After traveling to Raleigh, the men in Lynch's company were sent home and later dispersed to other units.[14]

At times the war seemed remote. "We hear nothing about conscription at all; desertion nothing," Franklin McNeill wrote his father in March 1863. "We hear nothing at all about the war up here—it seems to be a very bad place to hear news, although the railroad runs by the place." In the same letter McNeill noted that the Steward's Hall managed to provide biscuits two or three times a week. While he thought that "it ought to suffice," this level of frequency marked quite a change from previous years, when biscuits appeared at every meal.[15]

Signs of rising costs and increasing scarcity can also be seen in the acceptance of Steward's Hall's fees of twenty dollars per month and even higher rates at the private houses for considerably less food, when only three years earlier the students had vigorously protested twelve dollars. A classmate of McNeill's, Franklin J. McDowell, recalled the scarcities of his college years: "The table fare was necessarily meager and scant. Flour bread was very scarce, corn dodgers all right, turnip pudding and dried apple pies acceptable, ginger cake a cherished luxury, and rye coffee and sorghum molasses called 'long sweetening' were as inseparable as the Siamese twins. Only invalids and the elderly were allowed a taste of sugar and genuine coffee. Dandridge Burwell, class of 1863, remembered "only one store open, [with] next to nothing in it, kept by a Mr. Henderson."[16]

The town did gain a few new faculty who arrived to replace those leaving for war duties. An example was Professor John Rennie Blake, who joined the faculty in the fall of 1861. Davidson's forty-nine "white" houses were not sufficient for all of the village's families of European descent. Rebecca Neal Lynch, daughter of Professor William Lynch, recalled her mother's roughly three years in Davidson. Arriving immediately after her marriage in 1861, she made her first home in the Helper Hotel. She and her husband later lodged in the homes of Professor and Mrs. McIver, and then with the Thomas Sparrow family before their departure in 1864.[17]

Other families moved into town to seek a refuge from war-torn areas or safety as fathers and husbands left for war. Some new residents found the housing in Davidson inadequate. One woman wrote to her family, "We are living in a little wooden house with the same number of rooms . . . , but with the disadvantages of there being but one fireplace in the whole house, and if we do not succeed in getting some stoves before winter sets in I'm afraid we will stand in danger of freezing, as this house sets quite near the ground and is not plastered." Her slaves experienced additional difficulties:

> At present all the cooking, washing and ironing are done outdoors.
> . . . Evelyn gets along very well with her washing and ironing but
> Betsy grumbles very much about the winds and the caterpillars
> from the walnut trees, and cooks most of the time in a house . . . in
> this yard without any floor in it. She always makes me uneasy for
> fear she will set the building on fire.[18]

The village still had no distinct neighborhoods. Businesses and homes could be side by side, or even in the same building. Mrs. Lynch would have found herself sharing a dining room with students, townspeople, and travelers. Servants and slaves would have lived in relatively close proximity, and livestock continued to forage in yards and on the campus.

Overall, Mecklenburg and nearby counties were buffered somewhat from the extreme poverty that affected other parts of the South by the region's relative prosperity before the war and by the fortunate absence of any military campaigns. Soldiers passed through town from time to time, and increasingly as the war neared its end. Julia Holt McIver wrote of her mother's memories of feeding soldiers and the determined efforts of village women: "Mrs. Kirkpatrick . . . was by far the best forager. With a small Negro boy to drive, she went the country over in search of food for the soldiers. There was no money, so when persuasion failed, off came her brooch, her collar, or any article of dress that could possibly be spared in exchange."[19]

Even though no battles were fought in the area, residents still experienced periods of fear and concern when rumors of troops in the area spread. The arrival of General William Sherman's troops in North Carolina in January 1865 and General George Stoneman's raids crossing the area from Boone to Salisbury that March brought images of devastation and looting, as did reports that Confederate cavalry under General Joseph Wheeler was approaching. In the last weeks of the war, reports from western North Carolina had made Wheeler's troops almost as dreaded as Sherman's.[20]

George McIver's memoirs contain only two accounts of troops in Davidson. The first was in late 1864, when about forty Confederate cavalry came to town and performed an exhibition drill for the residents of the village. While most of the troops were furloughed and allowed to return to their homes, a few men remained to care for the horses. The troops returned in the early spring of 1865, and the villagers soon watched them leave.

The second was just after the end of the war, when a unit of Federal troops camped outside of town for several weeks. McIver described one encounter with a Union soldier:

> On the day of their arrival, a young soldier, very mild looking and unarmed, came to our front door and asked politely if he might buy some milk. On seeing his approach to the house, I was very much alarmed, not from any personal fear but from fear that he was going to take away a discarded Confederate carbine I had recently found which had become my most cherished possession. I felt better when I found he [lacked] interest in the carbine.[21]

An incident at the college warrants notice. President Kirkpatrick reported to the trustees that "in . . . May [1865], on the occasion of a visit to this place by a detachment of United States troops, sent for the purpose of removing some government supplies which were here, some of the soldiers, by breaking open the doors and windows, entered the recitation rooms and chapel of the college and did considerable damage to the apparatus and damaged some laboratory equipment."[22]

Kirkpatrick's report did not specify what "government supplies" were housed at the college, and previous trustee minutes do not mention any contracts or agreements related to storing supplies. Because Charlotte became the site of the Confederacy's main naval yard, the "government supplies" might have been materials related to those operations. The commanding officer issued an apology for the damages and some of the equipment was recovered.[23]

Long before the end of the war, dissension over the state's involvement began to grow. In July 1863 peace rallies were held across the state. As pro-Confederate women were trading brooches and tending farms in order to send supplies to soldiers, both soldiers and ordinary citizens began to question the war's purposes. For many, the Emancipation Proclamation changed the conflict from the noble idea of protecting states' rights into a fight to preserve economic rights for slave owners, thus making the cause less universal and more focused on benefiting a smaller portion of the state's population.[24]

Franklin McDowell captured the discouragement of the war's last weeks as he wrote about his experience in Davidson:

> Near the surrender of the Confederacy, when people were disheartened and soldiers demoralized, the students became so homesick and anxious they could not study; and at a gathering under the balcony of Helper's store, A.J. Morrison of Lincoln [county] and Robert Shipp of Gaston [county] were the first to leave the meeting, starting home on foot for their homes, others soon following. The Alabamians, having purchased a horse and wagon from John H. Reid of Mt. Mourne, thus started on their long and eventful journey [home], the boys walking while Howard, the crippled soldier, drove the wagon which carried their belongings.[25]

It is easy to imagine the dust rising up around each of the departing young men, pulled home by the need to be with family and begin working to restore family farms and businesses. Surely the faces of the villagers watching them leave reflected similar discouragement as they pondered the possible fates of the college, their businesses, and their families.

For both black and white residents, there also had to have been hope and determination to meet the coming changes, combined with much uncertainty. Freed blacks were facing an especially complex future, with few resources for obtaining housing or employment. It is not surprising that some would choose to stay with the families they had served, at least initially, and perhaps longer if they became paid servants. George McIver noted that Patience, the mother of Ben and George's "mammy," stayed with the family for two or three years after the war, and that another former slave, Amy, remained with the family for ten years.[26]

Postwar Recovery

William Woods Holden was appointed provisional governor of North Carolina in May 1865, and federal troops arrived in Charlotte the following month. They would remain until December 1867. The state and its towns and rural areas slowly began their recovery, reestablishing governments, businesses, and schools. The recovery was slow because losses were ubiquitous: the loss of able-bodied young men killed and wounded in the war, destruction of property and the loss of tax revenue, and the total loss of the value of Confederate money. Affluent families lost their fortunes and banks, colleges, and other institutions faced bankruptcy because of the worthlessness of Confederate and state bonds.

In 1865 Davidson had neither cotton nor a railroad to spur its recovery. But it did have the college and a public thoroughfare. The college had stayed open during the war years, often closing earlier than planned and with the students in the pre-college preparatory program at times outnumbering regular students. After the war ended a significant number of trustees and employees made sacrifices to ensure the college's survival. Among these sacrifices were those of Trustee Robert McDowell, who advanced personal funds for several years to bolster the college's finances; of John Rennie Blake and Elijah Rockwell, who filled the void created when John Kirkpatrick resigned the presidency—Blake temporarily filling the role of faculty chair until George McPhail arrived to assume the presidency and Rockwell, as bursar, carefully watching college expenditures; and of Amos Caldwell, former slave of John Blake and "servant of all work" who added long hours making repairs to college buildings to his regular duties.[27]

The town's main street continued to be a thoroughfare for farmers carrying crops and livestock to market. In 1866 villagers sent a petition to the

John Rennie Blake

trustees asking to "change the location of the street or public road." The trustees recorded their denial of the petition, but not the reasons for the request or the denial. Perhaps an event similar to the stampede vividly remembered by Lucy Phillips Russell raised questions about safety. Russell's family moved to Davidson in 1868, when Lucy was four years old. Their house was known as "The Oaks" and faced the campus from across the main street.

One day a drover brought a herd of cattle from the mountains through town on their way to market in Charlotte. One of Russell's neighbors had butchered a cow the same day and the smell of blood set the cattle off. She recalled that "with blazing eyes and clashing horns they milled around the [neighbor's] lot bellowing hideously, snorting, pawing the ground and charging the men who attempted to control them. . . . It was late that night before a crowd of men and boys armed with clubs and pitchforks drove the maddened beasts out of town, moaning and bellowing as they crowded through the narrow street."[28]

Russell also recalled wagon loads of apples and chestnuts as well as droves of sheep, hogs, and turkeys being brought through the town every winter. When Anne Sampson, wife of Latin and French professor John Sampson, arrived in town several years later, the main street still had no sidewalks and, she recalled, to "cross the road to the chapel on high rocks was a fearsome thing."[29]

To recover fully not only from the isolation but also from the economic effects of the war, Davidson needed (1) the college to survive and grow, (2) the railroad to once again bring people and transport crops to market, (3) new businesses in town and area farms to return to full productivity, and (4) employment and housing for former slaves as well as white laborers.

To recover fully from the political and social effects of the war and Reconstruction years, Davidson would have to have had a greater vision of racial equality than was possible at the time. The town did recover sufficient economic stability to survive and prosper as a small town, but it succumbed to the racial and class divisions of its time and place and formed patterns that left their traces on future generations.

As noted earlier, the college was aided by individuals willing to share what funds and experience they could to keep it functioning. Their task was challenging. In explaining the college's condition in 1866, President Kirkpatrick identified serious problems affecting recruitment and enrollment. He mentioned the general scarcity of money, the need for young men to assist on farms now without slave labor, the large number of young men who had entered the military before completing their schooling and who now were unprepared to enter college, the increasing competition for young men from "the unprecedented number of classical schools which have sprung up in every part of the country," the lack of faculty which created both an inability to teach a full curriculum and an unfavorable comparison with competing institutions, and the poor condition of the college grounds about which "[s]trangers who visit the place do not hesitate to express their surprise that so expensive buildings and so capable grounds should be left in so rude and uninviting a condition."[30]

In the fall of 1860, the college had six professors, two acting professors, and 105 students. In the fall of 1865, there were four professors and 29 students. One year later, enrollment rose to 70. Two years later enrollment dropped back to 29, and in 1870 the college dropped to only 27 students. In 1871 the number doubled to 54 students, and in 1872 enrollment finally surpassed 1860 numbers with 121 students on campus. These fluctuations reflected the unsettled economic conditions throughout the region and nation.

One change on the faculty reflected regional political conflicts. Professor Alexander McIver was excused from his classes in late 1865 and early 1866 to serve as a member of the state convention called by Governor

Eumenean Society members in 1866

Holden to prepare a new state constitution. McIver's willingness to work with white and black Republicans—and in 1868 to support the Republican presidential candidate, Ulysses S. Grant—cost him his position at the college. Writing later to a friend, McIver reported that after telling President George McPhail that he intended to vote for Grant, McPhail informed him that "no one who would vote for Grant could receive the support of five members of the Board," and that McIver's politics were keeping students from applying to the college.[31]

New challenges arose with the opening of North Carolina State University, the closing in 1876 of the college's Steward's Hall due to lack of patronage, and the national economic crisis of 1877. In that year the trustees, with a touch of pride, placed equal blame for lowered enrollments on the "reputation of our college for a high standard of scholarship, which is supposed to render it more difficult to enter our classes." Three years earlier, the college had felt confident enough to prepare a study comparing Davidson to four respected northern institutions, Chicago, Lafayette, Princeton, and Yale.[32]

As the trustees and faculty struggled with finances and with finding ways to attract new students and enhance the curriculum, they also worked to improve the campus. Between his duties in the state convention and his dismissal, Alexander McIver took his mathematics students onto the lawn to lay out a great circular driveway and pathways. The driveway gave both elegance and a semblance of order to the campus. The curve's being slightly elliptical and starting at the north and south on Main Street later gave rise to the expression of being on the "D."[33]

The college also continued the practice of having students plant trees. One of those students was Thomas Woodrow Wilson, the son of a Presbyterian minister who spent his freshman year (1873–74) at Davidson before transferring to Princeton University. Wilson brought distinction to Davidson first as a political science professor and college president at Princeton, and then in 1913, when he became the nation's first president since the Civil War who had been born and raised in the South. During his generally unremarkable time at the college, Wilson was known for "dressing and reaching [required] chapel in minimum time."[34]

The Railroad Returns

Being on a rail line again was of critical importance. Anticipating the return of the Atlantic, Tennessee and Ohio Railroad, the college included a reference to being "situated on the line" in the 1869 catalog. The next year the board approved a report to the presbyteries that placed the return of the railroad on equal footing with the return of prosperity in increasing admissions, donations, and the number of faculty. In 1871 the president of the AT&O Railroad spoke to the trustees, urging them to invest in Mecklenburg County bonds designated for rebuilding the line. The board did invest, but it took until 1874 for the line to begin running again. Townspeople turned out to celebrate the train's return, waving flags and cheering as the cars rolled into the depot.

In 1875 William Withers, a young physician, returned to Davidson and a railroad stockholders' meeting by riding on the top of the train. He reported that those riding with him "fared quite sumptiously both with a pleasant breeze and an abundance of dust." In another letter Withers provided some perspective on the phrase "easy of access." He noted that the schedule had changed—something that would happen with increasing and frustrating frequency in subsequent decades—and that travelers from western counties often had to plan an overnight stay in Statesville in order to make the connection to Davidson and Charlotte.[35] Still, traveling and shipping by rail was faster and, if one rode inside the train, provided better protection from the weather than traveling by wagon, buggy, or horseback.

The 1870 Census

The 1870 census offers a few insights into the Davidson area's slow recovery. For this census Davidson was included as part of Deweese township, which existed only on paper. Using a concept from the Ohio state constitution, the 1868 North Carolina constitution created townships as a new unit of county government. However useful they were for counties, they made the census once again less precise than might be wished. Still, it is possible to get a general sense of the village and surrounding area.

The township's total population, including college students, was 1,605, with 975 white and 630 black residents. Most white and black male adults were farm workers; only 103 white males and eight black males worked their own farms. Other than farm workers, occupations of white men included physicians, cabinet makers, shoemakers, professors, store clerks, carriage maker, merchants, confectioner, postmaster, chair makers, and minister, with black males working as day laborer, domestic servant, college waiter, blacksmith, and apprentice carpenter. Most women, black and white, were listed as keeping house, with four white women working as domestic servants, one as a fortune teller, and thirteen attending school. Black women were much more likely to work outside the home: forty-nine black women worked as domestic servants, seven as farm workers, four as washerwomen, and only three attended school.

Following the pattern of the rest of the state, most of the population had been born in North Carolina, thus reinforcing the regional character of the area. Of the 122 people from out of state, 88 were connected to the college, thus making the town more cosmopolitan than the surrounding area.

The Recovery of Businesses in Davidson

Lucy Phillips Russell described the town in 1868 as having "only two stores . . . , Mr. Helper's and that smaller one kept by 'Gran-pap Allison,' and later Mr. Scofield opened another. . . . Everybody was poor because the whole South was; nobody had a carriage, no fine clothes, no fine houses."[36]

When Anne Sampson arrived in 1879, there were still just three stores—now being operated by Mr. Scofield, Mr. Thompson, and Mr. Sloan. There was no market. Instead a "beef-man" came through town twice a week selling beef and pork. Sampson reported that the boarding-house owners often purchased a whole quarter at a time, leaving house-keepers empty-handed. She also noted that "'Going to Charlotte' was an event and we shopped and marketed for each other," and that large wag-ons still came down from the mountains carrying fruits and vegetables. With many families keeping chickens, "eggs were plentiful and cheap."[37]

Merchants needed the farmers, housekeepers, and students to buy goods. In 1873 Dr. Withers reported that farmers were recovering but that merchants were still doing "very little business."[38] A few boarding houses continued to attract students, although the practice of private boarding clubs remained a necessary economy for many students.

Boarding houses were becoming increasingly a woman's business. Al-though the cooks had long been black women, the owners were often men. Increasingly, instead of Mr. Sparrow or Mr. Alexander, students now boarded with Mrs. Holt, Mrs. Scofield, and Mrs. Williams. Anne Samp-son remembers Mrs. Holt as "a good businesswoman" who helped her physician husband "become quite wealthy for Davidson."[39]

Few Davidson merchants could hope to attain the wealth of their coun-terparts in Charlotte or Statesville, but by combining enterprises—stores and boardinghouses or schools and renting rooms—families were able to prosper. Hanson Helper was even able to add the somewhat whimsical improvement of a widow's walk to his hotel in 1871. Helper also was able to lend money to the college during these years. In contrast to Helper's success, the Brady store failed in 1876 and townspeople watched as workers for Charlotte merchants took goods from the store to cover debts.

Some townspeople ran smaller businesses, including doing laundry, chopping wood, and hauling goods. In 1874 laundresses were charging $1.25 a month, while boarding houses were down to $10 per month and firewood sold for $2 a cord. The town still had no barbershop; instead, a barber came from Charlotte once every two months and spent a very busy Saturday.[40]

Main Street business in 1875

For merchants the college was a critical but not guaranteed or uncomplicated source of income. Even though students needed to furnish their rooms with everyting from beds to bathing tubs to lamps, students often resold these items to one another. It would seem that local businesses would need to maintain good relationships with the college to ensure sales and room rentals to students and faculty families. But this apparent need did not prevent at least two townspeople, Thomas Sparrow and Mr. Dickey, from suing the college, or the college from pursuing cases against individuals and businesses. Not surprisingly, the college's suits against local businesses primarily concerned the sale of alcohol, but others involved property disputes.[41]

The lack of clear records relating to the college's original deed created some conflict over boundaries and town lots. In 1870 bursar John Blake reported that "several persons are trespassing upon college grounds, and in some cases seriously affecting the convenience of the village by stopping back streets, etc." Because of these problems, he urged the college to settle its boundary disputes. He also suggested selling more lots, especially those near the rail bed and along a new street on the south side of the campus.[42]

Agreeing with Blake, the trustees appointed committees to settle the boundary disputes and to sell additional lots, a process with important implications for town growth that took several years. The last boundary dispute was settled by 1873, and the college sold six lots and the Sparrow storehouse to seven men during 1873 and 1874.

The sale of these properties created opportunities for new businesses and homes. In October 1875, Dr. Withers made an optimistic report on the town's prospects, noting that "the merchants of the village have all returned with their gorgeous supplies; farmers are busy bringing in their cotton and produce generally, making the market of our little place quite lively." Withers also observed that "Davidson College has got to be quite a heavy cotton market. I think there have been as many as one hundred bales of cotton bought and sold here this season." As was the case in much of the South, the town's economy had grown substantially since its nadir ten years earlier.[43]

Employment for Former Slaves

Black women continued as cooks in the boarding houses and even free-lanced in student-founded boarding clubs. Black men cleaned the buildings, brought firewood, and maintained the college grounds.[44] These were humble tasks, but vital to the college and town; without them the faculty would have had few students to teach or useable rooms. Their labor and low wages were an integral part of the college's recovery from its financial losses.

Although Davidson blacks had few choices in employment, they remained capable of creative responses to the limitations they faced. Professor William Carson offered two examples in his reminiscences. Once in his position of superintendent of grounds he was petitioned for a permit to enter the campus, a requirement for permits being instituted after a series of "petty pilfering" incidents. According to Carson, the petitioner "had recently acquired a horse and cart" and "was planning a huge monopoly in transportation." Carson refused to grant a permit because of suspicions about the supplicant's character.[45]

On another occasion Carson sought information about why the college had trouble hiring servants despite paying "somewhat more" than area farms. He questioned one of the college janitors, asking him to speak frankly. The janitor informed Carson that "the trouble lay in the mental strain to which a janitor was necessarily subjected that a man who plowed or chopped 'don't have to study about nothing' but that this would be very far from the case with one who had 'to dust, or sweep, or take up ashes.'"[46]

The tone of his reminiscences suggests that Carson did not recognize that the "mental strain" might have had less to do with the complexity of the tasks than with the complexity of the relationships. Local blacks were considered likely suspects for any crime; college janitors would have known that suspicions would fall easily upon them and that proving their innocence would be difficult. To keep a college job would require some study to learn proper forms of deference and self-protection. This janitor appears to have learned very well how to manage Carson, providing an honest (and witty) answer without giving himself away.

Other blacks chose to find work elsewhere, leaving townspeople and area farmers to take on unpleasant tasks formerly assigned to slaves. "In common with my neighbors, I find it difficult to keep myself provided with servants," Professor William Martin complained in 1871, "and it has often been . . . cause of serious inconvenience that the water for family use has to be brought from a neighbor lot." Lacking cheap black labor, his family chose to "use water with an economy that is neither healthful nor pleasant" rather than wear themselves out obtaining larger amounts. In contrast, William Withers was able to get "all the Negroes on our farms now that I want," but his success was "more than many others have done."[47]

Racial Tensions and White Supremacy

In a private letter written a year after the war ended, President Kirkpatrick offered an insightful assessment of the racial tensions and social challenges facing the town and the surrounding area at that difficult time:

> I can hardly give you an idea of the condition of things in our
> country. We are yet under military rule, which although we have
> not suffered directly from it, is heavily complained of . . . where

the garrisons are stationed. . . . The Negroes are doing better than might have been expected. For a while they were perfectly crazy with the idea of being free. They are now much sobered down, and for the most part . . . have gone to work to make a living. But they look miserable, many of them suffering for food and other comforts. Some are trying to live by stealing, in which they are assisted by unprincipled white men, and in some places many have perished and more will perish for the want of the care which their masters once bestowed upon them, and which the Negro knows nothing of bestowing upon himself for his family. The whites are so reduced that they cannot help the Negro, where they would desire to do so. It is as much as they can do to feed their own families; for last year the crops fell short through the want of labor to work and gather them. Another year we hope will put a different face on things.[48]

Among Kirkpatrick's themes were white people's distrust of federal troops, antipathy aroused by emancipation, lingering white paternalism, and sympathy for the losses experienced by all southerners. In another passage Kirkpatrick referred to military rule as "this evil," which it was to many white southerners not only as a reminder of military defeat but also because it and the Freedman's Bureau embodied the federal government's efforts to protect blacks.

In Davidson, an altercation between a black man and Davidson students resulted in four students being fined $50 each by the head of the Charlotte Freedman's Bureau. The fine was a heavy one, and Kirkpatrick helped to obtain the money for the students. Other whites sought revenge by firing into the home of the freedman for three nights in succession, stopping only when he was chased from the village.[49]

County historian D.A. Tompkins claims that the "Ku Klux Klan played no part in Mecklenburg affairs, and though there were a few members in this section, there was not an organization in the county." Another local historian, Cornelia Shaw, notes that there was a white supremacist group in Davidson comprising students and store employees under the direction of a "Lieutenant Verner," who had been a member of the Klan elsewhere. According to Shaw, the men "frightened the colored community into good behavior. The group had all the ghostly paraphernalia which was part of the intimidating scheme." The alleged catalyst for organizing was a black man's speaking rudely to a professor's daughter.[50]

Racial tensions remained strong enough in 1875 that some students petitioned to "keep out of the college campus all colored persons to whom express permissions had not been given to enter or labor there." The faculty granted the request, adding an exception only for those blacks still attending church services in the college chapel. A few weeks later two men, Jim Burton and George Wilson, were designated as "colored persons worthy to be laborers about the college buildings and campus."[51]

At the same time, some of the students at the all-white college and white women in the town worked hard to provide a weekly Sabbath school for black residents that also served as a rudimentary school for adults as well as children. The organizers taught former slaves to read and write and also presented Presbyterian theology. Although this effort was worthwhile, it is instructive that whites at the Presbyterian Church's Board of Publication in Philadelphia, in sending reading materials to the church and to schools in Davidson, assumed that blacks were not advanced enough to read adult-level books except for the Bible.[52]

The major effects of the racism that continued in Davidson after the Civil War was a white community that felt entitled to maintain its power over blacks, on the one hand, and a cautious and subservient free black community, on the other. Whites carefully regulated social interactions to maintain their power and privilege, both through the intimidation that led to a black man feeling forced to leave town and through the relatively benign means of limiting reading materials for blacks in the Sabbath School. With local blacks facing few employment opportunities beyond working as servants or day laborers, the best hope for economic and educational advancement lay in moving to cities with more opportunities. It thus is not surprising that the percentage of blacks in the local population fell from roughly 40 percent in 1860 to 27 percent in 1900.

Religious Life

The appointment of John Blake as chairman of the faculty in 1871 created an unexpected situation in the college church. While his title was chairman, his responsibilities were those of president, including serving as college pastor. Every president prior to Blake had been an ordained minister; Blake was not. Thus other faculty would have to conduct the chapel services.

In 1878 Andrew Hepburn assumed the college presidency. With the return of an ordained minister to that office, the old pattern resumed, and he took over as college chaplain. But discontent was growing. Anne Sampson recalled that Hepburn's "mind was so upon the students that he would say 'young gentlemen' sometimes instead of 'brethren.'" Some town residents thought that "we got the crumbs from the students' table." While they might have been "mighty good crumbs," families increasingly felt "outside in that chapel."[53]

Another problem was that the "old chapel," built in 1837, was dreary and uncomfortable. By 1879 some members began "talking church" and raising funds to build a new building.[54] The process would take until 1885, but the first steps had been taken in creating a new relationship between the townspeople and the college church. While the college and congregation would remain linked, villagers attending Davidson College Presbyterian Church increasingly had an identity separate from the formerly student-dominated assemblies.

All of the faculty families attended the church, but some of the other villagers traveled to outlying churches to attend Methodist or Baptist services. Across the nation congregations became increasingly segregated as blacks either left established churches to form their own congregations or denominational governing bodies established separate churches. In Davidson, several white families attended the Methodist services at Mt. Zion. William P. Williams, soon to be Davidson's first mayor, became a lay minister and taught Sunday school there.[55]

Some black families traveled to Torrence Chapel A.M.E. Zion Church. Begun in the mid-1860s, church services were held in a brush arbor until a frame structure was built in 1869. Others, attending services in Davidson conducted by college students and women from the college church, became the nucleus of the first black church in town, originally known as Davidson United Presbyterian Church.[56]

In addition to Sunday services—sometimes lasting all day, especially for black congregations—annual camp meetings remained popular in the area. Mainly Baptist and Methodist, the meetings usually were held for one or two weeks in the late summer after harvest. Building on the camp-meeting traditions of earlier eras, the meetings were held outdoors in spaces large enough to accommodate dozens of tents. Within traveling distance of Davidson were Torrence Chapel (Mecklenburg County), Tucker's Grove (Lincoln County), Rock Springs (Lincoln County), and Balls Creek (Catawba County). Camp meetings banned alcohol from their gatherings. In 1879 a Davidson resident, Munroe Byers, almost landed in jail before convincing the authorities that the liquor found at a camp meeting was not his.[57]

Duncan Buie attended a camp meeting while a student in 1860 and wrote home to describe it:

I went to a camp meeting some time ago [and] saw lots of folks. It beat any place for women, babies, Negroes, and dogs. . . . almost every woman had a babe and every Negro a dog. When the good breatherin and sisterin began to sing and shout the babies (poor things nearly scared to death) began to cry and the dogs to howl to the sharpest shriek. I think such things as camp meetings are a nuisance to a community and should be stopped either by the good citizens or by law.[58]

While Buie found the experience too colorful for his tastes, most camp meetings after the 1870s were more like family reunions than extended revivals. They also followed the patterns of segregation, with black and white camp meetings at times located within a few miles of one another.

Health and Health Care

In February 1861 Davidson's only physician, Dr. W.L.D. McLean, committed suicide by drinking laudanum. Fortunately for a town without a doctor, Davidson was spared serious outbreaks of fevers during the war years. The college's annual reports for the years 1865 to 1879 cite only a few cases of mumps and measles in 1866, some fevers in 1869, and the death of one student from "the epidemic sweeping the country" in 1879. The general wellness of the students was echoed in the broader population. Dr. Withers commented at times about having "nothing to do, . . . as there is no sickness."[59] Of course there were illnesses and deaths: Dr. Withers lost his twenty-year-old sister to illness just as he was beginning his medical practice in Davidson, and records show that three children were buried in the college cemetery during those years. But at least the area was relatively free from the spread of deadly infectious diseases that it had experienced earlier.

The town also lacked a dentist during the war years. Dandridge Burwell, class of 1865, recalled visiting town merchant James Henderson for help with a dental problem: "I sought his services, as he had the only pair of forceps in the village, to remove an aching tooth. He removed it and a part of my jaw bone with it . . ."[60]

Schools and Education

Partly because the state government provided no funds to assist local governments until 1897, there was minimal public funding of education during the 1860s and 1870s. In Mecklenburg County in 1874, the budget was $5,346 for 46 white schools with 1,702 children and $2,948 for 34 black schools with 1,814 children. In the case of the black schools, all the money that year went for construction, leaving no funds for paying teachers.[61] Most of these schools were in the southern part of the county. Children in Davidson attended private schools or made do with Sabbath schools.

During the war years, two women who moved to Davidson opened schools. George McIver attended classes conducted by Mrs. Taylor, who had fled from Charleston after its capture by Union troops. Mrs. Holt, whose husband was an army surgeon, opened a school for girls. According to Cornelia Shaw, "pupils came [to Mrs. Holt's school] from nearby towns and the surrounding country. Some of the texts studied were Cleveland's *Grecian Antiquities*, Alexander's *Evidences of Christianity*, and *History of Belles Lettres*, which stood for polite and elegant literature." As befitted a female academy, her students also studied fine needlework.[62]

Mrs. Taylor left Davidson for Tennessee after a year or two, but Mrs. Holt remained, and after the war she and her doctor husband made Davidson their home. But she closed her school shortly after her husband's return. Lucy Russell recalled attending a private school held in the Masonic Hall. Her teachers were college students who alternated teaching and attending school.[63]

Because the school term lasted only four months, leaving time for children to help with farm and other work, Sabbath schools were an important supplement for both black and white children. Lucy Russell recalled long hours on Saturday afternoons in the college chapel going over Bible verses and the Presbyterian "shorter catechism" under the tutelage of faculty. For black children, Sabbath school occurred on Sunday afternoons with college students assisted by women from the town.[64]

There are no records for private academies for black students in town, but the 1870 census listed a number of black children as attending school. Some were old enough to be attending the newly founded Biddle Memorial Institute in Charlotte (now Johnson C. Smith University) and Scotia Seminar in Concord (now Barber-Scotia College). One of the students from Davidson listed in Biddle Institute catalogs was A.E. Houston.

A few faculty families continued to send daughters to Winston-Salem or Raleigh to boarding schools. A hard-working, capable young woman from the Mt. Mourne area, Mary Scofield, wanted very much to take classes at the college, but Elijah Rockwell turned down her father's request.[65] Other young women, especially the daughters of President Kirkpatrick, had easier access to college classes, thus opening the way for more young women to take classes at the college. Although there were rarely more than three or four "co-eds" at any time, none of whom were permitted to graduate, they reflected the acceptance and encouragement given to some women to pursue education beyond high-school Latin and fine needlework.

Clubs and Entertainment

Mary Scofield was not the only assertive young woman in the area. Lucy Russell noted that her older sister and several other girls, including Mary and Lily McPhail and Mary and Sue Anderson, formed a "secret society." They called themselves the "I.S.H.H." which some interpreted as "I shall have a husband" but which really meant "Independent Seekers of Health and Happiness." They pursued both goals by taking long walks every afternoon.[66]

Faculty wives also enjoyed socializing on long walks. Anne Sampson recalled that they often took long walks on the railroad ties, and whimsically named two large pines along their path "Gog" and "Magog." But village life was not entirely provincial: the return of the Latimer family after a year in Europe brought a bit of the world to Davidson, and not just in the form of Mrs. Latimer's much admired Paris bonnet.[67]

While Anne Sampson remembered that "[s]ocial life was almost nil," townspeople could and did find many diversions. For the more literary minded there was a Friday evening "Reading Circle." And a music club was formed for the musically inclined. Its members not only served as the choir in chapel but also were adventurous enough to carry their instruments to the cupola of the Chambers Building and perform open-air concerts.

Young women in the college church skirted restrictions on dramatic plays by adopting the delightful nineteenth-century practice of tableaus. These consisted of arranging constumed scenes of historical or religious events. No one spoke lines, but narration was permitted to identify and explain the scene. Because tableaus were intended to be educational, they were acceptable enough to be presented regularly in the chapel. The young ladies no doubt had great fun in preparing constumes and planning the evenings.

The first mention of baseball in college or town records appears in 1871, when students requested permission to play a Charlotte team. The request was denied, but games in town continued unabated. George McIver remembered students taking up the game in the fall of 1865. He had been told that Confederate soldiers, having learned the game in northern prison camps, brought it back to southern towns and campuses. In the winter, young townspeople would carry their skates to ponds two or three miles away; in the spring and summer, croquet matches were popular.[68]

Circuses and fairs in Charlotte remained popular, and the centennial celebration of the Mecklenburg Declaration of Independence on 20 May 1875 drew huge crowds from all the surrounding towns.[69] While Fourth of July celebrations generally became less popular across the South in the 1860s and 1870s, county residents added extra emphasis to the already popular May 20th observances.

Within the town, commencement weekends, holidays, and national elections provided occasions for celebrations. Commencement of 1871 was a somber affair because college president George McPhail died during the week. But other years saw hundreds of people coming into town for fellowship and diversions—and, not least, to congratulate the graduates and wish them well. Along with the speeches and musical programs, visitors could enjoy concession stands selling ice cream, soda water, and other refreshments.

A decade earlier, President Kirkpatrick expressed his concern to the trustees about the "disorder" in the weeks preceding the Christmas break. Recognizing that it "is simply impracticable to dispense with the Christmas recess," he sought ways to limit the pranks stemming from a contagious "Christmas in the bones" levity. No doubt villagers shared his concerns. Typical pranks involved creating as much noise as possible. Duncan Buie admitted to being in a band called the Davidson Busters, playing an instrument "called the lionet—It makes a noise resembling, very much, the roar of a lion. . . . At every house we would sing a song before we left." Another band member, James Greenlee, described a "masquerade" held one night: "a party of about twenty of us with paper masks and pillow slips on our heads and blankets and sheets over our shoulders, and banjos, tambourines, fluid cans, and tin pans in hands sallied forth to serenade the faculty and ladies."[70]

Letters from postwar years suggest that Christmases generally became quieter. The season did offer occasions for festive socials and suppers, although apparently not enough to suit Joseph Rankin, who found the 1869 Christmas in Davidson very dull because none of the young ladies had invited him to any of the suppers. Dr. Withers had better luck in 1875, attending "tea parties and one jolly dance."[71]

Conclusion

In November 1876, students and townspeople held a torchlight parade to celebrate Democrat Zebulon Vance's election as governor. With seventy-five torches, a barrel of rosin, and signs declaring "Grantism is dead," "Zeb the true Tar Heel," and "Freedmans Bank," they formed a procession "with several Negroes in the front ranks. . . . We first went up the street toward Dr. Hepburn's, then turned and went to Mr. Williams, where Dr. Thomas Moore gave us a good little talk. We then marched around for about half an hour, then concluded with throwing up a lot of fire balls." The balls were made with rags soaked in kerosene. According to participant H.E. Fries, "The boys threw them in all directions, and as they were all at different heights, it made a very brilliant display."[72]

At the end of its fourth decade, Davidson could not be called much of a display, brilliant or otherwise. Main Street still made a rustic backdrop to improvised fireworks. But the village was beginning to come more fully into its own. Having survived the losses of the war and beginning to adapt to the resulting economic and social changes, its economy was reasonably stable.

With this stability came clearer social divisions, not only between blacks and whites but also within each group. While blacks and whites might join together in an occasional parade, their work and educational opportunities were increasingly defined by economic status and by the overt favoritism for whites that endured for many decades after the end of Reconstruction. As the town moved toward incorporation, it was pulled along by the region's political, economic, and social tides.

3 The Town Incorporates and Grows, 1879–1900

That the town of Davidson College . . . is hereby incorporated into a body politic and corporate by the name . . . of the town of Davidson College, to have the usual powers of such corporations to sue and be sued, to plead and be impleaded, contract and be contracted with, and to make all needful rules and regulations, bylaws and ordinances for the government of said town, not inconsistent with the constitution and laws of this State and of the United States.[1]

On 11 February 1879 Davidson entered a new era. On that date the North Carolina General Assembly officially incorporated the town of Davidson College. A new mayor and five commissioners took office on February 17. Taking seriously their change to manage this new legal entity, they quickly enacted several ordinances designed to bring order and direction to the rambling village. Over the next two decades, the town government's decisions concerning roads, health and sanitation issues, telephones, businesses, cotton-weighing regulations, law enforcement, and the town's name cumulatively, if sometimes unintentionally, encouraged a new sense of community identity.

Despite the undeniable significance of the new government, there was at least as much continuity as change in the town's life from 1879 until the end of the nineteenth century. Among the elements of continuity were the community's rural grounding, its racial hierarchy with whites above blacks, the centrality of the college as an employer and source of town identity, and a dynamic mix of communities based on race and social class combining to form the whole. But the town also saw significant changes

Advertisements from the *Davidson Monthly*

with the establishment of a medical college, cotton mills, new churches, and schools.

The town's growth, whether measured in the number of buildings and businesses or in relative sophistication, was built upon its rural character. The town's incorporated area included farm land, and many families maintained stables and livestock as a matter of course. Town merchants continued to rely on area farmers as customers. J.D. Brown's advertisements listed grain cradles, mowing scythes, packages of Pape and Company's "celebrated" horse and cattle powders alongside hats, shoes, groceries, and tinware. Similarly, M.W. Cranford's stock of buggies—plus saddles, collars, and harnesses for the horses who pulled them—required customers from outside of the village and college.[2]

The college still provided a sense of distinction, setting Davidson apart from surrounding communities. Other area towns could boast of private academies, but the college gave residents opportunities to hear distinguished lecturers and also provided both the elan and influence of professors, many of whom had studied in Europe. The arrival of new professors and the travels of faculty families lent a certain cosmopolitan polish to the community. The number of faculty members hovered around six or seven during these decades; but as the student body approached two hundred, the number of jobs the college generated, directly and indirectly, expanded.

With the coming of the mills, the town's mix of communities expanded. Professors, laundresses, merchants, and mill workers still lived in close proximity, partly because many families continued to take boarders. But economic and racial divisions were becoming more apparent. Both blacks and whites were expected to work on the college cemetery even though no blacks could be buried there. Mill housing put these white families in a separate neighborhood on the west side, and their children had fewer opportunities to attend school. And while most married white women listed their occupation as keeping house, most married black women worked outside of their homes. More often than not, while also maintaining their own households, they were employed as servants or cooks, or they took in washing.

The creation of a town government complemented the already established pattern of civic cooperation. With a street committee and an ordinance allowing work on roads to substitute for taxes, the town government provided a better structure for large projects such as road maintenance. But it did not supplant or diminish the activities of civic groups to improve the town and assist one another.

Many of the civic groups were connected with the local churches. With no theaters or saloons in town, and no community hall, churches provided welcome social outlets and encouraged service and charity work. The King's Daughters and Junior King's Daughters of Davidson College Presbyterian Church creatively combined fund-raising for charitable projects with entertainment. Revivals and camp meetings continued to provide excuses for extended visiting, and church dinners gave townspeople a chance to gather, sometimes across congregations, sometimes within. Sunday schools might not have been children's preferred form of recreation, but they did provide time for being with other children and the possibility of refreshments.

Establishing a Town Government

The first mayor and commissioners received little compensation for their work. The mayor received two dollars per day when working on tax lists, reimbursement for office rent and stationery, and fees for conducting trials as the town's acting judge. The commissioners got no pay except for the treasurer and clerk, who received nominal sums. The board's responsibilities included establishing town ordinances, levying and collecting taxes, electing the town marshal, and supervising improvements to public property, with roads being their main concern for many years. The first ordinance for the town set a monthly board meeting to be held the first Tuesday of every month at 7 p.m., but that schedule was rarely followed. In their first full year of meetings, the board failed to convene together for five months out of the twelve.

Reflecting the diverse character of the town community, the initial board appointed by the General Assembly included William Williams, a Methodist lay minister; William Martin, a college professor; Hanson Helper, a farmer and former merchant and innkeeper; Robert Query, another farmer; and S.T. Thompson, whose occupation is uncertain. Thompson, who died within two weeks of taking office, was replaced by James Allison, a grocer and confectioner. This board served from February to May 1879, when the town held its first election and the entire board was returned. While all male and all white, the board did represent differing occupations and churches.

Bylaws and Taxes

After electing John Johnston marshal, the commissioners adopted a set of bylaws for the corporation. The first section set up rules for the board, including setting the monthly meeting date, establishing the board's right to assess taxes, granting the mayor the power to punish any persons refusing to comply with town ordinances, and requiring that the commissioners and marshal put the town streets in good order "as soon as practicable." Levies included a dog tax and a poll tax of one dollar for all men between the ages of twenty-one and fifty, with an exception allowing two days' work on the streets to substitute for the tax and—in a telling reminder of the lingering effects of the Civil War—an exemption for all "maimed and halt persons."[3]

The second chapter of the "Laws for the Corporation" included ordinances regulating residents. Among others, these included making the sale of intoxicating liquors within town limits a misdemeanor punishable by fines up to $25 or up to thirty days in jail; forbidding "fighting, quarreling or . . . disturbing the peace and quiet of the village," "using profane . . . or vulgar language, or singing obscene songs, or making indecent exposure of their person"; firing a gun within two hundred yards of any street in town or running a horse or mule through the streets; and regulating smoking and the storage of flammable materials around the railroad station.[4]

The college's influence was evident not only in the banning of alcohol sales but in the size of the fines. All of the other offenses—disturbing the peace, firing pistols, creating fire hazards—were fined only fifty cents to five dollars. The image of the village established by these laws is of a bustling market town with some rough edges, but orderly overall. The fact that the marshal could be assigned the time-consuming tasks of street work and tax collecting reflects a fairly low concern about crime. Annual audits of the marshal's account bear out a low crime rate (or a very lenient sheriff), for fines collected rarely exceeded twenty dollars.

The first tax assessment showed a total property value of $71,737, fifty-four men eligible for the poll tax, and nineteen dogs. The first tax levied was at the rate of one-sixth of one percent (about seventeen cents per $100 valuation), making the town's operating budget $196.62. The marshal set to work and collected $142.75 in cash and $26.04 in work, with the remaining $27.53 still to be collected as of 1 May 1879 and $23 still to be collected that November. The original act of incorporation limited the tax rate to not more than thirty-three and one-third cents per $100, a limit that was reached briefly in 1882 and then for a much longer period in the 1890s.

Reflecting the generally low incomes and modest businesses and homes in Davidson compared to many northern towns and cities, the village's budget rarely exceeded a few hundred dollars. The primary expenses were the marshal's salary, lumber for sidewalks, and street repair costs.

Contemporary Elections

During the years 1879–1900, five men served as mayor. William Williams had the longest tenure, serving from 1879 to 1889 and again from 1891 to 1895. Three of the others—Robert Shelton, John Brown, and Frank Knox—were involved in the cotton business, thus reflecting the growing importance of cotton for the town. The number of candidates for town commissioner varied: in 1887, for example, ten candidates ran for the five commissioner positions, whereas in 1894 there were only six candidates. Black as well as white men voted in town elections, at least in the 1890s. The list of the forty voters casting ballots on 7 May 1894, for example, includes the names of at least twelve African-American voters.[5]

National elections appear to have generated greater excitement than local elections. When Grover Cleveland was elected in 1884, thus becoming the first Democratic president-elect since the Civil War, students launched a torchlight parade using oil-soaked rags tied to sticks. When Democratic vice-presidential candidate Adlai Stevenson spoke briefly during a train stop in Davidson during the 1892 election, college students greeted him with a paraphrase of the college yell: "Rah! Rah! Rah!!! Whoop-la-run! Democracy! Stevenson!" As further proof that the town (including the college) had become largely Democratic in its politics, the celebration of Cleveland and Stevenson's victory in the 1892 election included bonfires, fireworks, a parade, and impromptu speeches by Reverend M.A. Smith, Reverend Alfred Graham, and Dr. John Dupuy.[6]

Renaming the Town

When the town was first incorporated in 1879, its leaders willingly chose the familiar, well-established name of Davidson College. The shared name led to some good-natured humor, as when the editor of the *Davidson College Magazine* complained that, with the college, village, and post office having the same name, "All the elopements, fights, etc., that happen [with]in a mile or two of the college are placed by the reading public to the credit of *us innocent* students."[7] (italics in original)

Whatever the minor confusions, by the early 1890s the village increasingly had an identity separate from the college. The commissioners acknowledged this change by proposing to rename the town as part of a larger charter revision. The first mention of a new charter and possible names appeared in the 6 January 1891 minutes when the board "went into a committee of the whole on town charter and a new name for the town." During this and subsequent meetings, several names were bandied about, starting with Hempstead but also including Canton and Brandon. Eventually the board passed the charter unanimously with Hempstead as the new name for the town. Even after that vote, a new member of the board, Dr. John Munroe, tried to change the name back to Davidson College.[8]

Dr. Munroe's effort failed, and the town board sent the charter, including the new name of Hempstead, to the General Assembly, where the proposed new name sparked yet another debate. While evidence is lacking, it seems reasonable to infer that North Carolinians unhappy with the proposed name change, perhaps including some town residents and alumni who lived in Charlotte and Mooresville, contacted their representatives to express their displeasure. Whatever the specific reasons, a story in the Statesville *Landmark* reported that "there arose quite a discussion" during the third reading of the bill. A representative from Charlotte, R.A. Grier, proposed an amendment requring that the people of the town vote on the change, and an amendment offered by T.J. Williams of Mooresville replaced the name "Hempstead" with "Davidson."[9] After both amendments were adopted, a new town charter for "Davidson" was approved. There is no record of the town voting on the name. Nonetheless, the final choice was an apt one. The village was still tied closely enough to the college to make a name such as Hempstead artificial and even awkward. But it also was becoming established enough to justify some distinction in names between town and college.

The Town's Roads Gradually Improve

Roads were critical in the town's development and in its ongoing relationship to the college. Prior to incorporation, the college controlled the location of streets through laying out and selling lots. While Mecklenburg County undertook some improvements, overall road conditions remained primitive.[10] The commissioners began addressing town roads at their first meeting; the subject would remain central in the next decades, taking up a large portion of the board's time and the town's budget.

In addition to the ongoing needs of general maintenance work, the town tackled larger projects, including twice straightening sections of Main Street, putting in street lamps, putting in plank sidewalks and rock crosswalks, laying out Concord Road (the town's second major road) in 1886, and hiring a lawyer to recover the road tax previously paid to the county.[11] An 1883 editorial in the *Weekly Enterprise*, "The Town Awakes from its Rip Van Winkle Sleep," praised the board's road improvements, especially the installation of street lamps.[12] Largely due to financial constraints, however, progress remained slow over the next several years.

A major step forward occurred in 1887 with an amendment of the charter granting the town the right to condemn private property in order to build new streets and widen existing ones. It also provided for a system of arbitration to settle compensation disputes. Town voters approved the measure by a vote of 69 to 27. Praising the decision, the *Davidson College Magazine* commented that the town soon would be able to "open new streets" and "assume a more business-like appearance."[13]

Within weeks of the 1887 charter approval, commissioners were meeting with local landowners about acquiring property for widening streets; within six months they were appointing arbitrators to set property values. The opening of streets not only allowed for future growth by providing access to lots but also permitted the town to place taxes on "all vacant lots . . . on streets kept open by the town."[14]

Yet the condition of town streets remained primitive well into the 1890s, largely due to the high cost of acquiring a rock crusher and macadamizing roads. Life in the village was still rustic. With red clay streets, alternately dirty or muddy, rock crossings, plank sidewalks, a line of wooden storefronts, horses and wagons tied up along Main Street and livestock pens next to homes, Davidson looked more like a Dodge City with farmers and students instead of cowboys than a pristine college town of dignified homes and orderly appearance.

In April 1897 the student magazine deplored the condition of Main Street:

> Whenever you leave the campus on [the west] side, you must jump across a zigzag gully, partly filled with stones and all manner of debris from the town and college, while over all the rankest weeds and creeping vines run riot in every direction; or you must cross by stumbling over some decayed broken-down footbridge. The whole street is an eyesore and detracts enormously from the otherwise beautiful sward beyond. Cannot something be done soon to rectify it?[15]

Mayor Knox was able to procure use of a road machine, and by June 1897 Davidson streets showed some improvement. But soon enough the rain and sleet of the winter months again made the streets muddy and dangerous.

In 1899 the town issued $6,000 in bonds to macadamize the streets and improve the sidewalks. That November the *Davidson Monthly* reported that "the long talked of macadam" had partially replaced "the inimitable Davidson red clay" on the town's streets.[16] "Since the town macadamized Main Street, the once familiar term 'Red Sea' has become obsolete," the same publication noted three years later. "With the other roads completed, the horrors of the red mud of Davidson should live henceforth only in legend and history."[17] In addition, the bonds made possible the brick sidewalks that the town board had considered "impracticable" earlier.

Improved Sanitation and Wells

While addressing the mud and dust of the streets, the commissioners also addressed sanitation issues, often with the same slow pace toward improvement. In June 1886 they passed an ordinance regulating privies and hog pens or any "other building which . . . is a nuisance to persons living in the vicinity."[18] Three years later the college faculty urged the town to look into additional sanitary measures, but it took the town until 1895 to establish a Sanitary Committee and finally to expand on the 1886 ordinance, levying a tax from April to October for the maintenance of privies. The first contract for cleaning the privies went to the mayor, J.D. Brown, with fees of one dollar a day for the first cleaning and $1.50 per week after that. Longtime resident Ralph Johnson remembered Andy Byers operating the town's "sugar wagon" in addition to his blacksmith shop. The ordinance also banished pig pens from within 200 feet of Main Street, and required that all pig pens be cleaned weekly during the summer months.[19]

In 1890, at the request of the college's sanitary commissioner, Henry Louis Smith, the board appointed a Low Land Drainage Committee to investigate local swamps and ponds. Townspeople's response to this committee fell short of the usual standard for civic cooperation. After visiting several sites and meeting with the property owners, the committee reported that the owners "refused to contribute anything as to defraying expenses." The town board responded by ordering J.G. Hood to drain his fish pond and having ditches dug on the Hood and R.M. Armour properties.[20]

The college took the lead in providing safe drinking water. In 1898 the college hired an artesian well firm from Atlanta to dig a well to furnish water for college, town, and railroad. The firm worked from fall 1898 through the following spring, and by June 1899 the college was able to supply water to the town. The commissioners willingly gave the college permission to lay water pipes throughout the town.[21]

The impetus for the new works came from a typhoid epidemic at the college in the summer of 1898. In response, the college closed the existing two wells on campus and sought to provide a safer water supply to ensure student health. Walter Lingle, class of 1892, noted in his memoirs that, in conjunction with the new wells, the "first shower bath, or bath of any kind, in the history of the college was installed."[22] It was attached to Morrison Hall, the college YMCA and gymnasium building.

Upholding Law and Order

In addition to public health concerns, the town board increasingly faced public safety issues. In 1883 the commissioners ordered the first guard house to be built—an 8 by 16 foot, two-room building not to exceed $50 in construction costs. How much this tiny building was used is uncertain. In 1896 the mayor was instructed to "build a suitable guard house," but with the usual slow pace of town government, no further action was taken until 1899, when a committee was appointed to oversee the construction of a new guard house with a "steel cell."[23]

A few instances of crime appeared in the *Enterprise* and other contemporary records. In June 1883 Edwin Taylor abandoned his barber shop after being accused of stealing shoes from E.B. Sloan's store and reselling them in Charlotte. In 1884 two area residents, Suel White and Henry Hunter, were arrested for stealing pork from Mr. Mull's smokehouse. Two other residents, J.G. Hood and J.W. Summers, faced possible imprisonment for disturbing the peace, but the town commissioners spared them after the board concluded that "they have suffered sufficiently at the hands of civil court."[24]

The goal of many town ordinances was to regulate and, in some cases, to protect and promote town businesses. In 1889, for example, the board approved a $5 fee for non-residents wishing to sell confections during Commencement. The revised charter of 1891 greatly expanded the list of license taxes, although most of the new levies were again intended for non-local enterprises such as peddlers, circuses, theatricals, and rope dancers. Davidson's first Sunday-closing law appeared in June 1893 with an ordinance making the selling of any goods on Sundays "except for burial purposes or for sickness" a misdemeanor. Such laws reflected concerns about commerce and morality. And because streets and sidewalks were never far from the commissioners' minds, it is not surprising that fines were imposed for obstructing sidewalks with merchandise or displays.[25]

Cotton Weighing and the Founding of Cornelius

One of the most significant decisions affecting business occurred in 1886, when the town board, prompted by Charlotte's decision to regulate cotton weighing, held a special meeting and voted to appoint a cotton weigher for Davidson as well. Heretofore two businesses, the R.J. Stough Company and Sloan Brothers, handled the weighing, with customers coming from as far away as Lincoln County. The board's action created a split in the town, and R.J. Stough moved his scales outside the town into what is now Cornelius. He soon opened a store in conjunction with his cotton weighing operation.

The significance of this ordinance is that Stough's move proved to be the beginning of a new town in Mecklenburg County. Cornelius, as it came to be known, played an unintentional role in the life of its neighbor, Davidson. To generalize public perceptions in Davidson, Cornelius was to be the mill town to Davidson's college town. Even with an overlap in populations, with some families crossing town borders, the two towns developed very different characters. Reflecting the familiar human desire to feel superior, some Davidson residents, including even school children, soon began to consider themselves "better" than their "inferior" neighbors to the south.[26]

Davidson's First Cotton Mill

Considering these feelings of superiority, it is ironic that Davidson itself had a cotton mill from the 1890s until the 1950s. The initial pattern for textile manufacturing in North Carolina was to establish small villages near streams and rivers. With the advent of steam engines, cotton mills also were established in a few towns and cities. It was not until 1881 that the first mill was built in Mecklenburg County, but by 1900 there were seventeen mills in the city of Charlotte and 300 within a 100 mile radius of Charlotte.[27]

The firm that built the first cotton mill in Davidson, the Linden Manufacturing Company, was incorporated in 1890 and built on the west side of town on land purchased from the college. It was truly a local company, as shown by the fact that all six of Linden's directors had served on the town board. Two of them, Henry Louis Smith and W.G. Graves, were professors at the college, and the other four were local merchants. Some of the six were related by marriage. Given the fact that all six directors were prominent residents, two of whom were serving on the town board, and given the widespread links between politics and business in America at the time, it is not surprising that in 1891 the town board granted the company a twenty-year exemption from having to pay local property taxes.[28]

By November 1891 the *Davidson College Magazine* reported that the town's "cotton mills are still booming. . . . There are 2,800 spindles running all the time, and the [company's] president informs us that more are to be added shortly. The machinery . . . has all the latest improvements. An automatic fire extinguisher will be put in during the next few days. They already have electric lights in full running order." Another report a few months later noted increased success: "The hum of our cotton mills can now be heard both day and night, thus giving Davidson the sound of progress and prosperity. . . . The president of the mills tells us that their product is of the very highest grade, and is readily disposed of at the top of the market."[29]

The cheerfully lauded prosperity was good news for the town, and the jobs offered increased incomes for former farmers and laborers seeking steady employment. For those who worked long hours and graveyard shifts, however, the jobs came at a price. Mill workers were segregated from their neighbors by the hours they worked and also by limited access to activities and services in the town, especially schools and churches. Mill managers, especially Joseph P. Munroe, responded to these needs by creating housing, organizing a mill chapel, and encouraging college students to help with educational programs.

Mill Hill, as it was known, was not a mill village in the usual sense. The directors built rental housing for mill families, but there was no company store—or, as in the original pattern in North Carolina—a separate village with the mill as its center. Instead, the mill and the small houses nearby were located within the boundaries of the already established town.

Patterns of interaction within the town reflected the shifts and continuities in southern society, with the college and businesses forming professional and semi-professional social strata, blacks forming a servant and working class, and white mill workers forming a separate working class. The dividing lines were not necessarily stark. Nevertheless, despite close relationships between black servants and affluent white families and the interaction of students with mill workers, the social and economic divisions between the groups were deepening. The unspoken understanding of difference and station was reflected in clothing, language, homes, and churches.

While Davidson's cotton sales occasionally matched Charlotte's, having on one day marketed 147 bales to Charlotte's 148, a substantial, multicompany mill district never developed. Instead, the three additions to the town's manufacturing and commercial operations in the 1890s were a cotton gin built on Concord Road, a brick warehouse for storing cotton constructed near the depot, and a cottonseed processing firm, the Southern Cotton Oil Mill Company, located on South Main Street near the southern end of town. According to a contemporary report, "the oil mill processed the byproducts of [cotton] ginning—lint and seed. The lint was used for bedding material or gun powder, while the seeds were cooked and the oil pressed from them. The oil was shipped to a New Jersey refinery, and the remaining hulls and crushed seeds went for livestock feed."[30]

Changes on the Business Scene

The incorporation of the town and the work of the commissioners—as commissioners—created the necessary frameworks for the village to grow, while individual commissioners—as businessmen—brought new industries and technologies to town. Following the pattern of the cotton mill, two commissioners—Joseph P. Munroe and William J. Martin, Jr.—served on the board of the first telephone franchise, established around 1898. Telephones first appeared in Raleigh in 1879, in Charlotte in 1883, and in Asheville in 1886, so Davidson was late in establishing this service.

Alongside businesses dependent on cotton, the town's longstanding trades continued to serve students, townspeople, and families from the surrounding countryside. During the 1880s and 1890s, enrollment at the college grew from 88 to 190 students; the town population also more than doubled, from not quite 400 to just over 900. Outside of town, Mecklenburg County's rural areas continued the shift toward smaller tenant farms, with roughly 60 percent of all farms occupied by whites and 40 by blacks.[31] Attracted by steady work in Davidson's factories and other businesses, some farm-to-town families from Mecklenburg and neighboring counties contributed to the town's growing population.

Serving students at Davidson College and the new Medical College, boarding houses remained a fixture in town but ownership shifted frequently. A boarding house that opened in March 1889, for example, closed in January 1890. The wives of Dr. Wooten and Rev. Luther Wilson added to their family incomes by opening boarding houses in 1895. Laura Alexander ran the boarding club at the Brady house from October 1896 until her marriage in December 1898. Mr. and Mrs. McLeod took over her house, but no one took over the Sloan house when it closed in 1899.[32]

The merchants serving students and others in town also experienced substantial turnover. The Thompson store, a town fixture since 1852, changed hands with John Thompson's death in 1892. His son, W.H. Thompson, added his initials to the store sign, but sold out a year later to W.G. Sawyer. Two years later Sawyer moved into a new building. His move followed that of Lee Sloan, who in 1895 opened a new grocery store in what was Mr. Cranford's old store, Mr. Cranford having moved into J.G. Hood's business, Mr. Hood having moved to Charlotte. Then and later, operating a store in Davidson often was a risky, unremunerative venture.

The town apparently was ready for a new lawyer in 1889. Owen Brown, son of merchant and town commissioner John Brown, passed his exams and opened a practice in the village in that year. Other additions included a sawmill in 1895 and a livery stable in 1896. While not a new enterprise and only occasionally dependent upon economic conditions, the town's post office added considerably to the Main Street alterations. Its location changed at least four times between 1888 and 1898.[33]

Race Relations in the Jim Crow Era

The Jim Crow era deepened divisions between blacks and whites and institutionalized segregation in the South as most of the gains made by blacks during Reconstruction were lost. The *Charlotte Observer* published news stories and editorials that disparaged blacks. Members of the Young Democrats Club, mostly rising businessmen in Charlotte, paraded downtown on horseback while wearing red shirts, flashing weapons, and, one historian has noted, "proclaiming the superiority of the white race."[34]

In Davidson, the political currents were less dramatic, but there was at least one incident of racial violence and an increasing pattern of ignoring black concerns and isolating individuals. In 1889 the college trustees put off the request by "a committee of the colored citizens" for "a grant of land for a burying ground." And the college continued its policy of restricting access to the campus. "Only a select few . . . colored citizens will be allowed the privilege of coming on the campus this year," the *Davidson College Magazine* reported in October 1892. "The superintendent of grounds, Dr. Smith, [sees] this as the best method to be adopted, as a preventative against trouble, in the way of petty thieving, etc., which arose last year."[35]

Despite the restrictions, on one occasion the administration granted

African-American staff at the college in 1895

permission for two black baseball teams to play on college property. Unfortunately the game ended in violence. Walter Lingle described the altercation in his memoirs:

> The game went on beautifully for a while, but unfortunately a Negro spectator from Concord got in front of a hot-tempered [white] student from the town of Davidson. The student ordered him to get out of his line of vision. As he didn't move promptly the student cut him with a riding whip. He got out of the way and said nothing, but another Negro took it up and used some abusive language to the student, and made as if he was ready to fight. The student drew his pistol. The Negro ducked into the crowd with the student right after him with drawn pistol. He did have sense enough not to shoot into the crowd. As the Negro emerged from the crowd he was right under the window where I sat, with the student a few paces behind. When the student was immediately under my window he fired at the Negro, who was running in the direction of the Richardson athletic field. Fortunately he missed him. . . . In the meantime pandemonium reigned supreme. Some students got hold of the baseball bats and were swinging them right and left. The field was soon cleared and nobody was really hurt. Later the Concord team sent a friendly Davidson Negro to the students asking if they might have their bats and sweaters. The request was speedily granted and the incident was closed. But it might have been terrible, and all on account of a hot temper.[36]

The incident might be chalked up to one hot-tempered person, but underlying the conflict was an assertion of white privilege and the expectation of subservience. Even though the students "speedily" returned the bats and sweaters when asked, it is noteworthy that they had to be asked. No doubt there was a range of attitudes toward race relations among the students and white townspeople. Nevertheless, while the student magazine republished several articles from other college papers advocating segregation, no articles appeared that challenged those views. Presumably no challenges came from the pulpits of "white" churches, either.

The Vitality of Organized Religion

Christian churches were in transition. Locally, there were new buildings and new congregations; nationally and regionally, while still dealing with the effects of the divisions of the Civil War era, churches were faced with shifts in theology with the rise of the Social Gospel movement, the arrival of evolutionary theories in biology and historical criticism of Scripture, and a public with a growing acceptance of science and scientific methods and a willingness to entertain new questions. The Social Gospel movement encouraged church members to work to improve the lives of the poor—not just through charity, but also by addressing social and economic issues. A renewed interest in prohibition also brought an overlap in religious and political spheres.

Religion remained central to the lives of people in Davidson and the surrounding area. Mecklenburg County stayed predominantly Protestant, with nearly 200 Protestant churches but only one Catholic church and one recognized Jewish community (but no synagogue). The county was known for its large number of white Presbyterian, Methodist, and Baptist churches, and for the equally impressive presence of black Methodist congregations. Well before *Plessy v. Ferguson* (1896) made "separate but equal" a legal standard, religious segregation had been firmly established in North Carolina, partly because African-Americans wished to control their own churches.[37]

In Davidson, Presbyterians were preeminent, especially among whites. Within the town limits, four new church buildings were constructed between 1885 and 1897, two for black congregations and two for white ones. The black churches were Davidson Presbyterian Church and Reeves Temple African Methodist Episcopal (A.M.E.) Zion Church; the white churches were Davidson College Presbyterian Church (DCPC) and the Mill Chapel. While the Mill Chapel initially was not affiliated with any specific denomination, most of the leadership was Presbyterian.

The new church buildings helped to maintain the influence of religion in the town. Churches were not just for Sunday sermons or Wednesday Bible study. They contributed directly to education and entertainment, provided structures for many organizations, were conduits for charity, and marked social boundaries between classes as well as denominations.

The grandest of the new structures built in this era was DCPC. The resignation of Andrew Hepburn as the college's president in 1885 opened the way for the church to separate from the college. The college donated land for the church with the proviso that the "building be a neat and substantial brick structure costing not less than $2,500." When completed, the church cost $6,318, with all the funds raised by church members—even the Children's Society contributed funds for a chandelier and bracket lamps. The college also provided land for Davidson Presbyterian Church, whose members not only raised funds but provided labor to construct the

Davidson College Presbyterian Church, 1885–1950

building. In contrast to the brick DCPC, Davidson Presbyterian, Reeves Temple, and the Mill Chapel were all simple wooden structures.[38]

None of the buildings afforded much comfort. The plea of *Weekly Enterprise* editor Robert Sparrow to heat the new DCPC with a furnace instead of stoves—because stoves caused "extremes of heat and cold in different parts of the room"—apparently went unheeded. In 1892, church services moved back to the old chapel for a month after a large stovepipe broke. "Someone has said that the Lord builds churches, but sometimes the devil gets the contract for heating, lighting, and ventilating," Walter Lingle quipped years later. "That saying seems to apply at least to certain areas in the old church at Davidson."[39]

After several years of short-term and supply pastors, including even an occasional Methodist minister occupying the pulpit, the Reverend Alfred Graham arrived in May 1891 and, happily for the congregation, remained until 1907.[40] By April 1894 the church's membership had grown to 172, with thirty-two joining in the past six months. Yet church budgets and ministers' salaries remained low, and pastors often had other jobs such as teaching or tailoring to supplement their incomes.

Davidson Presbyterian Church

Although it is likely that not more than half of the villagers were members of a church, churches were important organizations for the town. In addition to religion, their roles extended into education, civics, philanthropy, and recreation. Even more than their white counterparts, black churches supported the educational, political, and business activities of their members.

The oldest of the black congregations is the Davidson Presbyterian Church. The congregation formed in the 1870s and erected a church building just west of the railroad tracks in 1894. The college trustees' action in donating land for the church anticipated the decision of the Presbyterian General Assembly's Committee of Colored Evangelization in 1897 to establish a separate church for "colored people."[41]

One of the church's earliest pastors was the Reverend Baker, who also worked as a tailor. When he left in 1892 for a church in Lincolnton, the editors of the *Davidson College Magazine* called his departure "quite a loss" since "he and his family were Davidson's only tailors and they did their work well." In an example of that era's paternalism and condescension by whites, the editors noted that they could "pay him no better compliment than to say that if all the colored race were as thrifty, as honest, as polite, and as courteous as he, our South-land would have much better prospects before her."[42]

An A.M.E. Zion congregation was established in Davidson in 1897. Called Reeves Temple A.M.E. Zion, the congregation began as members of Torrence Chapel A.M.E. Zion Church. They constructed a frame structure on Eden Street and their minister, Reverend Johnson, served as the teacher for black children in town and may have organized the first black Masonic Lodge as well.[43]

A few white villagers also began attending the newly formed Hopewell Baptist Church, located in a rural area about two miles east of the town center. The congregation started with a Sunday school held in a brush arbor and constructed their first building, a small weatherboard structure, in 1880. Local Episcopalians' hopes to build a church were less successful. Articles in 1889 and 1891 suggested that the small number of Episcopalians in Davidson were close to building; but no building was erected, nor would one be for another sixty-five years.[44]

Traveling evangelists stirred up religious fervor in the 1880s and 1890s, and visiting missionaries offered glimpses of exotic cultures. The missionaries' programs combined education and religion, and if their presentations sometimes stereotyped the peoples of Mexico, China, or Africa, they nevertheless exposed their audiences to a larger, more diverse world. In addition, many of the missionaries had family connections in Davidson and remained in town for several weeks, further extending opportunities for education. April 1893 was an especially busy month for missionary lectures, with four different men offering talks on Japan, China, and Greece.[45]

Town residents also had opportunities to hear female missionaries. The Presbyterian Church began accepting women as missionaries in the mid-nineteenth century, not just wives assisting their husbands but also single women. Despite the difficult conditions they faced, these women did not see themselves as pioneers for women's equality. They worked very much within the bounds of social conventions that held women as protectors of the home and men as protectors of women, not always recognizing how much their work challenged those very conventions.

The traditionalism played out in Davidson with the women missionaries speaking mostly to all-female gatherings. The propriety of women speaking to mixed or "promiscuous" audiences was still a matter of serious debate. In 1897, for example, the college's president, John Shearer, spoke out against women addressing mixed audiences.[46]

DCPC children were also involved in mission activities with special "Missionary Days" that included recitations and songs and the formation of a Junior Missionary Society to help raise funds. Reports of missionary visits often included references to donations gathered. One talk at DCPC by the financial agent for Home Missions in the Synod of North Carolina raised more than $900, prompting the comment that the large amount was "almost marvelous for such a small church."[47]

Mission Sunday Schools

As this donation attests, DCPC's interest in missions was not limited to foreign ones. Inspired by both compassion and religious obligation, members of the congregation continued to sponsor Mission Sabbath or Sunday schools for outlying communities and the new mill community in town. In the 1860s, Sunday schools in the area focused on sermons and singing hymns; by the 1880s, the classes were providing instruction in reading and other basic skills. According to historian Tom Hanchett, Sunday school sessions, which "offered the basics of modern education to working people who could only attend school on their single non-working day . . . taught reading, writing, and arithmetic and—as importantly—attempted to instill the value of hard work, thrift and obedience that factory owners thought their employees lacked."[48] DCPC's Sunday schools targeted both blacks and whites newly employed in local cotton mills. The intent was not to raise factory workers, whether white or black, to a higher social status, but only to improve conditions within their prescribed lots and to make them more reliable employees.

Whatever the motives, town residents took great interest in the schools and especially enjoyed the annual celebrations. In the mill school the programs usually included speeches by local leaders, including Linden Cotton Mills president John Munroe and DCPC pastor Alfred Graham, and music selections and skits performed by factory workers and young women from the college church. There are few descriptions of the programs at the black schools, but in 1893 one student recorded that "[o]ne of the most enjoyable events of the season was the exhibition of the colored school at the close of the session, December 22nd." He also noted that, even though there was a major exam the next day, "about one-third of the audience was composed of students."[49]

At first the Linden Sunday school classes were probably held in the textile mill, but in 1894 a separate chapel was built for both church services and the classes. Construction was managed by Munroe and completed that November. Although the building was a simple wooden structure, its costs exceeded the contributions in hand. Munroe appealed to students and other contributors for additional donations, noting that otherwise he would have to sell his bicycle to make up the difference. In addition to organizing schools and making speeches at the annual celebrations, in 1892 Munroe opened his home to mill children for a Christmas gathering and helped sponsor annual Christmas programs in the mill chapel for many years.[50] Munroe provides an example of the concern for others and commitment to community service that are major themes in the history of the town and college.

Health and Health Care

Economic and social divisions also played a role in differences in health and healthcare. Although town doctors offered their services without regard to race or economic status, inadequate diets and poor housing conditions meant that those with lower incomes generally experienced more health-related problems. And even though doctors were available, calling on the doctor often was a last resort for poor residents.

For all town residents, fevers and epidemics remained a serious threat. Three college students died of typhoid fever on the same day in 1882, and in 1887 measles spread throughout the village, causing one death. Whooping cough took Agnes Currell, daughter of English professor William Currell and his wife, Sarah. One young woman died when typhoid fever returned in 1895, and another died during another episode of that dread disease in 1899. The town also experienced minor outbreaks of diphtheria and meningitis, and influenza, described at the time as the "much-dreaded monster, 'the grip,'" visited the town regularly in the 1890s.[51]

A special town board meeting was called in January 1898 to consider reports of smallpox in Charlotte. The board passed an ordinance imposing a fine on "any tramp, vagrant, or other person with no visible means [of support] who shall remain in the corporate limits of Davidson longer than is necessary to pass directly through it." The *Davidson College Magazine* reported that "owing to the recent smallpox scare everyone is very much excited over vaccination, and Dr. Munroe is kept busy giving points on the arm."[52]

North Carolina Medical College

Healthcare in Davidson expanded dramatically in the 1890s with the establishment of the North Carolina Medical College, which emerged initially from the interests of college physician Paul Barringer. A grandson of college founder Robert Hall Morrison, Barringer came to Davidson in 1886 and, along with his college duties, began to offer private lessons in

North Carolina Medical College circa 1898

anatomy and physiology. Dr. Barringer's classes became so popular that the "Old Danville" building in which his classes were taught soon became known as "the medical school."[53] Barringer left Davidson in 1889 to teach at the University of Virginia. John Munroe, his successor as college physician, shared his interest in medical education. Under Munroe's direction the medical program grew from a fledgling operation into a college and clinic.

The medical school was incorporated as the North Carolina Medical College in 1893, and the course of study was expanded to three years.

Enrollment grew from 12 students in 1890 to 62 in 1897. To accommodate growth, the medical college moved first to the Maxwell house on South Main Street in 1889 and then in 1897 to a new facility on Concord Road.

A report in the *Charlotte Democrat* on the opening reception for the new facility provides a glimpse of some of the social patterns in town. For guests, the somberness of the tour of the lecture room and library was balanced by "sweet music being discoursed by the college Mandolin-Guitar Club." And to balance the largely male atmosphere, a group of young ladies assisted in the "large hall from which tea was served from three separate tables." The article also noted that "[t]he rooms were lighted by colored incandescent lamps and electric chandeliers and tastefully decorated with vases of flowers and festoons of ivy."[54]

The medical school's hospital opened in October 1899 in a "new cottage . . . at the lower end of town." The *Davidson College Magazine* noted that "[p]ersons desiring to enter a hospital for treatment can do so here at a very moderate cost for board and incidentals and receive the best of nursing and medical attention." A story two months later noted that "[a]t least a dozen patients" had been treated at the hospital since it opened on October 20.[55] The hospital did not benefit all residents equally, however. The closest hospital treating African-Americans was the Good Samaritan Hospital in Charlotte, which opened in 1891 through the efforts of three Episcopal churches.

The hospital in Davidson also played a part in a sad and gruesome chapter in town history—grave-robbing. The need for cadavers resulted in students robbing graves from local black cemeteries.[56] While there was not a black cemetery in town, black cemeteries were connected to area churches including Torrence Chapel A.M.E. Zion, Huntersville United Methodist, and Rockwell A.M.E. Zion.

In 1900 classes were added in diseases of women, and in 1902 advanced students began doing clinical work in Charlotte hospitals. In 1907 the school was moved to Charlotte, where it operated until 1913. The last classes of students completed their work at the medical school at Virginia Commonwealth University. With the departure of the medical school, higher education in Davidson again meant an undergraduate liberal arts curriculum at a college centered in the Chambers Building.

Local Schools

Like churches and hospitals, schools were another area in which Davidson followed regional practices. The failure of state and local governments to provide adequate funding for public schools after the Civil War contributed to the fact that the state's literacy rate in 1880 was lower than it had been in 1860. The 1900 census recorded more than 10,000 illiterate people over ten years of age in Mecklenburg County, including 88 in Davidson over age 10 who could neither read nor write. Not surprisingly, the highest percentage occurred among those born in slavery. Public schools continued to be inadequate to meet the needs of area youth: in 1880, for example, only ten African-Americans ranging in age from 10 to 19 were identified as "attending school."[57]

In that year, white students in Davidson whose parents could afford tuition of $1.25 to $4.25 per month could attend Miss Lucy Jurney's school. Others might have received private tutoring, and still others attended schools in Statesville, Concord, and other nearby towns and cities. A few young women still took classes at the college, including four who studied French there in 1890 and another four who studied the same language in 1894.[58]

In 1892, members of DCPC decided to establish a school that would provide four months of free education for area children from farm and mill families and six months of classes for those whose families could afford to pay tuition. Mr. and Mrs. R.W. Shelton donated land on South Street. By 1893 the school had both a two-room wooden building and a six-room brick structure. The wooden building served younger students and the brick building, which became known as the Davidson Academy, was used for older students. During the four months of free schooling, as many as eighty-five to ninety students attended, requiring some classes to be held in the Masonic Hall.[59]

Apart from the Sabbath schools, the first mention of a "colored school" in Davidson appeared in a report in the college magazine in January 1893.[60] By 1897, classes were conducted at Reeves Temple A.M.E. Zion Church. After the construction of a black Masonic Hall, classes were held there as well.

Educational Clubs, Literary Societies, and Men's Groups

Educational opportunities were not limited to classrooms or even to young people. In 1891 William Currell, the college's first professor of English literature, formed a Chautauqua Literary and Scientific Circle for the white "ladies of the village." They met weekly in members' homes. Eleven women joined at the first meeting and, not surprisingly, the topic for the year was English history and literature. The group, which fre-

Jennie Martin, founder
of Booklovers Club

quently included college students, occasionally hosted lectures open to town residents.[61]

College students and young women from the town attended another group that studied Greek mythology. While enjoying opportunities to socialize with prospective husbands, the young women took their participation in the club seriously. At the second meeting, for example, six women presented papers on various versions of the Prometheus legend. A "Correct Speaking Club" also appealed to the younger set.[62]

Jennie Martin, the wife of the college president, formed a women's book club in 1899. Initially called the Women's Book Club or Ladies Book Club, the group met semi-monthly and discussed books with titles like *Familiar Studies of Men and Books* and *Marie Antoinette*. Typical of the many women's literary societies that formed in America from the 1870s through the 1890s, this club, eventually settling on the name Booklovers, was the first of many women's book clubs and literary societies in the town. Its formation reflected an increase in leisure time for at least some middle-class women in the town. With membership by invitation, the club provided a form of social distinction as well as an intellectual outlet. Black women and working-class white women were not considered for membership.

Masonic lodges permitted some men to socialize and work together. In 1898 the white masons helped to organize a Knights of Pythias chapter for their younger counterparts in town. The black Masonic lodge formed in the 1890s; its members built their hall behind the newly established A.M.E. Zion church. The town also briefly had a chapter of the Farmer's Alliance, a national organization dedicated to improving the social and economic condition of farmers. The group held at least one public program in 1891, but it did not have a lasting impact on the town.[63]

Social Gatherings, Fund-raising, and Parlor Theatricals

The small size of the town lessened the effects of the kinds of social divisions among whites that were developing at the time in Charlotte. As Janette Greenwood has argued, the rise of a group of wealthy manufacturers in Charlotte led to the formation of a social network of upper-class families that distanced itself from the less fortunate and focused on "social events . . . that displayed their wealth."[64]

In Davidson, however, the social circles remained more fluid than in Charlotte. While the town's leading businessman, John Munroe, occasionally hosted fashionable evenings featuring young white ladies attired in silks and satins, diamonds and pearls, the guests could be found working with others in the town on charity fund raisers the next week.[65] Further, the centrality of the college meant that social prestige did not equate simply to success in business.

Faculty wives and daughters, while rarely wealthy, held considerable social power. They remained active in church and civic causes, including the Ladies Benevolent Society of the college church, founded in 1880 to provide support for missions. The members raised funds through ice cream suppers and oyster dinners. Along with making donations to foreign missions, they purchased a bell for the church, helped furnish the parsonage, and contributed to the college YMCA.

For African-American women, church-related organizations remained a central social and civic outlet. As with the white churches, women made up the greater part of the congregations. Their work within churches and fund-raising efforts were critical to the churches and to their community. These activities also gave women experience in leadership and allowed them to participate in town issues, albeit on a limited scale. In contrast, because the mill chapel was used primarily as a Sunday school, taught by college students and ladies from DCPC, mill women had few if any opportunities to take part in fund-raising or socials, thereby limiting their participation in the wider community.

For college and merchant families, social events typically revolved

An informal gathering of students and young women of Davidson.

around visiting guests or receptions for students—or both, as in the case of Professor Harding in February 1890. According to the college magazine, "Dr. Harding gave quite a successful reception to the senior class . . . [a] delightful party . . . given in honor of Miss Nannie Harding of Farmville, Virginia, of Mary Ramseur, of Milton [N.C.], and of Miss Berry of Virginia, all three of whom have for some time been the guests of Mrs. Harding." Typical of such events, the evening included music and recitations; this program also featured the debut of the college Glee Club. The magazine's editors pronounced it "one of the most enjoyable events ever recorded in Davidson's social annals."[66]

A month later the magazine reported that "[d]uring the past month there have been three social gatherings, one for the older and two for the younger people." One such event a month, perhaps two, would have been normal; but three socials in one month was unusual. The fact that two of the three hostesses were faculty wives accurately reflected their leading roles in such social events.[67]

This is not to suggest that college-related socials in Davidson were invariably formal academic affairs. While Dr. and Mrs. Currell once offered a "symposium" party that required teams of guests to answer questions, Mrs. Harding hosted a "tacky party" with guests appearing in "ridiculous, side-splitting, verdant, hayseedy costumes," a masquerade featuring sheets as costumes, and a well-received domino party. In 1897 Anna, Mary, and Nellie Sparrow surprised their guests by offering a small play or parlor theatrical during the evening. "The idea of a parlor theatrical on social occasions is a rather novel one in Davidson," a guest commented, "but the admirable success of this one has shown it to be worthy of imitation."[68] Although families in the black and mill communities generally had less money and leisure time, young girls gathered to share gossip and play games, and church events provided occasions to spend time with potential suitors.

Music and Plays

Music remained a primary source of entertainment. Families sang at home and during church services, church choirs rehearsed and presented programs, and visiting vocal and instrumental artists performed on campus. For musically inclined young people whose families could afford the fees, a variety of classes were offered periodically, including lessons for mandolin, guitar, and voice. After graduating from the Statesville Female College in 1892, Helen Stinson began teaching instrumental music. Additional classes were offered in 1896 by Gertrude Williamson and Eulalia Cornelius. Public recitals allowed students to show off their newly acquired skills.[69]

The greatest musical excitement of the era came in 1890, when Charlotte hosted a Grand Music Festival. Townspeople organized a twenty-five-member chorus, with hopes not only of participating in the festival but also of becoming one of "Davidson's permanent institutions." The chorus gave several public performances before the Charlotte festival, but disappear from the records after their "banner" appearance in the Queen City.[70]

Any artistic void was filled by performances of the college's Glee Cub and Jug Band and by the continuing theatrical and fund-raising efforts of the King's Daughters of DCPC. Over time, tableaus gave way to singing concerts, skits, and plays. One popular set of skits was "The Peak Sisters," which included traditional songs like "The Last Rose of Summer" and "Mary Had a Little Lamb." In addition to offering several versions of "The Peak Sisters," the King's Daughters also staged the plays "Old Maids Made New," "At the District School," and "A Davidson Art Gallery." Because the plays were comedies with joking references to townspeople and events, they overcame local scruples about theatricals.[71] During these years the college generally ignored its prohibition of theatricals, permitting programs sponsored by the King's Daughters and the junior and senior classes.[72]

The Sporting Life

Sports offered important outlets during these years. Especially for young people, tennis, skating, and biking joined baseball as favorite pastimes.

The irrepressible Henry Louis Smith found time to promote new forms of exercise. One of his most ambitious projects was the creation of Lake Wiley, a fourteen-acre pond on the east side of the campus. Built in 1893, it had two bath houses, "one for the boys and the other for the girls," seven boats, and a water toboggan. The toboggan was a large wooden slide that was used in summer to send a sled full of young people splashing onto the lake and and in winter to send them flying across the ice.

The lake quickly became a popular hangout for students and townspeople alike. Unfortunately, storms broke the dam three times within four years, and it was finally drained in 1909 to accommodate the needs of the new sewer system.

Another of Smith's projects was the opening of a skating rink in 1889 on the upper floor of one of the town's store buildings. He ordered seventy pairs of skates to be rented out for thirty cents per month. Two years later the college included a skating rink in the new YMCA building, Morrison Hall. In order to encourage use of the facility and to provide social outlets for the all-male college students and young women of the town, the rink was open on Saturday afternoons to both genders. The rink also hosted a series of skating contests and parties, including costume parties.[73]

The town's young women also found their way onto newly constructed lawn tennis courts and took to riding bicycles. The college magazine teasingly reported that "Miss Lucy Martin has a new wheel. It is a beauty and is causing many of the girls to break the tenth commandment." Some young women even found their way onto the baseball field, or at least set up baseball diamonds in their front yards. One spring Lucy Martin served as captain of the "Blues" and Maggie Brown as captain of the "Reds." Their teams won praise from college students, who noted "the heavy hitting and clean base-running of Misses Hall and Martin for the 'Blues,' and the neat [play at] shortstop by Miss Brown for the 'Reds.'"[74]

These women's participation in sports, with its mixture of the social and the athletic, reflected complex changes in women's lives. At the same time that they were finding more freedoms, they were still relegated to a narrow sphere of social and educational roles. Women could play sports as long as they remained genteel. Because Davidson was a small town and because the college embraced the new emphasis on physical activity, young women in town, especially those with ties to the college, often had considerable freedom. Thus Lucy Martin, daughter of professor and former college president William J. Martin, not only could participate in genteel skating parties, but also could take up bicycling and even baseball. Still, some social boundaries remained and, as girls grew into women, sporting activities were curtailed and courtship rules became more stringent. Breaking the informal social rules, Mrs. Harding once shocked her neighbors by skating with a college student.[75]

For young men in town baseball remained popular, with town teams of white players challenging college teams. Softball was especially popular with African-Americans. When football arrived in the late 1880s, it was mostly played by college students. For younger boys, marbles and slingshots, referred to as flipps, found their way to Davidson by 1890.[76]

Sports even changed some holidays. Thanksgiving afternoon, for example, became a time for playing football or tennis. In 1893 townspeople gathered on Thanksgiving afternoon to watch a football game between the college's sophomore and junior teams. By 1898 townspeople were traveling to Charlotte on Thanksgiving day to watch football games. Surely few townspeople in 1879 would have imagined that Thanksgiving afternoons would soon be devoted largely to sports.

Conclusion

The college catalog in 1880 proudly proclaimed that "[f]ew places are so free from temptations to vice and extravagance. The . . . college is remote from towns and large villages." Six years later, the college magazine declared that Davidson was a "flourishing little town. . . . The large, well-stocked stores, the handsome residences that have been erected, and other signs of development speak well for the progress of the place." By 1900 the town had earned a reputation for "progressive spirit and elegant homes and beautiful grounds." Its eleven stores were reported to have a "good trade," and, befitting its location in a cotton-growing region, "two thousand bales of cotton" were sold annually.[77]

Some residents probably wished for even greater development. But circumstances during these decades ensured that Davidson would remain a small college town. Despite the return of the railroad, the founding of a mill and a processing plant, and the opening of a medical college, the reality was that Davidson would remain a train stop, not a transportation hub. The establishment of Cornelius ensured that the area served by Davidson's retail stores and cotton buyers would remain small. National and regional economic conditions slowed Davidson College's growth, which in turn limited the town's economic prospects.

Internally, the residents established a government and thus deepened their civic identity, gathered on Main Street to shop and in their various churches to worship, and although often imbued with paternalism, deepened the ties of civic cooperation and charity. With the turn of a new century, Davidsonians saw themselves as part of a progressive era. Having weathered the political transition after Reconstruction and having seen the town advance economically during the previous twenty years, they generally faced the future with more hope than foreboding.

4 Modern Conveniences, Traditional Social Patterns, 1901–1920

During the first two decades of the twentieth century, the United States as a whole was changing much more rapidly than Davidson was. While America's population grew by 39 percent between 1900 and 1920, from 76 to 106 million, the town grew by only 28 percent, from 904 to 1,156. Although Davidson attracted some new businesses, including a new cotton mill, it remained much less dynamic economically than the rapidly growing cities and towns in the state, including Winston-Salem, Charlotte, and nearby Mooresville. Influenced by Progressive Era thinking about the positive role of government in solving the nation's problems, the town government continued to address issues relating to sanitation, education, transportation, and public service. Relatively new products based on technological innovation—notably cars and trucks and many products that used electricity (e.g., telephones, kitchen appliances, and motion pictures)—probably did more than anything else to alter life in Davidson during these years, especially for those who had the money to buy them or, in the case of motion pictures, to pay to see them. National and international developments in the 1910s—especially the election of a former Davidson College student, Woodrow Wilson, as president in 1912, followed by World War I and the influenza epidemic of 1918—left their marks on the town.

The arrival of a substantial number of cars during these years greatly increased the mobility of Davidson's middle class, especially for local women who often had more leisure time than men. Although faculty wives and

Main Street around 1910

daughters had a long tradition of traveling and visiting, cars facilitated these activities, for they could travel directly between a house in Davidson and, say, a house in Charlotte with a convenience that trains could not match. Having started as passengers in cars, women soon became drivers. Not only could Minnie Cranford "motor up from Charlotte" for weekends with her family, but mothers, daughters, and sisters could now drive with relative ease to towns and cities within a sixty-mile radius of Davidson (e.g., Winston-Salem).[1] And middle-class men could take hunting, fishing, and golfing trips by car that would have been impossible earlier.

While new products such as cars and new games such as Rook were coming into widespread use in the town and national and international developments were affecting its residents, the patterns defining the town's character continued to be reinforced and refined. As earlier, the college played a significant economic and political role in town life even as new partnerships and tensions emerged between town and gown. Social stratification deepened between and within the town's black and white communities. And churches continued to help mark these divisions as congregations offered social as well as religious identities. The activities of civic groups expanded, while public education struggled to get established.

Following regional patterns, the town disfranchised black voters in 1900. This regrettable act probably did not make much practical difference at the local level because the white majority was not going to permit a black candidate for a town office to get elected and because local elections were rarely contested during this era. Indeed, the number of candidates typically matched the number of offices to be filled. From one perspective, this tradition encouraged a political civility that fostered a sense of community and cooperation; from another, it reinforced the status quo by limiting political power to a small group. Political leadership was understood to come from white males with business experience or with college connections.

A Tragicomic Student Riot in 1903

Rivalry between the graduating classes, including upper-class hazing of freshmen, was an established tradition at all-male Davidson College. The student riot of 1903 grew out of the rivalry between the classes of 1906 (freshmen) and 1905 (sophomores). Traditionally, sophomores intimidated freshmen as part of their initiation into college life. But the class of 1905 had the disadvantage of being almost half the size of the class of 1906. The sophomores also had pledged not to haze. After a loss to the freshmen in a baseball game, however, they let it be known that they intended to beat up the freshmen after a banquet on February 13. Their resolve was strengthened after four freshmen painted the score of the game on a fence. Realizing that a fight was coming, "about 25 or 30" freshmen, including H. Smith Richardson, decided to "resist" on "the upper floor of the Spence building . . . occupied by fresh[men] only, and reached by one narrow steep stairs." Richardson noted that the upper floor "was armed by plenty of tubs of water, rocks, [and] sticks," and two barrels filled with rocks were placed at the head of the steps ready to be rolled down. Richardson recalled what happened when the sophomores attacked:

> When the sophs came roaring in with paddles ready and belts
> unbuckled, the first few who dashed up the steps to eat up the
> fresh got wet and retreated. The sophs saw they could not go up
> those steps and so sent back for the whole student body. No men,
> however, could have gone up those steps. Finally a compromise was
> made: each fresh was given twenty-five licks as hard as they could
> be made.[2]

Unfortunately, the matter remained unsettled. The sophomores announced their intention to exact more punishment, and the freshmen decided it was best to leave the college. They were gathered at the train station in Cornelius when, according to Richardson:

Davidson class of 1906 as freshmen

About twenty minutes before train time Bill Joe [Professor William J. Martin] galloped up on horseback, then came Wooley [Professor W.R. Grey] sprinting on his wheel [bicycle], the Dandy Jim [Professor James Douglas] and Tommy [Professor Thomas Harrison] raced up in a buggy. You never heard such pitiful appeals as those poor profs put up. Anyhow they persuaded us to return. Bill Joe swearing that if a f[reshman] was touched it would be over his dead body. He also mentioned his trusty six shooter; . . . you can understand how everybody was worked up.[3]

Over the next few days classes were suspended to give the students time to cool off and conduct negotiations. By February 18, five days after the fight, calm had returned. Meanwhile the college and town had to bear the embarrassment of accounts in newspapers across the state, including a headline in the *Charlotte Observer* proclaiming "Freshmen on Rampage: Serious Trouble at Davidson."[4]

This riot marked a turning point in the town's history: it was the last time that a large group of students took steps to desert the college. Even though the class of 1906 intended to stay away for only a few days, unlike the students in 1855 who left permanently, the college's reputation was at stake and, by extension, the well-being of the town. Despite the addition of other enterprises, the town remained dependent economically on the college's success. Although town-gown relations would remain complex, thereafter the town was spared large-scale student threats to leave.

Downtown Fires

More serious than student conflicts, fires occurring in 1901 and 1906 destroyed whole sections of the downtown business district. The 1901 fire began in Monroe Potts' livery stable. It quickly grew out of control and burned Manly Cranford's three-story department store and several small wooden buildings that housed William Sawyer's grocery store, Abraham McCullough's barber shop, Sallie Lafferty's millinery shop, and a meat market. The estimated loss was $15,000, and only Cranford had insurance. The 1906 fire began near the intersection of Concord Road and Main Street and traveled south, stopping this time just before Cranford's new store. Construction on new stores began within a year after the 1901 fire, but recovery from the 1906 fire took longer.[5]

The first buildings constructed after the 1901 fire were a drug store and a new Knox and Brown store. Manly Crawford built a new two-story structure in 1902. John P. Munroe continued to expand his business interests, first erecting a new pharmacy next to Cranford's store and then enlarging the building in 1903 to accommodate the town's first bank, the Southern Trust Company. After another building went up in 1903, no further structures were added to Main Street until a small construction boom occurred in 1908. Reflecting the town's tenuous prosperity in the early 1900s, several stretches of the business district remained empty until the 1920s.

Town commissioners responded to fires with ordinances that established a fire district on Main Street. The ordinances prohibited the construction of wooden buildings in the area and required all new buildings downtown to have metal or stone roofs. Livery businesses were banished from the fire district as well as near the train depot and the Davidson Academy building on South Street and along the full length of Concord Road. While these ordinances did not prevent the 1906 fire, they did help to limit the damage. The 1906 fire stopped at the edge of where the brick buildings following the new codes began.

Other New Ordinances

In addition to addressing safety issues, the town commissioners continued to concern themselves with regulating businesses, maintaining roads, and improving sanitation. Compared with big cities such as New York and Chicago, Davidson experienced the problems of urbanization on a very small scale. But the commissioners still took their duties seriously, altering and adding ordinances to address changing economic and social conditions. In 1901 the board established fees for merry-go-rounds, shooting galleries, and street vendors of fresh meat, fish, and oysters. A decade later, fortunetellers no longer were seen as a sufficient moral hazard to be banned from town; instead, they were added to the license-fee list.

Motion pictures caused more concern for the commissioners. In addition to requiring an annual $25 license, the town board decided in 1915 that "as many as two of the town commissioners (including the mayor) as censors shall first pass on the pictures before being exhibited." The ordinances also record the beginnings of an even more significant cultural change: fees were set in 1914 for "automobiles kept for hire," the fees for livery and dray businesses were dropped in 1918, and a fee for individual car owners was set in 1920.[6]

The advent of automobiles ensured that road maintenance stayed on the board's agenda. The first "locomobiles" were spotted in town in the fall of 1901. In 1911 Henry Louis Smith could be seen riding his new motorcycle about town, and in 1915 the *Davidsonian* occasionally noted townspeople taking motoring trips for shopping and visiting nearby towns.

Under the direction of the Street and Light Committee, new portions of roads, including Depot Street and a stretch of Concord Road dubbed "a five thousand dollar running track," were macadamized. Cement walkways gradually replaced the worn wooden sidewalks. The committee also helped to align the northern end of Main Street with the public highway running from Mooresville to the Mecklenburg County line.[7]

A 1904 ordinance made littering unlawful "upon any of the streets, sidewalks, alleys, public squares, or in any place where [littering] would be unsightly or a menace to health . . ." Compliance with this and similar ordinances passed the same year appears to have been sporadic. A 1912 ordinance, prompted by a petition from the women of the Civic Club, ordained that

> all sweepings, papers, boxes, barrels, straw, banana peelings, watermelon, muskmelon and cantaloupe rinds, and other trash or refuse . . . accumulating in [or near] any storehouse or . . . any residence in the town should be placed . . . in cans, barrels, or boxes and kept in the buildings or premises until removed. All shavings, refuse, and trash from new buildings or buildings being repaired shall not be thrown on the streets or sidewalks, but shall be removed directly from such buildings by the contractor or owner.[8]

Livestock in town remained a concern. In 1909 the Sanitary Committee investigated complaints about a slaughterhouse near the home of

Dr. Z.K. Justice. Upon finding "bones and hoofs in sufficient numbers to attract buzzards," town leaders ordered the offending hog pen removed and passed an ordinance banning slaughterhouses within the town limits.[9]

In 1917 the board, spurred by a scarlet fever scare and the Civic Club's pledge to pay part of his salary, appointed Dr. Justice to be the town's health officer and passed nine new health ordinances. One of the ordinances set fines for people "attending [a] public event [while] knowingly having a contagious disease." These actions followed a national pattern: in the 1910s local and state governments passed a plethora of laws addressing health concerns.[10]

In 1912 the board expanded an earlier ban on Sunday sales to prohibit the opening of any shop or store except for drug stores dispensing medicines. Yet three years later, after being petitioned by Harlon Helper, the town established limited Sunday hours for restaurants, cafes, and lunch rooms. They could be open before 10:30 a.m., between 12:30 and 2:30 p.m., and from 5:00 to 7:00 p.m.[11]

Along with motor vehicles, health challenges, and blue laws, town officials continued to grapple with new technologies. The board's Light Committee spent six months considering the college's proposal to provide electricity to the town before granting the college "the privilege of erecting a pole line through the town." Work began on the power plant in May 1904. The college operated the plant until 1908, when the Southern Power Company took it over.[12]

The town also allowed the college to expand its water and sewer lines to much of the town on and east of Main Street. During these decades, however, such utilities generally were not extended to the African-American and "mill" families who lived west of Main Street.

Law and Order

Although new regulations added to the duties of the town marshal, Davidson continued to have a one-person police department. Local business owners petitioned the board in 1902 to add a night watchman, but no action was taken. In addition to police duties, the long-serving marshal, James Johnston, was the town's tax collector, dog warden, and cotton weigher and inspector.

By 1917 traffic control increasingly occupied Johnston's time. On one Sunday he counted forty cars speeding through town, at least five of which belonged to townspeople. The first recorded accident involving an automobile occurred in October 1917, when a car driven by Marsh Potts of Davidson collided with a horse-drawn hack driven by another town resident, M.M. Hampton. Fortunately, the *Davidsonian* reported, neither man was "seriously injured."[13]

The most serious crimes Johnston faced were robberies, a small riot, and two killings. The first death was that of Dr. Wooten who was shot to death on 10 February 1914. After a much publicized trial, his business partner, R.M. Jetton, was declared not guilty. In May 1915 a selective thief took several pairs of shoes, some neckties, and a few hats as well as a small amount of cash from Goodrum's store. That same night two barrels of flour were stolen from the depot.[14]

The riot proved that, despite the college's continued emphasis on temperance and local laws forbidding the sale of strong drink, alcohol was readily available. One Saturday night in 1918, a small crowd of drunks gathered on North Main Street. After an altercation involving pistols, buckshot, and pokers, Johnston, assisted by soldiers from Camp Greene in Charlotte, moved the drunks to the town jail. More sadly, a fight that started at the cotton oil plant and finished late on a Friday night in 1919 left mill employee George Patterson fatally wounded.[15]

A Growing College

Although the North Carolina Medical College's move to Charlotte in 1907 hurt the town, the decision of Davidson College's trustees to expand the student body soon offset any damage to the local economy. The college grew from 160 students and eight faculty in 1901 to 454 students and fourteen faculty in 1920. The near-tripling of the student body during these years virtually ensured the college's continuing viability.

To accommodate the new students, the college needed additional buildings. Along with three dormitories—Rumple in 1903, Watts in 1906, and Georgia in 1909—the college built a lovely Carnegie library (today a comfortable guest house) and a new gymnasium. College newsletters highlighted innovations, noting that Rumple was "heated by steam, has two bathrooms [for sixty students] with hot and cold showers on each floor" and that Watts not only had a "lavatory with running water in each room" but the entire building was "heated by steam and lighted with electricity."[16]

To finance the new library building, the college raised funds to match a $20,000 grant in 1908 from the Andrew Carnegie Foundation. From 1881 to 1917 the Carnegie Foundation gave more than $43 million to help build two thousand libraries in towns and colleges around the world. Da-

Students studying in Carnegie library

vidson's facility, open only to college students and employees, was one of ten Carnegie libraries in North Carolina. The only other library in town was in the white public school until 1920, when the ladies of the Civic Club established a small circulating library with an initial purchase of $21 worth of books.[17]

The Alumni Gymnasium, made possible by donations from former students, reflected the growing importance of sports in the life of the college and, by extension, in the life of the town as well. Another, much smaller building constructed in 1919 changed town-gown relations in a different way. The establishment of a college laundry service in a town where more than fifty women, all but one black, earned or supplemented their family incomes as laundresses cut into their income, and only a few of these women took jobs with the college.[18]

For the women managing and cooking for boarding houses, the increase in students brought more opportunities to earn money. In the fall of 1915 the student newspaper listed fourteen houses. Mrs. Nannie Barnes ran the largest house, which served fifty students. The other houses had from twenty to forty students each. Monthly fees ranged from $9.50 to $16.

In 1917 in response to dire conditions in Europe caused by World War I, Herbert Hoover, the coordinator of relief efforts, urged Americans to observe one meatless day per week. Students at Mrs. Manning's boarding house responded promptly, voting to observe one meatless meal per *day*. With some students at other boarding houses reluctant to make sacrifices, a *Davidsonian* editorial in October 1917 called for greater participation:

How about that meatless, wheatless, and sugarless day? Some of the boarding houses have made this response . . . readily. All have not done it. We appeal to you once again [to do it]. This is on the same principle as Liberty Loan Bonds. Do It Now.[19]

Downtown Businesses

From 1901 to 1920, the downtown area remained a combination of homes and small shops strung along the west side of Main Street. Slowly, as brick buildings replaced wooden structures, cement sidewalks took the place of wooden planks, and gas pumps appeared, the business district took on a more modern look befitting a new century.

In addition to the bank mentioned earlier, new businesses on Main Street included a hotel, a meat market, cafes, drug stores, and a movie theater. Little is known about the hotel beyond a notice in the student paper that a local stock company had been organized to build a hotel with "all the modern improvements" and that the hotel served as the site of the post office for a year after the 1906 fire. That it was not as successful as the bank is shown in renewed calls for a new hotel in 1923.[20]

While dry goods stores and groceries were familiar downtown fixtures, town residents either raised their own livestock or bartered with street vendors for meat. With the opening in 1908 of the first meat market, the village saw the start of a transition away from pig pens and peddlers.

Although many families continued to keep chickens and even horses in town, slowly urban customs replaced rural ones. The lack of fashion Mary Rice Lacy noted in 1858 gave way not only to events at which fashionable bonnets could be worn, but also to the ability to purchase them in town. In 1914 a Miss Rude moved to Davidson and opened a millinery shop within Goodrum's department store. Her business was continued in 1917 by two other women, one from Tennessee and the other from Pennsylvania.[21]

One custom that did not take hold easily was dining out. Two cafes opened in 1915 and 1916—one called the Flyless Restaurant, perhaps reflecting sanitary concerns—but each lasted less than a year. Fortunately for students and townspeople who liked non-alcoholic beverages and sweets, a tea room, a confectionary, and three drug stores with soda fountains opened on Main Street.[22]

In 1915 the Civic Club brought the first motion pictures to Davidson. The league raised funds by showing films in Shearer Hall on Saturday evenings. While no one seemed to think this an odd use of the old chapel building, insurance regulations ended the shows after a few weeks.

Students soon filled the void by remodeling the building on Main Street south of Long's grocery store. "The Palace" opened its doors on 4 May 1916 to a large and enthusiastic audience. The student operators promised "two performances . . . each night of the week, at 7:15 and 8:00 with matinee on Saturday at 3:00 p.m."[23]

Eventually the students' ambitions outran their abilities. By 1919 the daily shows had been replaced by weekly ones operated by the college YMCA and occasional offerings by the Civic Club. Enthusiasm for films remained high enough that, in one week, the Civic Club made $45 on a showing of "Seventeen" with Jack Pickford and Louise Huff on Thursday night and the YMCA had a good turnout on Friday night for "The Goose Girl" starring Marguerite Clark.[24]

The arrival of automobiles also created new business opportunities. By 1914 Carlyle Sloan had purchased a new car and used it for a local taxi service, while J.F. Carter opened a garage on Main Street. The *Davidsonian* reported that he was "kept busy with work." At the same time, livery stables, drays, and blacksmiths had less and less work as horses and buggies gave way to autos. While these changes affected both blacks and whites, more new jobs were opened for young white men who became mechanics and drivers than for young black men.[25]

A concern for local merchants was the creation in 1916 of an "auto bus line" between Mooresville and Charlotte. The bus actually was a "very attractive twelve-passenger Buick" that made two trips each way per day, passing through Davidson en route. The "bus" line, added to the existing train service, gave town residents more opportunities to shop in Charlotte and Mooresville, thus potentially taking business away from downtown merchants. College students also found it easier to visit young women at Queens College in Charlotte.

One of the most significant transitions in Davidson in the 1910s was the closing of Scofield's general store in 1916 and the death of its owner, Stephen "Skit" Scofield, the following spring. A town institution since 1870, the store had been especially popular with students who, according to the *Davidsonian*, looked "upon the closing of his store with genuine regret." The *Davidsonian* article highlighted Scofield's contributions to the college and the town:

> Mr. Scofield was the builder of the linen mill and also helped lay out the telegraph lines in this community. For years he was the efficient station agent for the railway company. . . . He was employed in the building of both the Y.M.C.A. building and the church, and

Skit Scofield (second from left) with family

has probably done more in [the] "upbuilding" of Davidson than any other of its citizens.

Partly because of its relatively small size, Davidson has always been a place where seemingly ordinary people have made extraordinary contributions to the community. Skit Scofield was such a person, and in a real sense an era of town history ended with his passing.[26]

Manufacturing and Other Jobs for Men, Women, and Children

Manufacturing saw the creation of several new businesses and the expansion of others. The new businesses included a flour mill opened in 1901 by the Davidson Roller Mill Company, a second cotton mill in 1907, and a corn mill in 1915. These firms provided some jobs but did not displace education as the main focus for the town.[27]

The Delburg Cotton Mill Company built a new cotton mill on land purchased from the college. The company added a large cotton warehouse in 1914 and a building "sixty-five by seventy-six feet, two stories high" in 1917. The 1917 addition doubled the capacity of the mill and created more than 100 jobs. Although the mill was important to the town during the first half of the century, there were much larger cotton mills in Charlotte and other nearby communities.[28]

As was true elsewhere in America at the time, children often worked in the mills and in other businesses during these years. The 1900 census shows Davidson children under twelve years of age working in mills, and several under twelve worked as servants, farm laborers, and cooks. A 1917 state law raised the minimum age for employment to fourteen, and children between the ages of eight and fourteen were required to attend school throughout the school year. Despite efforts to end child labor, the 1920 census listed a ten-year-old Davidson resident, Alice White, as a dishwasher at the Henderson Hotel.[29]

Census data show that, in the families of Davidson College faculty and white merchants, only the male head of house worked for pay, but that in most other households several family members were gainfully employed. The children of carpenters, electricians, farmers, mill superintendents, bank cashiers, and sales clerks often worked in the mills or as sales clerks or office assistants. Three young men, aged 17, 16, and 12, were the town's first generation of soda jerks—or, as the census called them, "soda dispensers." The children of college caretakers and laundresses worked in the same occupations or as laborers, shoeshine boys, and telegraph messengers.

During the first decades of the new century, the range of employment for black males expanded somewhat, with gardener, fireman, barber, driver, plumber, tailor, butcher, and laborer at oil and saw mills included in the list of occupations. As in the past, black families generally reported that most members of their families worked for pay, with fathers, mothers, and children all needing to produce income. In 1900 about half of black families in the census showed the wife at home; in 1920 only three families had wives not working outside the home.

Nationally as well as locally, women—among whites, largely unmarried women—began entering the workforce in greater numbers around the turn of the twentieth century. As educational opportunities increased, more women found jobs in teaching and nursing. Women also gained acceptance as bookkeepers, stenographers, and sales clerks; in Davidson the daughters of faculty, merchants, and even carpenters worked as stenographers, insurance agents, and office assistants. Locally, domestic work remained one of the few options for black women and girls. While doing laundry remained the most common occupation for black women, the census shows a teacher, Issie Norton, and a midwife, Pattie Harris. Although mills provided employment for many young women, in Davidson most mothers in mill families did not work outside the home.

Among white women who worked for pay in Davidson, in addition to the milliners mentioned above, were Minnie Cranford, a stenographer; her sister Charlotte, an assistant in the post office; Louise Sloan, an insurance agent and the 1920 census taker; Cornelia Shaw, a college librarian who was the first woman holding a professional job at the college; and Hattie Thompson, the assistant to the college treasurer. A number of women from Davidson became teachers in other places, mainly in North Carolina. Harriet Hill served as an Episcopal missionary in China and later became a nurse.

Although Davidson's economy between 1900 and 1920 was characterized by modest growth and considerable stability, the town's manufacturing—and hence its population—grew much more slowly than Mooresville's. With better road and rail service, and without a college that set the social and economic tone for the town, Mooresville boasted four cotton mills, two flour mills, two cottonseed oil mills, a furniture factory, a large lumber mill, a bottling plant, an ice factory, and a mattress factory. By 1910 Mooresville's population reached 3,400, and in 1920 it was 4,315 to Davidson's 1,156. For many local residents, perhaps especially for college families used to thinking of the college as the town's focal point, Davidson's more modest growth may have been just fine.

Regional Patterns in Social Life Continue

Not surprisingly, Davidson continued to follow regional patterns in racial and class relationships. Jim Crow segregation grew stronger through daily practice and unquestioning acceptance; and, as mill populations increased, social divisions between middle-class and working-class whites grew. In Davidson there were separate recreation programs and a separate chapel for mill families. And while there was never a separate mill school, the town continued to offer only four months of free schooling with additional months offered for a fee, thereby creating a two-tiered system that disadvantaged mill children. The student publications that reported frequently on the activities of young women in town focused on the eligible daughters of faculty members, other professionals, and merchants. Rare was any mention of the daughters of mill workers—or even the daughters of supervisors.

The attitudes of white residents toward their black neighbors followed the regional pattern of group discrimination and individualized paternalism. While there are no recorded incidents of white-on-black violence in town, news of lynchings and intimidation arrived through area newspapers and local grapevines. Most black families continued to rent rather than own homes in town, and the town government did not extend amenities such as sidewalks and water service to their neighborhoods. Despite these limitations, the black community worked to keep schools operating, created an aid society, and sponsored social events.

Blacks did so against a regional backdrop that included fear, charity, protest, goodwill, and paternalism. In 1901, an "evangelist of colored work" from Alabama, a Reverend Lilly, gave a "very instructive talk on the duty of the church toward the Negro." Central to his talk was a listing of "the natural deficiencies of the Negro's nature" and suggestions of ways to ameliorate them. The white audience almost certainly approved of the talk's appeal to paternalism.[30]

In 1903 the members of Reeves Temple A.M.E. Zion Church received a very different message through the denomination's newspaper, the *Star of Zion*, published in Charlotte. An editorial decried individuals "who are telling the white men of the South that the Negroes are . . . satisfied with Jim Crow [train] cars and disfranchising laws." It declared that such statements were lies "and the white men know it. Who can be satisfied to be humiliated?"[31]

In 1907 the state legislature extended segregation to public transportation. Ralph Johnson, a Davidson resident, recalled taking the train into Charlotte in "the Negro passenger car up front next to the baggage car." The car's location meant that "smoke from the engine whirled in the open windows," thus causing discomfort for the passengers.[32]

Looking east from train station in 1900

The 1917 obituary of Hiram Potts provides a telling example of local white attitudes. Potts, known to students as "Uncle Hiram," worked for the Southern Railway before becoming a servant first to the William Martin family and then to several other faculty families. He began working for the college in his sixties and was described as "always courteous and obliging" and as one who "considered the 'white folks' as his friends, and what they did as right." Davidson students showed their affection for him by raising money for a tombstone. But in keeping with their view of what was appropriate for a servant, the stone was to be "a simple slab with his name and other details" rather than one of the elaborate memorials used for students buried in the town cemetery.[33]

Potts and his family were buried in a separate cemetery, one established by the local chapter of the Christian Aid and Benevolent Society. The Davidson society focused on providing help in emergencies and maintaining a local cemetery for African-Americans. In January 1905 the society purchased two acres of land for the cemetery from H.M. and Hattie Sloan for $150.

One year after Potts's death, another speaker appeared on campus and gave "a very interesting stereopticon lecture on 'The Negro Problem.'" The Rev. John Little was inspiring enough that after his talk "a canvass of the student body was made and seventy new men signed up for a study of the Negro problem." Those seventy joined another twenty-five who had "already been making a study of this subject."[34]

While well-intentioned, the very act of defining their neighbors as a problem prevented students and town residents from seeing the underlying causes of segregation. The result was the continuation of the odd division of personal from general race relations. Students could admire a man enough to buy his tombstone, but not question laws requiring his family to ride in a separate train car. Black residents might read and agree with the protests against segregation in the *Star of Zion*, but they could discuss this perspective only within the black community.

New Churches and Other Changes in Religion

For town residents attending church services, these decades brought noticeable changes when two new churches opened and two others temporarily disbanded. The new churches, one African-American and one white, were Gethsemane Baptist and Davidson Methodist Church. The first service for Gethsemane was held in a house on Depot Street in 1905. The congregation moved into a new building on Potts Street after church

Davidson Methodist Church, 1906–59

member Julia Connor, a widow with three children, approached Mayor J. Lee Sloan and asked for his help.

Davidson Methodist Church grew out of Mt. Zion Methodist Church in Cornelius. By 1906 the congregation was large enough to build a new church in Davidson. The church was built on South Main Street on a lot donated by J. Lee Sloan. Like Gethsemane Baptist, it was constructed primarily by church members. The church's first pastor, R.S. Howie, arrived in November 1907. By then the women of the church were already organized and had held their first fund-raising bazaar. Starting with 100 members, the church grew to 150 by 1910.

The Methodist Church's growth was fueled in part by the closing of the Mill Chapel. Members of DCPC long supported the Mill Chapel, but once plans for a Methodist congregation took shape, they decided to end their support. Mill families were invited to join the new Methodist congregation. The two congregations overlapped until 1913, when DCPC member Frank Jackson reorganized a mill Sunday school. Jackson served as supervisor until 1924 and was assisted by women from the church, including Nan Gray and Hattie Thompson. The Sunday school included a Sunday afternoon program and a Thursday evening prayer meeting.[35]

DCPC also underwent changes to accommodate the college's growth. In 1903 renovations increased the seating capacity to 700, and the church installed a new pipe organ. The first church service in the renovated building took place on 1 February 1904. Longtime pastor Alfred Graham left in 1907 and was replaced by Charles Richards, who stayed with the congregation until 1926. Davidson Presbyterian Church also replaced a long-serving minister at about the same time.

Despite the ongoing interest in missionary work at DCPC, there were fewer public events or lectures by missionaries than in years past. As women began to form more civic groups outside the churches, fund-raisers for mission work became the work of committees rather than involving the entire congregation.

Two other changes marked new directions for women in DCPC. A 1915 constitution changed the Ladies' Missionary Society to the Womens' Missionary Society. The two names had been used interchangeably since 1913, with the more old-fashioned "Ladies'" finally disappearing. The members also voted in 1914 to end their practice of meeting in one another's homes and instead to use the new Civic Club hall on Main Street.

Health and Health Care in the New Century

The new hall demonstrated the determination of local white women to influence the town's civic life. It also provided a way for women to cross denominational lines and form new partnerships. Participating women took up a number of causes, with health and education issues paramount. Health concerns included public sanitation, clean-up days, epidemics, and the loss of the medical college. These decades saw increasing scientific knowledge and a devastating international flu epidemic.

The loss of the North Carolina Medical College and its clinic obviously reduced the amount of medical care available for area residents. But the town was not without resources. The 1910 and 1920 censuses show at least three physicians, one dentist, two pharmacists, and two public nurses. New medical discoveries relating to contagious diseases meant that the town had fewer deaths from scarlet fever, measles, and typhoid fever, despite the recurrence of scarlet fever in 1907, 1914, and 1917.

The town began reporting vital statistics in 1912. In that year three deaths were attributed to dysentery and one each to pellagra, pneumonia, and tuberculosis. Until flu epidemics in 1918 and 1920, 1914 had the most deaths, with twenty-one deaths from disease and one each from gunshot wounds and a train wreck. Five of the deaths from disease were infants within four weeks of birth. "Let us not forget . . . as we start to work in the new year," the town's report concluded, "that during last year [1914] three little ones died because conditions in the homes or in the town were not what they should have been." Despite that warning, in 1915 there were four infant deaths, and seven children under eighteen months died in 1917.[36]

The year 1917 was a pivotal one for health in Davidson. The town board ordered a clean-up day that required residents to "drain all marshy places and see if the guttering retains any water." The order further noted that

> Mosquitos breed in stagnant water. . . . No standing water, no mosquitoes. If stables are kept clean there will be no flies and no typhoid in Davidson. Our death rate in 1914 was 23 to 1,200 people. In 1916 it was 12, with some increase in population. Efforts to have more sanitary premises have paid. More effort will pay more.[37]

In addition, the local school board began requiring that all children have a health certificate before enrolling. The local school board also paid Dr. Justice to provide examinations for school children. In 1918 he received $7.50 for examining "30+ colored children."[38]

Despite the precautions, Davidson was no more prepared to handle the flu epidemic than any other city or town. In September 1918 alone roughly 10,000 Americans died from the disease, and many more died in other nations. Davidson had more than two hundred cases, including students, in the fall of 1918. The campus newspaper reported on October 23 that

> through Sunday over 100 cases had been reported in town, with a number of pneumonia cases. It was a serious question combating the disease in town, as patients could not be brought to a central hospital, but had to be treated in their . . . homes. Last Wednesday evening in the Civic [Club] hall a citizens' meeting was held, presided over by Mayor Sloan, in which the epidemic was reviewed and several committees appointed with which the Red Cross should cooperate in an effort to see that there should be no neglect of the sick who are unable to have proper nursing . . . , especially because [they are] unable to find a nurse where most of the family is down with the disease. Both of the cotton mills were silent for several days as the electric power was not being furnished, but the Linden had to shut down the day before on account of the absences of sick operatives.[39]

At least five people died in Davidson, as did a nurse, Rose Stevenson, who contracted the flu while volunteering in Davidson but died in Charlotte.[40] Three of the five who died in town were African-Americans. As the situation improved, the *Davidsonian*'s student reporter showed surprisingly little sympathy for mill workers and blacks. For the former, the reporter noted that a "few convalescent employees" were hindering production. For the latter, the reporter condescendingly referred to ignorance and superstition:

> at the outset of the epidemic, due to their ignorance of modern sanitation and care of the body, the disease was most prevalent in their section. And among [blacks] are several who . . . resorted to such methods as shaking a little sulfur in their shoes and other unique proceedings at the suspicions of a cold, in the hope that the disease could be avoided by such beliefs.[41]

Folk-medicine practices certainly lingered throughout the town. Even with scientific advances, many people still valued grandmother's remedies and farmers' almanacs. More than reliance on folk cures, less access to education and poorer living conditions contributed to the higher death rate among blacks. Clean-up days did not necessarily encompass the entire town; and, as noted earlier, sewer and water lines were limited to the college and merchant neighborhoods.

Flu returned in January 1920. Within days of the first reported cases, the women of the Civic Club hired a community nurse with Red Cross training. While the number of cases was smaller and overall the epidemic was less severe, local businesses, churches, and schools closed briefly. A headline in the *Davidsonian* urged calm: "SIT STEADY, FELLOWS, THERE'S NO CAUSE FOR A 'FLU' PANIC."[42]

On a lighter note, town residents were disappointed to miss a Saturday evening movie and a program by Opie Read, a well-known humorist. The college physician cancelled both events because of the risk of the disease spreading in crowded rooms. When the movies resumed, the student managers ran two shows per night, one "especially for the town people" and one for college students only.

Advances in Local Schooling

Along with health concerns, education was the main focus of town women. Although men continued to serve as trustees and principals, women worked to improve schools and provide recreation for children. In 1900 children's education was still a church affair. Most white children attended the school established by DCPC, and black children attended school in the black Masonic Hall taught by ministers of Davidson Presbyterian and Reeves Temple A.M.E. Zion churches. The change from private to public schools occurred in 1911 with the passage of the graded school law for Davidson.

This change almost did not happen. The voters split 68 to 66 on the measure. Why a college town would be so reluctant to adopt a public school program is unclear. Perhaps voters believed that the current system was adequate, or perhaps they wanted to avoid state regulations or additional taxes. Whatever the concerns, a two-vote margin permitted public oversight and public funds. The first taxes for the schools—a property tax of 48 cents per hundred dollars valuation and a poll tax of $1.44—were levied in August 1911. Six local men served as the first school trustees. Section 11 of the Graded School Law for Davidson required the trustees to "establish graded public schools for the [town's] white and colored children," and to provide "each equal school facilities, due regard . . . being had to the cost of establishing and maintaining the graded schools of each race."

Information about the expenditures on the schools has been lost, but contemporary accounts show discrepancies between the schools. The white school continued to meet in a two-story, multi-room structure and had college graduates, male and female, as teachers. The black school moved from the Masonic Hall to a small one-room schoolhouse on Sloan Street. "No particular academic requirements were necessary to qualify teachers for our school," Ralph Johnson recalled. "It was assumed by the white board of education that employed them that they were qualified to teach us if they were preachers, or if they came from a 'good' Negro family and had themselves finished a grade school."[43]

Local women, especially the members of the two civic clubs, assisted the public schools. Their projects included (among others) sponsoring essays, providing equipment, planting bushes, and hosting receptions for teachers. In April 1913 the Civic Club hosted a public meeting featuring six speeches by prominent citizens; over the summer they added sixteen closets in the white school building. In her annual report, the club president took the liberty to editorialize, noting that the cost of the closets would appear "in the treasurer's report for the year. The expenditure in time, nerve-strain, and patience by the committee can be computed by anyone who has tried to get anything built in Davidson."[44]

By 1915 the white school could boast of a library installed with "neat book cases," a literary society, a regular column in the *Davidsonian*, and a well-received burlesque production of Shakespeare's *Merchant of Venice* that was deemed "far above average, especially for amateurs."[45] Although the black school had no library and was almost invisible in terms of local news, it played a central role in the lives of the students and their families.

The two schools had at least one thing in common: overcrowding. The white school grew from 160 students in 1914 to 210 in 1916, and the black school had more than fifty students. Trustee efforts in 1917 to "either enlarge" the white school building "or build a new one" failed due to a lack of funds from the town.

In April 1920 "mothers of the town and teachers of the Davidson Graded Schools" formed a Parent-Teachers Association. The PTA and the trustees pressed for improved facilities for the schools, but it took another three years for construction to begin. By 1924 the white school had a new building or, as Mary Beaty aptly described it, "a school building which was new in front but still 1893 as to its rear section." Around the same time a second small building was added for the black school.[46]

In addition to the public education available in town, several private schools operated in Davidson in the 1910s, including two schools for young children that lasted only a short time. In October 1913 Maude Vinson, a young graduate of Converse College, opened a girls' seminary. Intended for post-high school education, the seminary won the enthusiasm of Davidson College students because, the college magazine noted, the "campus has ever had a hearty interest in every educational move—and incidentally, has ever felt that the town has none too large a following of girls."[47] Unfortunately, the seminary closed in 1915, thus leaving the college's male students once again with too few women their age to date. With the seminary's closing, Vinson began what would be a lifetime career when she joined the teaching staff of the Davidson High School in the fall of 1915, taking over the 7th and 8th grade classes.

There also were evening schools for the children of mill workers and for black men. The mill school, with three teachers and twenty students, met for one hour twice a week and featured what the *Davidsonian* called "the good, solid, old-fashioned subjects, spelling, reading, writing, and arithmetic." Mrs. John Reid, perhaps as a result of her Civic Club study of the "Negro School," helped to organize the black school. College students taught the school's twenty-seven students.[48]

Other Educational Programs and Literary Events

During these years the Booklovers Club expanded from the original eight members to twenty. Most members of the club were connected to the college as wives of faculty or as members of the college staff. Their reading lists maintained an academic tone; several books were selected for discussion each year on such topics as Shakespeare, Russia, the Ottoman Empire, U.S. history, and women writers of the eighteenth century.

The college and the Medical College (until 1907) continued to offer public lectures, with appearances by notables such as William Jennings Bryan, one of the leading orators and Democrats of his generation, and Malcolm Patterson, a former governor of Tennessee. The Civic Club also hosted speakers and forums on a wide range of local and national issues, including education and woman suffrage.[49]

Town businessmen entered the education realm by forming a Chautauqua Committee. The Chautauqua movement began in Chautauqua, New York, as a summer program of lectures and classes. By 1900 there was an active lecture circuit. In preparing for Chautauqua's first appearance in Davidson, on 23–24 September 1920, more than thirty volunteers worked on committees with tasks as diverse as tents and grounds, locating pianos, advertising, seating, children's hour, and hospitality. Eight ticket committees were formed, most of which covered a portion of the town, including the "mill division." Notably absent in this list was any reference to the mainly black parts of town.[50]

The 1920 Chautauqua in Davidson was held in a large tent on the village grove (now the village green). The program included lectures on the English language, the U.S. government, and foreign cultures, plus humorous readings, magic tricks, and musical programs by the Neopolitan Quartet, the Oakley Concert Company, and the Kraft Trio. The two shows a day came at a price of fifty cents per performance or two dollars for a "season ticket."

Civic Organizations Largely Flourish

The community effort for the Chautauqua visit reflected Davidson's basic pattern of civic cooperation that alternately crossed and reinforced social divisions. Town residents organized around projects such as church building, fixing schools, sanitation days, or entertainment. While some causes were largely local, others, such as the Red Cross and war bonds, stemmed from regional or national concerns. The results were often sporadic: clubs came and went as interest waxed and waned, and causes faded only to reappear a decade or so later. These decades saw the first two clean-up days, the first efforts to improve housing, and the first community dinner, held on 9 June 1920.[51]

Although interest varied and one group disappeared, there were more men's civic organizations in 1920 than there had been twenty years earlier. Both the white Masonic lodge and its junior organization, the Knights of Pythias, folded early in the new century. The Knights held oyster suppers and started a reading room over White's Drug Store, but interest waned and they surrendered their charter in 1908. The white Masons were able to reorganize in January 1915. Two years later three college employees and a merchant organized the Citizen's Club "for the benefit of the young men of the town." This club set up a reading room and recreation hall over Goodrum's store, using funds contributed by the first fifty members.[52] The black Masons continued to meet and maintain their hall, no longer needing to provide school space.

For young boys, the college YMCA introduced the idea of Boy Scouting. Scouting was brought to America in 1910 by progressives seeking to reinvigorate pioneer ideals and counter the perceived negative effects of industrialization and urbanization.[53] While Davidson's streets were hardly urban, the combination of outdoor skills and moral virtues appealed to YMCA members.

The first white troop in Davidson was formed in 1912. By 1914 twenty members were enjoying hikes and facing the challenge of writing the best essay on "How to Rid Davidson of Flies and Mosquitoes." In 1916 another club, part of the Pioneers of America, was established for boys between the ages of nine and twelve.

Ironically, the most industrialized section of town, the mill village, did not get a Boy Scout troop. As a substitute, Dr. Howard Arbuckle organized a "live boys' club" in 1914. Quite likely, the finances and schedules of the mill families could not accommodate the fees and time for hikes and overnights. The YMCA eventually extended Scouting to African-Americans, establishing a troop in 1932.[54]

At the same time that Scouting was introduced to American boys, Luther and Charlotte Gulick founded the Campfire Girls as a non-sectarian organization for girls. While the organization's focus was nurturing a sense of community, the members' activities reflected the increased acceptance of physical activity for girls.

In 1915 Irene Foreman organized the town's first Campfire group, named Wakichonze. The nine members—Willie Campbell, Birdie Christenbury, Dorothy Finlayson, Elizabeth Grey, Willie Henderson, Sarah Lingle, Eloise Martin, Katherine Potts, and Mary Thompson—were all daughters of professors or merchants. Despite issuing a challenge to the

Boy Scouts that they would "show them up" and producing a public program of folk dances and ballads, the group became inactive over the summer. Gordon Baskerville revived it in November 1916.

The most active and visible organization in town was the previously mentioned Civic Club. Founded in 1911 by educated white women, the club took on education, sanitation, beautification, and homemaking projects. During its first two years it organized a junior club with ninety members and an African-American club with twenty-seven members. It rented its first hall in 1913 and provided a community meeting space for several organizations, including the Boy Scouts. The club procured a new hall in 1915 after the old space was declared unsafe for large gatherings.

Funds raised through bazaars, flower shows, fancy dress parties, and oyster suppers were expended in many ways. Some went to pay a portion of the town health officer's salary, to reimburse a school playground director, to clean Main Street each week for one year, and to buy packets of flower seeds that were distributed to mill families. In addition, funds provided for trees and flowers at the train depot and prizes for essay contests, supported a canning demonstration, underwrote the costs of mailing to every home information on caring for outhouses, aided the white public school library and the town library, and nourished dozens of other projects. The Civic Club also organized a Red Cross Auxiliary in 1917.[55]

While Cornelia Shaw served as the club's president for many years, Clara Souther Lingle, wife of Professor Thomas Lingle and sister-in-law of Walter Lingle, then president of the college's board of trustees, was the group's most dynamic and visible member. In 1914 she represented both the Booklovers Club and the Civic Club at the North Carolina Federation of Women's Clubs at its annual meeting, and served as the president of the federation in 1915. Elected the first woman member of the North Carolina Conference on Social Service, she went on to serve as secretary/treasurer for three years. An active member of the North Carolina Equal Suffrage League, she lectured on such diverse topics as suffrage, parliamentary government, and South American politics, and published a story in *Woman's Home Companion*.

While living in Raleigh in the late 1910s during the time her husband was in Europe doing YMCA work for soldiers, Lingle was a leader in the University of North Carolina's extension division, organizing correspondence courses, study groups, and club programs for women. She also advised the university's twenty-five women students. Back in Davidson in the early 1920s, she sponsored a New Year's Eve party featuring the

Davidson Orchestra and served as vice-president of the Civic Club. Her contributions at the state level as well as in town would earn her a place on any list of Davidson's highly accomplished people.[56]

Davidson During World War I

After America's entry in April 1917 into what contemporaries called the Great War, Davidson's women combined to buy nearly $10,000 in war bonds (called Liberty Bonds). In addition to the Civic Club and the Red Cross Auxiliary, town women also formed a local chapter of the Women's Committee on National Defense. Using the Civic Club hall, members of the various groups rolled bandages, prepared gift boxes for soldiers, and reported that they had "done a greater work than any undertaken by any group between Charlotte and Asheville."[57]

The Red Cross Auxiliary held concerts and weekly sales of ice cream, tea, and sandwiches to fund their work. An article in February 1918 listed 134 women volunteers and another in March mentioned young girls who had "patiently and painfully cut scraps to fill comfort pillows for the use of the wounded on the battlefields. Many a little hand has been blistered, but very proudly borne for the sake of the Red Cross."[58]

The women's efforts made sense given that they saw not only their sons and husbands but also so many of the young men at the college off to war. Shortly after the U.S. declaration of war, roughly eighty Davidson College students were excused from completing the school year so that they could go home and help with food production. About twice as many Davidson students, 158, entered the armed services between 1 April 1917 and 1 September 1918.[59] White and black men from the Davidson area also volunteered, including 44 men whom the *Davidsonian* listed in September 1917. Because there was an effective military draft, many who volunteered would have been drafted into service had they not volunteered.

The war reached Davidson in other ways, most noticeably the shortage of coal (the main source of heating) in January 1918 and the previously discussed flu epidemic that often was brought home by soldiers. While the college was able to obtain enough coal to remain open, the *Davidsonian* reported on January 23 that townspeople were "urged to use the utmost economy in burning their coal" because there was "no certainty when the next shipment of coal will reach here."[60]

During the war white residents of Davidson, most of whom had joined the overwhelming majority of their fellow southerners in voting Democratic ever since Reconstruction, were pleased that an accomplished

Logan Houston while serving as a soldier in World War I

Democrat and former Davidson College student, Woodrow Wilson, was serving as America's president. Having taken great pride in Wilson's brief visit to campus in May 1916, local white men voted overwhelmingly to re-elect him that November. For its February 1918 program, the Civic Club invited Professor J. Moore MacConnell to lecture on "The War Aims of President Wilson," inviting "all the women of the town" to attend.[61] The town joined the nation in prayers after Wilson's massive stroke in September 1919.

Conclusion

For middle-class "college" and "town" whites generally, there was more change than continuity between 1901 and 1920. New products—especially automobiles, electric appliances, and movies—made their lives easier and more exciting. New job opportunities emerged, including the hiring of the first woman in a professional position at the college, and white women got the right to vote in time for the 1920 election. Golf, played mainly by white men, arrived in town when the Davidson Golf Club was organized in 1914. And new civic organizations, notably the Civic Club and Boy Scouts, increased opportunities for learning, adventure, and service to others. A worthy addition was the Methodist Church, which gave "town" whites a significant local alternative to the largely "college" DCPC.

Continuity more aptly characterizes the lives of most of the town's African-Americans and mill workers. Their incomes remained very modest, thus keeping them from enjoying most modern consumer goods, and their housing—almost entirely west of Main Street—remained much poorer than middle-class whites had on Main Street and on the town's east side. And while the education of their youth improved with the arrival of public schools, it remained inferior to that available to middle-class whites.

Socially, the town by the early twentieth century divided into four main groups: "college," "town," and "mill" whites plus African-Americans. Economically, however, the town was becoming increasingly two-tiered, with "college" and "town" whites constituting a broad middle-class, and virtually all "mill" whites and blacks forming an equally broad lower-class, including some families who lived in poverty. In what was to become a pattern throughout the twentieth century, adults and children in "mill" and black families who wanted to better themselves socially and economically often moved away from Davidson as part of their effort to do so.

5 The Relatively Prosperous 1920s and the Depressed 1930s

The decades of the 1920s and 1930s often bring to mind the flappers of the Roaring Twenties and the bread lines of the Great Depression. Like other small towns in largely rural areas, Davidson experienced these major social and economic changes to a lesser degree. After all, in a town where alcohol sales had never been legal, the national Prohibition of the 1920s and early 1930s was already the norm. Nor was the appearance of stills and rum runners a new experience, for students and townspeople long had found creative ways to get around the ban. Overall, the already established patterns that limited the town's commercial activities and population growth continued. Thus, compared with large cities, the town maintained the good fortune of dealing with issues on a small, human scale.

During these decades a new neighborhood grew up on the Shelton land off Concord Road. A goodly number of new businesses opened, although not all survived the uncertain economic times, especially during the Depression of the 1930s. Improved roads made getting to Davidson easier, but compared to Charlotte and other cities, the town still remained largely a place to pass through. The mill strikes that garnered national attention for neighboring towns and cities played out relatively quietly in Davidson. Still, townspeople, their government, and the college experienced changes and challenges that left their marks on the community.

After 1929 economic challenges grew, especially for those who lacked steady jobs at the college. In 1929 twelve-year-old Blanche Knox, well-known in town later by her married name of Blanche Parker, moved with her parents and six siblings into a rental house on South Street. Her father managed the Davidson Ice and Fuel Company, which had prospered in the 1920s. Like many businesses in town, Davidson Ice and Fuel allowed customers to open lines of credit, delivering ice and coal to homes and businesses with the understanding that bills eventually would be paid. By the early 1930s, Parker recalled, "people charged things and . . . couldn't pay their bills; they had no money." As a result, her family was unable to pay the rent on their home in Davidson, and had to move to a cabin north of town that lacked electricity and running water and was so "rustic" that "you had to blow out the lamp to get dressed because there wasn't anything between the logs."[1]

In addition to the economic hardships that affected many families in the 1930s, perhaps the largest contrast between the 1920s and 1930s was the much smaller population growth in the Depression decade. Whereas the town's population grew by 25 percent in the 1920s (from 1,156 to 1,445), partly due to a 25 percent increase in the size of the college's student body, it increased by only 7 percent in the 1930s (from 1,445 to 1,550). With regard to population and economic activity, Davidson largely treaded water in the 1930s.

Changes in Town Government

For the town commissioners, the new world of managing utilities, learning to deal with state and federal offices, and supervising staff took center stage. The passage of women's suffrage in 1919 should have increased voter turnout. At first that does not appear to have been the case: only 97 people voted in the 1922 town election. Voter turnout grew dramatically in 1925, when 261 votes were cast, and increased to an interwar high of 317 in 1937. Only two women held official positions during these years. Mrs. L. Brady was appointed an election inspector in 1921, and Hattie Thompson became town collector in 1935. Her starting salary was $50 per month.

Thompson's hiring as the person responsible for listing and collecting taxes grew out of the town government's growing responsibilities. Traditionally the town sheriff also had listed and collected taxes.[2] Several factors prompted the change. As the town took over utility services from the college, now managing water, sewer, and electricity, the need grew for regular access to town officials and staff. The town also needed more office space. The practice of using the mayor's business office as town hall ended when the commissioners voted in 1933 to rent a small building on Main Street for this purpose. A year later, the board specified office hours for the town collector, one hour in the morning and one in the afternoon. These hours proved insufficient. When Thompson started work, her position was full-time, from 8 to 5 daily with a generous one-and-one-half hour lunch.

Personnel issues with the town sheriff also played a role in Thompson's hiring. In the early 1930s the town's marshal and collector, James Johnston, had a drinking problem. In August 1931 the town board suspended him for fifteen days because, the minutes explained, he had "been drinking and under the influence of intoxicants for the last week or more." After Johnston returned to public service, he had additional drinking problems and was relieved of his duties in July 1932, though he did work thereafter as the town's sanitary inspector. Johnston was replaced by E.N. Linker, soon to be known respectfully by generations of residents and students as "Cop" Linker.

Thompson's hiring was just one example of increasingly professional management of town affairs and the public sector's expanding responsibilities. In 1925 the board set up a "proper" accounting system and, after commissioners increasingly attended governmental conferences, the town joined the North Carolina League of Municipalities in 1934.

The commissioners also increased their involvement in fire protection. In September 1933, the board, with financial aid from the college, ordered a new fire truck. That November they elected and appointed the members of a fire department for the town. Three months later, they adopted laws for the "erection and inspection of buildings and fire protection," thus re-establishing the fire ordinances for the town. In 1936 they authorized the purchase of a fire truck and three new fire hydrants, "one on North Main Street, one on South Main Street, and one in the colored section of town."[3]

Streets, Lights, and Sanitation

As in the 1910s, streets, lights, water, and sanitation were major concerns for the board, with the added burden of selling and managing bonds. Although most streets still were not paved and many also lacked sidewalks, the biggest concern was getting a new highway built through town. This road—an improved Main Street called the Davidson College Highway—was dedicated in November 1923. The *Davidsonian* noted that "traffic seem[ed] to be heaviest on Sunday afternoons, when hundreds of cars pass through."[4]

When the highway opened, few businesses could be open on Sundays to profit from the travelers. Requests for adjustment to Sunday-closing laws began to appear on town board agendas in 1921 and 1922. In No-

Main Street opening celebration in 1923

vember 1922 the board agreed to a minor change, allowing restaurants a breakfast hour in addition to the one hour each at lunch and dinner. In 1925 the board permitted an extra hour for each meal. Finally becoming generous in 1932, the board allowed eating establishments to stay open Saturday evening until 2 a.m. Sunday, with Sunday daytime serving hours of 6:30 to 10 a.m., 12:15 to 2:30 p.m., and 4:30 to 7 p.m.

In 1933 the board received a request from a major petroleum company to sell gas and oil on Sundays. The commissioners were more liberal than they had been with restaurants, requiring only that gas pumps be closed during church hours—10 a.m. to 12:30 p.m. and 7 p.m. to 8:30 p.m. Five years later, restaurants and drug stores were granted the same Sunday opening hours.

While the burgeoning numbers of cars and trucks brought in some revenue through local tags and licenses, roads and motor vehicles also prompted frequent requests for road repairs and new paving, the need for parking regulations and revisions thereof, and even traffic direction by the sheriff from 8 to 8:40 a.m. and 12:30 to 1:40 p.m. at the corner of Main and South streets. The town's first stoplight appeared at the corner of Main and Depot in 1937. Given the number of newspaper articles describing car accidents in town, it is clear that both the stoplight and the town's Highway Safety Committee were much needed. Things had gotten so bad by 1940 that the board decried the "growing menace of the traffic through the Main Street of the town," and "heartily" endorsed a proposal to build a bypass west of town.[5]

In addition to roads and traffic, sanitation and water issues demanded the commissioners' attention. By the early 1920s it was becoming clear that the college's water works were not sufficient for both the college and the town. Aware that major improvements in infrastructure could not be funded on a pay-as-you-go basis, the town board voted in April 1922 to issue bonds—$60,000 for electricity and water, $30,000 for sewer, and $30,000 for street improvements. In the ensuing weeks, mill owners issued a protest and 100 residents signed a petition demanding a referendum on the matter. The voting took place in October. With 229 of 290 registered voters participating and a serious drought affecting the region, the bonds passed easily with a seventy-vote margin.[6]

By December 1923 the town had what the *Davidsonian* hailed as an "up-to-date water system" that "is the very best that modern engineering can secure." It was sure to provide all the water needed and the "tank with a hundred thousand gallons capacity had been erected and the proper elevation to give sufficient pressure."[7] After a new pumping and filtering station were added in 1924, the water was safe to drink and the flow was sufficient to allow a contract to supply water to Cornelius as well as to Davidson.[8]

Addressing sanitation issues did not go as smoothly. Although the town was still surrounded by farmland, some residents felt strongly that the keeping of farm animals, especially hogs, should be prohibited in particular sections of town. The commissioners passed a new ordinance in April 1932 after S.G. Morgan presented a petition signed by twenty-one residents "complaining about offensive hog pens and cow stables located on certain back lots." Interestingly, the ordinance banned hogs and pigs only in an area of town west of Main Street and south of Delburg Street, where both the mill and the black communities lived.[9]

In addition to reflecting changing sensibilities among the "college" and "town" whites, the petition and the ensuing ordinance shed light on economic conditions during the Depression. While a significant number of mill and black families were relying on farm animals for food, relatively few "college" and "town" whites needed to stretch their food dollars by raising livestock for meat.

The town was approaching another divide in connection with sanitation. While homes and businesses near the college were now on a sewer system, many residents still relied on privies. In response to complaints about "sanitary conditions existing in certain portions of the town," in February 1925 the town board passed an ordinance requiring "[a]ll property owners abutting Main Street from Mrs. Brady's property line to Depot Street and Depot Street up to and including the property of the Southern Railway" to connect to sewer lines. This ordinance was expanded in August 1926 to include "every property owner in town that is within 200 feet of the water and sewer lines."[10]

The town board also began to explore ways to expand and improve the sewer system. In subsequent years they entertained proposals by engineers to add lines to connect to new neighborhoods as the budget allowed. This approach left parts of town, especially the mill homes and black neighborhoods, without access to sewers and kept privy inspections as part of the sheriff's job.

A breakthrough resulting in a greatly expanded sewer system occurred in the mid-1930s. In 1934 Davidson chemistry professor Howard Arbuckle and town commissioner W.W. Wood, after returning from a trip to New York City, offered the board the prospect of the town's being a test site for a new sewer system.[11] By being a test site, the town would pay about one-third of the normal cost. Called the Major Roder System and offered by the BioReduction Corporation of Brooklyn, the system was built after months of negotiations and engineering consultations, coming into operation in October 1935.

The new system worked well until the Davidson Cotton Mill was added. After the mill's dyes caused problems, the town insisted that the mill stop using the sewer plant. In 1941 the board made another demand, this time to the Carolina Asbestos Company on Depot Street across from the train station. Noting that "the open ditch emanating from [its] factory constitutes a nuisance and menace to health," the company was required to cover it immediately.[12]

Two other utilities were part of the commissioners' agenda, electricity and telephones. In December 1923 the board signed a new contract with the Southern Power Company to furnish the town's electricity. This agreement left the town still collecting payments, setting rates by use (e.g., motion picture machines and "Frigidaires"), and paying for damage to machinery caused by high voltages.

In December 1937 the town's telephone exchange was upgraded to the "dial system." The new monthly rates for businesses were $3.50 for a single line, $3.00 for a two-party line, and $2.50 for a four-party line. Home rates ranged from $2.25 for a single line to $1.50 for a four-party line. In 1938 Mrs. Thompson's duties were expanded to collecting telephone bills and surcharges for long-distance calls, with one-half of the proceeds going to the town.[13]

Other Town Projects—And the Challenges of Financing Them

The town's finances were managed carefully during these decades. In 1926–27, after the passage of the bond initiatives and before the economic crash, the town's projected budget came to $46,981.13. Eight years later, the town treasurer reported at a "mass meeting of citizens" that "the town had reduced its indebtedness $8,700 during the past ten years and had reduced its tax rate from $2.25 to $1.25 per $100 valuation in spite of the fact that the taxable values had dropped [due to the Depression] from $1,500,000 to $918,000." The budget for 1936–37 was $22,799.45, less than half of the one for 1926–27.[14]

Especially in the 1930s, the town board rejected or delayed many projects because of lack of funds. Street lights were not extended down Main Street, for example, and a weekly garbage pickup service was turned down. Still, the town managed reasonably well and found small sums to support local civic groups—e.g., buying two stoves for the Boy Scout hut, contributing $25 to a pre-maternity clinic, and paying for the heating and electricity for the town library branch.[15]

Two more costly town priorities were a new jail and a new cemetery. For the jail, the town in 1928 purchased property on Depot Street, and then purchased two cells from the county and had them installed in 1929. After a failed effort in the 1920s, in 1938 the commissioners purchased twelve acres between South and Walnut streets as the site for a cemetery for whites. They appointed the mayor, Thomas Griffith, and two commissioners to serve as the board of trustees and direct the operations of the newly named Mimosa Cemetery.[16]

Commissioners almost always have had additional ambitions—wish lists—for the town. As a result of President Franklin D. Roosevelt's New Deal beginning in 1933, at least some wishes could come true because of federally funded programs, especially programs of the Civil Works Administration. On 20 November 1933 the board met to outline projects to submit to the state superintendent of the CWA. These included:

1. Finish grading and surfacing the tennis courts and basketball court at the Davidson Graded School grounds, estimate of cost $350
2. Grading and surfacing sidewalks in the two mill villages, estimate of cost $500
3. Draining lowlands in and around the town, estimate of cost $1,000

4. Cleaning up and disposing of leaves, trash, etc., in the town, estimate $100

5. Putting down permanent sidewalks in the town, property owners to furnish all material . . . , estimate of cost $2,000.[17]

By late January 1934 work had begun on several of the projects. All the streams with headwaters in the town were being drained, and Louisiana, an old campus building that once had served as the president's house, was torn down, with the bricks being used to create sidewalks on both sides of Main Street. The town board also voted to spend up to $1,850 toward the building of a new gymnasium for the white Davidson Graded School. Although the gym project was not initiated by the town, it did affirm the wisdom of the board's earlier decision to turn the school over to the county.[18]

Starting in 1911, the town basically had two school districts. A town school board oversaw the Davidson Graded School, while the Mecklenburg County Board of Education was responsible for the African-American school. After seeing the county Board of Education succeed in getting funds where they had failed, and after the superintendent of the Mecklenburg County Schools came to the board in December 1932 with the proposal to the CWA for the new gym, the commissioners voted in January 1933 to relinquish the town's special charter and to deed the school property to the county in the hope that the county would get funds for the gym. The new gym demonstrated the value of town-county cooperation.[19]

The town also benefited from four more projects initiated by other groups. In August 1935 the board voted to cooperate with the town of Cornelius on a Public Works Administration (PWA) project that offered federal funds for labor to build sidewalks on each side of the highway if the towns would provide the necessary top soil or gravel. In 1940 Davidson participated in a Works Projects Administration (WPA) project for codifying ordinances and charters.

More significantly, the county Board of Education secured $18,000 for a new school building for black children in Davidson. Construction began in 1937. A report of the Charlotte-Mecklenburg Landmark Commission offers some insight into this project:

> County Board of Education minutes do not tell the story of the
> [Davidson black] community's involvement in bringing the school
> into existence nor the vital support the community played once
> the six-classroom brick building was completed. According to
> community members, teacher Ada Jenkins and P.T.A. president

Logan Houston led the effort to build the school, and the black community raised money for the construction of the school.[20]

This school was tied to the final federally funded project. A few years after the Davidson Colored School building was completed, the college YMCA built a small community center on the school grounds. Student volunteers and Civic Club members offered a variety of youth programs and adult education classes. In October 1940 the college YMCA, the Civic Club, and an African-American citizens group successfully applied for federal funding for two recreational workers for the community center. "Two WPA workers, Thomas Harshaw and Lester Hunsucker, have been secured to help in the work with the Negroes," the *Davidsonian* reported in January 1941. "They are . . . conducting a survey among the colored people to determine what kind of instruction they desire besides what is being offered by the YMCA."[21] Harshaw and Hunsucker developed several programs for the community before the nation's entrance into World War II put an end to their work.

Davidson College showed less interest than the town in federal programs, turning down a National Youth Administration (NYA) project request on the grounds that the college was not set up to teach any practical courses in agriculture or home economics. But college officials did submit proposals for student employment. In 1941 ninety-four students were able to supplement financial contributions from their families with federally funded jobs on campus.[22]

The college also provided some direct economic benefits to the town. In 1922, after a request from the town for assistance with payments on water, electricity, and sewer bonds, the college's trustees voted to provide $750 annually during the life of the bonds, with the stipulation that the town "puts in efficient water and sewerage systems, with water and pressure sufficient for the purpose." Shortly thereafter, the college deeded over land for a water tank.[23] A decade later, the college paid half of the cost of a new fire truck—this at a time when, except for the funds collected by student organizations for charity work in town, the college had few financial reserves to share.

Challenges at the College

Disaster struck the campus during the night of 28 November 1921. A fire destroyed Chambers, the main campus building, leaving students without dorm rooms, faculty without classrooms, and administrators

Ruins of Chambers Building after the fire

without offices. Despite the extent of the damage and the presence of students in the building, the most serious injury was a sprained ankle. With remarkable resiliency and the support of townspeople, the college managed to find housing, classrooms, and office space, restarting classes after being closed for just one day.

Although devastating at the time, the fire signaled a new beginning for the college. The once elegant building had outlasted its usefulness and was ill-designed for adapting to changes in higher education. The fire both opened up new possibilities and offered a dramatic opportunity for fundraising. It also provided brick for projects in many homes east of Main Street.

The college quickly launched a campaign, receiving letters of support from such national figures as Woodrow Wilson and William Jennings Bryan. Success in fund-raising enabled the college to start a small building boom. Three new dormitories were completed in 1922–23, and were soon followed by the south wing of the new Chambers building, completed in 1925. Work on Chambers, begun again in 1928, was finished in 1929. Meanwhile the college also built a new fraternity court facing Concord Road.

The college's determination to rebuild and grow received a major boost in 1924, when industrialist/philanthropist James Buchanan Duke created the Duke Endowment and included Davidson College with a 5 percent share. College president William Martin later acknowledged that having this annual supplementary income "created a stabilizing influence" that assured the college's long-term future.[24]

Although Martin retired from the presidency in 1929, he attended the dedication of the New Chambers Building in 1930. His successor, Davidson alumnus Walter Lingle, ably guided the college through the Depression years. Lingle began his presidency with high hopes to build upon Martin's legacy by making additional improvements in the college's physical plant in time for the college's centennial celebration in 1937. Lingle's hopes to raise nearly $2.3 million in five years proved unrealistic because of what he rightly called "the severity of the financial depression."[25] The campaign ended up raising less than $200,000, but the college still was able to build a new infirmary and endow several scholarships.

During the Depression the college, like many individuals and families in Davidson, had to make do with less. The budget for 1933–34, for example, was $25,000 less than the one for 1932–33, a substantial amount for that time. Even as funds from endowments and donations from Presbyterian churches dropped, Lingle held high standards for the college, regularly reminding the trustees of the need for new buildings, equipment, staff, and money for contributions to the new federal Social Security program. He noted in his 1939 report to the trustees that the college had ended another fiscal year "without any deficit," and encouraged them to integrate continuous, intensive fund-raising efforts into the college's planning for the future.[26]

Changes at the Mills—And in Other Available Work

The local cotton mills did not fare as well as the college. Despite the additions to the Delburg Mill and the merger with the Linden Mill, by 1923 President J.P. Munroe and the board of directors were resigned to selling the property. Because of unfavorable "conditions in the mill business," Munroe wrote the directors, the selling price might be "considerably below par."[27]

The Delburg company was sold to Martin Cannon of Cannon Mills in August 1923, and the older Linden Mill building was closed and converted into a warehouse. The Linden Mill building eventually was sold and reopened as the Carolina Asbestos Company in the early 1930s. The Delburg Mill continued to operate, but faced a deficit of $125,000 by 1936. That year a group of former employees sued the asbestos company after being

First shift of the Davidson Cotton Mill poses outside the mill in 1928

diagnosed with asbestosis. The courts eventually sided with the company because North Carolina's liability law was passed after the employees became ill.[28]

In the fall of 1934, a wave of labor unrest and strikes in the cotton mills arrived in Mecklenburg and Iredell counties. With memories of the bloody 1929 strike in Gaston County still strong, the United Textile Workers' call for strikes in August 1934 increased tensions both locally and nationally. The headline in the 6 September 1934 *Mooresville Enterprise* read "Strike Closes Local Cotton Mill, 2000 Idle." The article's tone was unsympathetic to the picketers. The *Charlotte Observer* reported on September 11 that, in its canvass of local textile mills, only 600 of 4,200 textile workers were on the job. On September 16 the *Observer* reported that President Roosevelt was thinking about intervening in the strikes.[29]

With only one textile mill with 200 employees operating, Davidson remained on the fringes of the strike movement. The Davidson mill closed for three days but was never picketed. If any workers sympathized with the unionizing effort, they kept their views to themselves. Indeed, at a special meeting on September 6, the commissioners heard that "the mill owners were willing to run the plant and give their employees work provided that their property was given the proper protection from the violence of the strikers and their sympathizers," and received assurances that the mill workers "were all willing and anxious to work."[30]

An unusual opportunity for women's employment appeared briefly in 1937. Edwin Lee of Philadelphia announced plans to open a branch of the Lee Paper Box Company. According to a news report the factory would "occupy two vacant rooms in the brick building next to the town fire station" and employ "white girls." The location proved convenient: a fire broke out in the factory on 25 January 1938, but was quickly put out with so little damage that the factory continued to operate without the need to close for repairs. Despite surviving the fire, the company appears not to have lasted much longer.[31]

For most women, employment options did not change much during these decades. Black women working outside the home were primarily cooks, laundresses, and house cleaners. The 1930 census also listed three as school teachers. The mills were the largest employers of white women, with the schools a distant second. Along with a few stenographers, telephone operators, boarding house managers, nurses, and librarians, one woman worked as an insurance agent, another managed deliveries for the ice factory, and one, Eugenia Potts, was listed as an artist.

White men found employment at the mills, in the stores along Main Street, in the relatively new automobile service stations, in other local businesses, and at the college as carpenters and supervisors as well as faculty. Black males found work in the mills, as janitors at the college, as barbers, cooks, and draymen, and with the railroad.

Developments on Main Street

While African-American barbershops on Main Street had long been a town tradition, their successes were not always welcomed. The *Davidsonian* reported on 21 March 1934:

> Last Wednesday afternoon at about 12:30 . . . the local firefighters were called to the building occupied by Johnson's Barber Shop, where a fire had been started by some unknown source. Twice later in the day, alarms were put in for blazes in the same locality. The first fire was believed to have been entirely extinguished, but about 3 o'clock another broke out and again at 7 o'clock flames were reported . . . in the rear of the building. The barbers declare that the last one was set on purpose, because papers soaked in some sort of highly flammable fluid were discovered at the scene of the blaze.[32]

Writing his memoirs sixty years later, Ralph Johnson recalled the fires and his fears of either losing his business to fire or being run out by neighboring businesses. Although no one was ever caught, the building's owners offered sympathy and support.

As barbers, Ralph and his uncle Hood Norton represented some of

New buildings on
Main Street in 1920s

the older businesses on Main Street, though longevity did not necessarily ensure continuing financial success. But advertising may have helped. Editors of the *Davidsonian* surely hoped so. The student paper published a praise-filled article on the Norton barber shop in 1933 that began with the statement "Norton's Barber Shop believes in advertising" and ended with "[t]he depression has cut off a good portion of their business which they expect to bring back by courteous service in a clean shop, and by following the example of the hen who, when she lays an egg, goes out to tell the world about it!"[33] The editors clearly hoped to encourage other businesses to buy advertising.

Davidson's business district grew noticeably during the 1920s. Construction of a new stretch of brick buildings took place in 1922. J. Lee Sloan added two of the buildings, one becoming the new home of Henderson's Jewelry and the new location for the post office. Sloan's buildings were joined by three storerooms erected by J.V. Knox plus a new car dealership and garage. The new buildings prompted a shifting of businesses and renovations: the New York Cafe moved into the old jewelry store space, and Smiley's restaurant added new equipment and advertised its renovation by boasting "You won't know it."[34]

In 1924 the business district expanded again with the opening of the Maxwell Chambers Hotel. Although manager Emory Wilson noted that the hotel was not intended "to offer competition to the various businesses already in town but to fill a long-felt need in Davidson," it not only offered a dining room capable of seating 200 but also advertised boarding for students.[35] Local boarding house owners were probably not overly concerned, for they were used to competing for students and mostly relied on student managers to recruit them. Local restaurants, too, were familiar with intense competition.

Despite its prime location on Depot Street, the hotel underwent a change in ownership and in 1930 became just another boarding house, the Davidson Inn. By 1937, again under new management, it was the College Inn and its prospects were uncertain at best.

Between 1922 and 1935 three gas stations and two car dealerships opened in town. S.L. Presson moved to Davidson in the fall of 1922 to manage a Ford dealership across from the Carter Motor Company. He quickly added a gas pump and was able to employ six men. Because Presson sold tractors as well as cars, his business served as a reminder of the area's continuing rural as well as small-town character. In 1923 J.M. Blue opened a Chevrolet dealership. Over the next few years, Lester Hannah put in a gas tank on Depot Street, Presson's became Crayton's, Otho Smith built a filling station on South Main Street, and the already existing Henderson filling station shifted its rental sideline from U-Push to U-Drive It Fords.[36]

There might have been even more auto-related businesses, but the college removed hundreds of potential drivers from the roads beginning in 1924 by forbidding students to have cars on campus. Students also were not permitted to keep cars in town, but a few tried to rent clandestine parking spots in town. The ban, with some modifications, remained in place into the late 1940s.

Although most students did not benefit from the new automobile services, they greeted new entertainments enthusiastically. A popular new business was the Stough brothers' movie theater on the east side of Main Street in the business district. In March 1926, a month before the opening, the college newspaper declared that "the heart of every Davidson student has been gladdened by the announcement that a picture show is coming to town." Students were not the only ones to benefit, for plans were made to project "Wild West" shows on Saturday evenings for mill workers and other local residents. The town's first talking movie—"The Trial of Mary Dugan"—was shown in the spring of 1929.[37]

While students were delighted not to have to drive to Mooresville for movies and mill workers were offered a time that fit their work schedules, black residents had to go out of town to see a film. The one exception was the barber Ralph Johnson. The Stough brothers patronized his barber shop and arranged for him to watch from a small room near the projection booth. "This was a fine arrangement for me," Johnson recalled, "and satisfied the requirement of segregation since I was there alone."[38]

In 1930 a miniature golf course made a brief appearance on Main Street in the space between the Stetson "D" Store and White's Drug. Longer lasting was the bowling alley located in the renovated telephone building. This business opened in the fall of 1938 and garnered the largest front-page headline for the October 5 issue of the *Davidsonian*. Later issues mentioned a popular series of tournaments and prizes of Whitman's chocolates donated by a local drugstore.[39]

If any students or townspeople were hoping to see gambling come to town, local officials were determined to disappoint them. In 1934, after discovering that local businesses were hosting slot machines, licensed as vending machines, the police ordered them removed. According to town board minutes, the main objections were "that they were causing students to spend and throw away money that they ordinarily would have used for buying things that they really needed," and that "a large number of small boys were playing the machines."[40]

Two local organizations provide contrasts between Davidson in the 1920s and 1930s. The first organization was overwhelming business in orientation, while the second was more broadly based, as befitted the New Deal's values and emphases. The Davidson Development Association, formed in March 1923, was filled with booster enthusiasm. Its initial dinner featured several local businessmen as speakers, with former college president Henry Louis Smith as special guest. The local speakers called for new business ventures, and Smith offered encouragement to the fifty men attending and "gave the association a big boost."[41]

The other organization was the local Compliance Board, established in September 1933 under the New Deal's National Recovery Administration (NRA). The Compliance Board was composed of representatives of various businesses and other elements of the community. It included Fred Fleagle, a college professor, as the chairman; another professor, Archibald Currie, representing the "professional class"; Mrs. E.G. Gaffney, representing consumers; C.C. Anderson, an executive at the asbestos plant; Oscar Gant, representing Delburg Mills; W.A. Jetton, representing druggists; and T.E. Lothery, representing the town's merchants. The board's mandate was to hear "complaints which may come to it regarding the misuse of the standard set by the Blue Eagle [a symbol of the NRA programs] or any violations of the [NRA's] code." Its role was to be available to hear complaints and be ready to pass them along to NRA officials, watching and doing its small part to end the Depression while waiting for times to change.[42]

Celebrations and Other Social Activities

Throughout Davidson's history public celebrations, at times organized mainly by the college and at other times primarily by the town, have been hallmarks of community life. In the fall of 1921 the college took the lead in organizing a celebration that combined Davidson Day, an annual event honoring the college's founding, with the new Armistice Day that recalled the ending of World War I on 11 November 1918 and the many young American men who were killed or injured in that conflict.

Although Presbyterian efficiency contributed to combining the two celebrations, male college students' enjoyment of the company of young women led the college's recently formed units of the Reserve Officer Training Corps (ROTC) to elect female "sponsors" to participate in the event. Thus, five of the students' favorite young women—Orrie Steele, Helen Gibbs, Sophie Richards, Dorothy Finlayson, and Eloise Martin—were

Davidson ROTC students marching in Charlotte parade in 1919

selected to attend the ceremonies and "cheer for their respective companies" as they each presented "an original stunt" of a military character. Held on campus in Shearer Hall, the ceremony included music, prayers, speeches recognizing Davidson men who had served in the war, and the ROTC stunts.[43]

The celebration of combined Armistice-Davidson days continued for only three years, during which time sporting events began to take precedence. In 1922 one-third of the student body left for a football game in Charlotte as soon as the ceremony ended at 11 a.m. In 1923 both the armistice and the college founding took a back seat to the opening of the Davidson College Highway and a high school football game. The following year the joint event, marked by a military parade and speeches, was more somber because of Woodrow Wilson's death earlier that year. In 1925 the college returned to celebrating Davidson Day in October, freeing students and townspeople to attend a special Armistice Day auto race in Charlotte. The local war remembrance thus ended as students and townspeople moved on with their lives.[44]

This is not to say that the town turned away from the world. Residents participated in the Golden Rule Observance days to raise funds for and awareness of the plight of orphans resulting from the Turks' slaughter of large numbers of Armenians during the war. This project was initiated by students and conducted through special boarding-house meals; encouraged by local churches, town residents also participated.

The town's religious heritage and engagement also insured that a steady stream of missionaries came to share their experiences in and knowledge of Mexico, Japan, China, Africa, Korea, Brazil, and the Philippines. Some came only for lectures, while others lived in the community for weeks or months.

With leadership from "college" residents, an Overseas Club was formed in 1923. For the more affluent, Europe was a favorite destination, especially in the 1920s. Faculty took students groups on summer tours in Europe in 1924 and 1925. Other faculty took their families along as they spent summers doing research. One such experience provided Mrs. W.R. Grey an opportunity to give a talk to the Civic Club. Some young single women also got to spend time abroad, with Orrie Steele going to Europe with Winthrop College, Mary Richards and Mary Black studying for a year at Oxford, and librarian Cornelia Shaw joining a group of friends sailing to Europe. Others traveled to more exotic locales: J.P. Munroe went to Cuba and Panama, for example, and Thomas Lingle's letters home describing his time in Egypt and Palestine were published in the college newspaper.[45]

The *Davidsonian* rarely carried national or international news stories unless they had a college tie. For news from the outside, residents relied on urban newspapers and magazines, newsreels at the movies, and radios. Radios were affordable for most families and even for students on tight budgets, and local residents could listen to WBT in Charlotte and a few other stations. "After dinner," Annie Mildred Lowery recalled, "the family might sit around and listen to 'Amos and Andy.'"[46]

As occurred in many parts of the country, especially in New Jersey, some Davidson students got caught up in Orson Welles' radio dramatization of H.G. Wells' *War of the Worlds*, which aired in the fall of 1938 and graphically described a Martian invasion of New Jersey. According to the student newspaper:

> Many of the students didn't realize that the play was a dramatization of pure fiction and rushed frantically to the rooms of other boys declaring that the world was coming to an end. Other boys joined them in their fears or . . . uselessly tried to explain that the announcements . . . coming in over the radio were from a fiction play and that there was no real danger at all.
>
> Several boys dropped to their knees and began to pray before the broadcast was over. A group of Davidson students returning from Asheville and listening to what they thought were news radio bulletins stopped their car along the highway and kneeled beside the road to pray fervently along with other people who had stopped their cars.[47]

Obviously, many listeners did not hear—or remember—the preceding announcement that what was to follow was entirely fictional.

Social Relations between East and West Davidson

During the 1920s and 1930s the town's continuity in social relations was most noticeable in the separate social spheres that were both reinforced and breached by charitable acts and civic cooperation. College students and white women's civic groups reached out to provide education and resources to the mill and African-American communities, but there was little questioning of working and housing conditions.

In October 1923 two local book clubs held a picnic during which part of the entertainment was the arrival of a mock group of Ku Klux Klansmen whose goal, the *Davidsonian* reported, "was to seek out the man guilty of removing scuppernong grapes from the vines of a Confederate veteran."

The "guilty" party was the town mayor.[48] Members of these clubs were the same women who taught adult education classes and raised money to supply equipment to local schools.[49]

As in the past, the town board was slow to extend water, sewer, and electric lines to areas west of the railroad track. Mill houses on Depot Street did not receive electricity until 1931, and Ralph Johnson's request in 1935 for a water line and a fire hydrant was tabled for a year. The commissioners did agree in 1937 to provide a sewage connection to the new Davidson Colored School building.

Minstrel shows with black-faced entertainers remained popular. It was without any apparent sense of contradiction that the college paper could run articles in the same issue announcing the junior class's intention to give a "Negro Performance" and describing a well attended lecture on campus by an African-American, William Mack Lee. Occasional articles on members of the college's janitorial staff reflected a similar dichotomy of affection and even respect, often undercut by mocking patronizing. References to particular blacks included "this darkey friend," "a dear old colored Mammy," and even "a small coon."

In the fall of 1937 one of the most popular football halftime shows at the college—even taken on the road to Harvard—had two young black boys "pick" cotton off the field. The boys did get to sightsee in three north-

Football halftime stars

eastern cities, and perhaps they saw the show as a lark, but it revealed how deeply ingrained stereotypes lived on.[50]

Working through the college YMCA, students sporadically offered a series of eclectic adult education classes. In 1921 fourteen blacks attended hour-long classes twice a week, the main course being Bible with additional twenty-minute sections on personal hygiene, history, and arithmetic. Unfortunately for any interested students, enthusiasm waned, not to return until evening classes were started for the mill workers in 1938 and for African-Americans in 1940. That fall members of the Civic Club and DCPC's Women's Missionary Society taught sewing classes for black women.[51]

White civic groups did make an effort to educate themselves on race relations: the YMCA invited speakers on interracial work, the Civic Club took as a theme "Our colored people, their value to the village," and the women of DCPC invited African-American speakers to their meetings. By 1933 local groups were beginning to address inequalities in the town, especially in the mill community, where the YMCA discovered "cases of actual want and suffering."[52]

In 1938 the college "Y" created a committee for "Colored Work" that started with scouting and sports programs for boys but soon expanded into creating a community center; they also returned to teach evening classes for mill workers. After investigating local housing conditions, the Civic Club bought land and built homes for poor black residents. Using frequent and creative fund-raisers, by November 1939 the club, the *Davidsonian* reported, had bought "eight lots and erected one house from its own treasury, has seen two houses built by individuals, and has three lots to sell to people interested" in helping black residents.[53]

It took the YMCA until April 1940 to have enough funds to build the community center. African-American adults helped to raise funds and worked on the construction; black children participated by finding and hauling stones for the chimney and fireplace. Blacks also helped to plan programs and used the space for club meetings. A young people's club ended its second meeting with plans to invite white students for an open forum focused not on race relations but rather on a "problem concerning both races."[54]

Local Churches Continue to Be Important

Churches continued to play an important social role for townspeople. Even with a new movie theater, a new bowling alley, and improved roads to get to out-of-town events, local churches, with their missionary societies, youth groups, Sunday schools, and respected ministers, were significant sources of entertainment and engagement. They provided community service as a value and practice and encouraged awareness of the needs of their neighbors and the world—even if they frequently failed to examine how and why those needs arose. While minutes and reports of missionary meetings in these years reveal good intentions, they exhibit little reflection about the work of these white, middle-class groups or how many similarities their members might share with the objects of their charity.[55]

These were quiet and steady years overall for town churches. As might be expected, several churches brought in new ministers and members of DCPC dreamed of a new building. The Women of the Church at times opted to meet outside the "cold church building." A 1929 report noted that the building was "inadequate in size, heating, and ventilation system, was uncomfortable, and was entirely out of keeping with the other architectural surroundings." The report also correctly predicted that, given the expected cost, no new building would be possible "for a considerable time."[56]

While this was not a time of grand new buildings or dramatic events, a famous evangelist visited the town, a church recovered from a fire, and a new church came into being. With the decline in male participation in churches a serious concern in the early 1920s, a movement known as Muscular Christianity sought to revitalize men's interest. One of the best known proponents was Billy Sunday, a former baseball player turned evangelist. Although he came on a Friday morning in February 1924, DCPC's pews were filled with an enthusiastic audience of college students, school children, and townspeople.[57]

Later that year, with encouragement from the denomination, a new experimental group, Men of the Church, was organized at DCPC. With an organization similar to the long-standing Women of the Church, its purpose was to give men a "definite program of work" within the church. The Women of the Church got an innovation as well: in 1921 they adopted the new "circle plan" that divided the women into small groups that were expected to meet weekly. In recognition of gradually changing roles for women, one group was called the "Business Women's Circle." The circles outlasted the Men of the Church. But with its strong ties to the college, DCPC never lacked for professors to teach Sunday school or serve as elders.[58]

The fire occurred at Gethsemane Baptist Church on a Sunday morning, just after a funeral service. No one was hurt, and the town's fire department quickly put out the fire, proving the value of the fire trucks and hydrants the town had purchased.

Proving a different kind of value, the efforts of students in the college YMCA to provide Sunday schools and chapel services for the mill community resulted in the organization of a new church. No longer the mill chapel, it became the Unity Church, moving from a one-room building into a modest $1,300 structure in 1930 and growing enough to have a log cabin added in 1932 for additional meeting space for church groups.

Central to this change was the commitment of a Davidson senior willing to serve as a full-time pastor in addition to regular class work. He and the other students from the college "Y" built up a congregation described initially as a "union of faiths in which are included at least six denominations." The name Unity Church thus was apt. Along with Sunday morning services and Sunday schools, the church sponsored adult education classes, youth groups, and boy and girl scout troops. The church also sponsored an eye clinic, with doctors from Charlotte examining sixty people in one day, and hosted a town-wide birthday party for revered community nurse Selinda Mayhew.[59]

Health Care and Education

The town did well to honor Mrs. Mayhew, for community nurses were important to the local area, assisting doctors and at times filling in for them. The latter role became more frequent, for the town's doctors reached retirement age during these years. With the closing of the medical school and its clinic, townspeople had grown accustomed to traveling to Charlotte or Statesville for surgeries and serious illnesses. By 1922 the fears arising from flu and scarlet fever epidemics had faded to the point that the same citizens who had asked for a public health officer were happy to see the position abolished. Tuberculosis became the next health concern. A public health specialist visiting Davidson in 1923 discovered twenty-one cases, none of which required hospitalization.

The departure of Fletcher Adams in 1938 left the town with only two doctors. One of them retired in 1939, and the other worked only limited hours. Following standard Davidson tradition, women in the town stepped forward and, in an impassioned letter to college president Walter Lingle, demanded the college's help in providing medical services to the town. They listed seven "classes of persons" who were suffering from inadequate medical attention.[60] Given the college's pride in its first infirmary, the Preyer Building constructed in 1938, the women clearly expected that the college understood local healthcare needs and had the facilities to provide some support for the town.

First grade at Davidson Elementary School, 1927–28

In education, the biggest changes during these decades came for public-school children: two new school buildings, added grades, and, for the Davidson Graded School, a longer school year. The students might not have noticed the change that occurred in 1933 when the town abolished its local school board, but the added years and months likely were greeted with a mix of pleasure and pain. Parents and civic groups demonstrated their strong interest in schools by raising funds, sponsoring essay contests, and hosting receptions for teachers.

The first new school building opened in 1924. Built over the summer, the $40,000 structure on South Street was dedicated as the Davidson High School on September 12. It boasted an auditorium with seating for 550, five classrooms, a library, laboratories, and indoor bathrooms. The existing school building was renovated for the lower grades and had six "excellent" classrooms. The schools had one teacher for each elementary class and four teachers for the high school.

A 1924 state law mandated classes through 8th grade, but the Davidson school offered classes through 10th grade. The buildings expressed a belief in the future, for in 1921 the graduating class had only 15 students. There were 27 graduates in 1934 and 30 in 1937, but in 1941 the number dropped to 19. Putting the auditorium to use, the school offered operettas, plays, concerts, and holiday programs for parents and townspeople.

Davidson Colored School students and staff in 1940s

The two buildings and the teachers became part of the county system in 1933.

The second school, mentioned earlier, was built in 1937 as the Davidson Colored School; it had six classrooms. Prior to its construction, black students attended school in two small frame buildings with four teachers. The schools, run by the county, were inadequate and offered classes only through the 8th grade. There were twenty-five students when the new school opened; each year the school added one more high school year until 1939–40, when it matched the new state requirement of an 11th year as the final grade. Although a smaller building than the new white school, the Davidson Colored School was a source of pride and involvement in the black community.[61]

Both schools offered some after-school activities, sports teams and music being the most popular. Davidson students served as coaches for athletic teams, which meant that the coaching staff often changed from year to year and that practice times could vary depending upon the time constraints of college students. Before 1935 all music lessons were private, with recitals for white students in the high school auditorium. In 1933 the college established a music department, and in 1935 the new assistant music director, Warren Babcock, organized a band for the white high school students, with a junior orchestra being formed the following year. It took until January 1941 for the Davidson Colored School to get a band, sponsored by the college YMCA with music majors as instructors. Fifteen students quickly signed up when the band's formation was announced.[62]

The extra month of classes for the white high school came courtesy of the college's teacher training program. In order to provide time for practice teaching, the college arranged to pay the salaries of the principal, four teachers, and the janitor for that month. In 1936 the salaries for the month totaled $599, an indicator of how low the pay of local public employees was during the Depression. In 1936 the cost was funded through tuition charges, but by 1939 the college was asking for assistance from a local school committee to cover the gap between tuition and costs.[63]

With or without an extra month, local students did well. In 1934 Blanche Knox won an honorable mention in a state-wide French contest, reflecting Maude Vinson's ongoing determination to instill that language in her students. Between 1924 and 1938, at least six young women from Davidson Colored School went on to attend nearby Scotia Women's College, and roughly a dozen female graduates of Davidson High School attended Converse, Salem, Peace, Agnes Scott, and the North Carolina College for Women (now UNCG). Sarah Lingle broke the usual pattern by first attending Smith College and then earning a master's degree at Columbia University. She became a professor at Converse.[64]

For most of the female graduates, black and white, teaching school and nursing remained the primary career options. For white boys who did not attend Davidson or another college, the 1938 *Ace Review*, Davidson High School's newspaper, provides a brief look at their early careers. These included joining the army, working for Firestone Tire and Rubber, working at Erwin Cotton Mills, and managing gas stations.[65]

Students of all ages had ample opportunities to attend a variety of lectures and performances. The popular Chautauqua shows returned in 1921 and 1922, and in any given year the college, churches, and clubs brought in dozens of speakers on diverse topics. In 1922 the Booklovers and the newly formed Thelemites Club joined with a student group to bring poet Vachel Lindsey to town, where he gave talks and met with the clubs. A popular speaker, he returned in 1931. Other speakers included Bishop E.A. Penick, North Carolina governors Cameron Morrison and Max Gardner, and writer Carl Sandburg. In 1935 the music department began a series of musical evenings, including a concert by the Boston Sinfonietta under Arthur Fiedler, from which the college's annual Artist Series arose. Another longstanding town and college tradition, Christmas Vespers, began in this era when the YMCA started to offer a musical evening of Lessons and Carols for the last Vespers service of the fall semester.

White residents also were fortunate to have a public library in town. A project of the Civic Club, it became a branch of the county system in 1929, at which time the club turned over the 930 books it had acquired over the years. During the 1930s, the town board supported the library by paying for janitorial and heating costs.

If there was ever a question about Davidson being a town of readers, the proliferation of book clubs between 1921 and 1940 demonstrates that interest. The Thelemites formed in 1921, As You Like It in 1922, Sorosis in 1926, the Twentieth Century Club in 1927, Tuesday Club in 1934, and the Centennial Club in 1937. All of these clubs were open only to women, and most of them met twice a month. In addition to the books read for the meetings, members were expected to discuss current events and to provide reviews of new books. Outnumbered but not to be outdone, in 1923 college faculty organized a men's reading and discussion group, the Quadwranglers Club, that included men from the town.

It should be noted that these men held their first meeting in the Civic Club Hall. In addition to creating the library, pushing for sanitation reforms, supporting all the schools, and teaching adult education classes, the women of the Civic Club held rummage sales and elaborate bazaars, ran a delicatessen sale at Goodrum's Store every Saturday morning, showed films, and cajoled contributions from friends and family. Adding up the income from these varied sources, they were able to buy and furnish a small brick building in 1926 for $3,658.94. That building hosted many club meetings and scout troops, and eventually became the space for the public library.

One of the groups using the hall was the Red Cross. Founded during World War I, the Davidson group in the 1920s first focused on tuberculosis-related projects and then began raising funds to alleviate poverty in the town. The chapter reported in late 1933 that, during the previous year, it had raised "$44.13 for food and $96.70 for hospital and medical service, including medicine," aiding a total of sixty families. It also had "distributed flour to 76 families, [clothing] to 23 families, and cloth to 90 families," and "contributed $38.00 for the undernourished school children, both white and colored."[66]

On the lighter side, the college's ban on dramatic productions was being lifted, first with the annual Wildcat Minstrels and then in 1923 with the Dramatic Club, which offered a series of one-act plays. With the establishment in 1929 of the Red and Black Masquers under the direction of English professor E.J. Erwin, the club produced eight full-length plays, including the ever-popular *The Importance of Being Earnest*. To balance the all-male college students and faculty, the Red and Black Masquers regularly included townspeople, especially women, in its productions.

Conclusion

The biggest production of this era was to have been the college's Centennial Pageant on 7 June 1937. The town and the college had made big plans for 100th anniversary celebrations. The town government had purchased ads in the *Charlotte Observer* and the college had spent much time and energy on an outdoor drama for commencement. The rehearsal went well, but rain forced cancellation of the performance.

In a way, the pageant's non-occurrence reflected the real Davidson of these years. The town was not about spectacles. Its heartbeat was steady work, day by day, much of it behind the scenes. During these years many local businesses faced struggles for survival, not only during the Depression but even in some cases during the 1920s. Recovering impressively

Rehearsing for Centennial pageant

from the fire that destroyed the Chambers Building, the college stayed financially conservative while undertaking fund-raising campaigns to ensure a brighter future. Like the college, the town board and local schools managed limited resources well. African-Americans overall made steady progress, especially in education, despite deeply entrenched discrimination. And members of civic groups, often living out their freely chosen obligations as Christians, took on projects large and small to enrich the lives of their neighbors, black as well as white.

6 Moving Forward Slowly, 1941–1960

During the 1940s and 1950s, the United States experienced huge changes. As a result of World War II and the subsequent Cold War, America became an economic, political, military, and cultural superpower. At home, the nation's steadily growing prosperity increased opportunity, especially for white males, but also to some extent for women and blacks. The Supreme Court's unanimous Brown decision in 1954, combined with a determined civil rights movement, dealt an ultimately fatal blow to racial segregation. Despite strict limits on immigration, the nation's population grew from 132 million in 1940 to 179 million in 1960, an increase of nearly 36 percent.

Compared to the nation as a whole, Davidson moved forward slowly during these years. Apart from students at the college, the town's population grew by less than 8 percent, from 1,550 in 1940 to 1,673 in 1960. And while the college grew more rapidly than the town, from 689 to 900 students, it stayed a small, all-male, predominantly southern college. Moreover, most of the town's whites remained socially conservative, determined to maintain racial segregation in the town (including at the college) even as progress toward greater racial equality occurred in other parts of the country. Nevertheless, the town and college experienced some changes between 1940 and 1960, partly due to the construction of a much larger Methodist church in the town and substantial new facilities—notably a library, a gym, and a stately church—at the college.

These and other new buildings are especially noteworthy because North

Carolina—and the South generally—remained well behind the rest of the nation economically. In 1952, for example, the largely rural Tar Heel state, with a per capita income of $1,049, ranked forty-fifth in the nation, roughly 40 percent below the national average of $1,639. Only three other southern states had lower per-capita incomes at the time.[1]

Davidson in the 1940s and 1950s remained a community in which people knew each other—especially within their economic and religious groups, but also frequently across lines of social class (due to mixing in such places as the Davidson School and in the stores on Main Street) and across the racial divide in a town roughly 75 percent white and 25 percent black. James Puckett, the son of a professor at the college, has an overwhelmingly positive memory of growing up in Davidson at the time:

> It was a place where the only lawyer in town was the trust officer at the bank, and a shaken hand or a person's word was as good as any signature. It was a time and place when groups of neighbors regularly brought out their lawn chairs on summer evenings and chatted amicably for hours while their children chased fireflies in the gathering darkness. There was a sense of neighborliness, trust, and reciprocity that I have not experienced in any other place.[2]

In contrast, Ralph Johnson, a successful barber of mixed descent whom most whites considered African-American, wrote movingly in his memoir, *David Played a Harp*, about the discrimination he faced from whites. During the 1940s some well-educated whites associated with the college wanted to "take control of the barber business out of the hands of the shop owners [including Johnson] and place it on the hands of the group [of local whites] who wanted to dominate it."[3] As the recollections of Puckett and Johnson show, memories of life in small-town Davidson during these years are diverse.

"Doing Our Part" During World War II

Japan's attack on Pearl Harbor on 7 December 1941 united the over-whelming majority of Americans in support of war against the Axis powers. The residents of Davidson were no exception. So great was the patriotic feeling that the college's recently installed president, John Cunningham, fearing that the institution he led might have to shut down, urged the students to continue to pursue their educations and not to rush to join the armed forces.[4]

Davidson graduates go from cap and gowns to uniforms, 1942

Cunningham was right to worry about the college. The enrollment of civilian students dropped below 200 by May 1943 and remained between 150 and 250 for the next two years. The decline in the size of the faculty, while substantial, was not as precipitous. This was partly because Cunningham was able to convince the War Department in Washington to send more than 2,200 young Army air cadets and other young soldiers to Davidson—typically in installments of 500—for a couple months of course work and training during 1943 and 1944 before they were assigned to the more intensive training that preceded service on the fighting fronts. Especially during academic year 1944–45, Cunningham sent urgent appeals to donors to help "avert a deficit" in the college's finances.[5] Despite substantial inflation, the pay scale for faculty remained frozen during the war, and indeed was only slightly higher than the pay scale in effect in the 1920s.[6]

Although the wartime earnings of others who lived in Davidson are not known, it seems safe to assume that incomes generally were going up, as they were throughout the nation at a time when the armed forces were employing millions and only wage controls kept salaries from exploding upward in the private sector. Economically, historian David M. Kennedy has noted, "[m]ost Americans had never had it so good. . . . They went to movies and restaurants [frequently]. They bought books, recordings, cosmetics, pharmaceuticals, jewelry, and liquor in record volumes. . . . Retail sales ascended to a record high in 1943 then went still higher in 1944."[7] In legally dry Davidson, of course, any and all liquor sales occurred illicitly.

At least one important Davidson business did well during the war. On 31 December 1943 the net worth of Davidson Cotton Mills stood at

$358,000—the equivalent of more than $3 million in 2010 dollars. The company's assets grew from $487,000 at the end of 1943 to $540,000 a year later—an increase of more than 10 percent.[8]

Improved economic conditions were gratifying, especially after the hardships experienced during the Depression. The community's deepest concern, however, was how many of Davidson's young men and women would be killed or wounded. The fact that a significant number of these soldiers were husbands and fathers added to the community's anxieties.[9]

According to a "service honor roll" published in a Davidson newspaper in October 1945, 218 residents—roughly 14 percent of the town's population —served in the armed forces during the war. Of these, 183 were white males, 30 were black males, and 5 were white women. Of these, 6 (all white males) died, including the brothers Edward and Phifer Erwin.[10] A much larger number of Davidson College alumni and students served—2,540, including 1,503 officers. Of these, 155 died in the war.[11] The 2.3 percent of the town's service personnel who died is much more similar to the percentage for the nation as a whole (2.5 percent) than it is for Davidson College's (6.1 percent).[12] With both pride and sadness, the college, with its high percentages of both officers and fatalities, lived up to such long-standing ideals for it students as developing effective leaders and "facing life with courage and nobility."[13]

To show appreciation for the townspeople who served, students at Davidson High School published a newsletter, the *Post Exchange*, that they sent to service personnel from Davidson. The newsletter provided chatty news from home and, whenever possible, addresses and other information about where people from the town were serving. In the spring of 1943, for example, the newsletter noted that "Laura Mae Gamble is to be one of the first women supply officers in the Navy. (She's a WAVE, you know.) At present she is at Radcliffe." Later the *Post Exchange* reported that "she is replacing a [male] lieutenant in the Supply Corps at Dahlgrew, Virginia."[14] In early 1945, the town government erected a large billboard on the east side of Main Street, a "Roll of Honor" listing the names of all townspeople who served, placing gold stars beside the names of the six who died.

For the families from Davidson and the surrounding area that lost sons, the grief often was deeper than words could describe. George Gunn, a Davidson College student, remembers the impact of the deaths of three sons of faculty members—the Erwin brothers and Jimmy Fulcher: "Sitting in class under these grief-stricken fathers left its mark on each of us."[15] Nancy Blackwell recalled that a Western Union employee brought the telegram with the news of her brother's death to her father while he was working at the cotton mill. Her father was furious—ostensibly at the embarrassment of receiving the telegram at work, but surely as well because of the devastating news. "[Our family] never got over it," she said simply.[16] In a small community where families often were close friends as well as neighbors, even a small number of deaths had a lasting impact.

While many of the service personnel faced life-threatening experiences, Davidsonians on the home front faced, at most, inconveniences. The most pervasive inconvenience was rationing, which included (among many other items) meat, sugar, shoes, and gasoline. Rationing seemed fair, Edith Ann Cashion recalled, because "everybody was in the same boat. My mother stretched hamburger meat by putting bread and onions in it."[17]

Rationing of gasoline resulted in one of the era's funniest stories. Tish Kimbrough learned it years later from her parents:

> My mother was pregnant with me in 1942, and Dr. [James] Woods, the town doctor, did not deliver babies. The hospital [Presbyterian] was in Charlotte. There were five ladies who were pregnant at the time, and they had to carpool to save gas. So they all made their appointments on the same morning, and one of the husbands would drive them into Charlotte. They went to the S&W cafeteria for lunch after the appointments, and here is my daddy with these five very pregnant women. And a strange gentleman went by the table and stopped and put his hand on my father's shoulder and said, "What a man!"[18]

Another inconvenience was blackouts, organized at the request of federal officials in early 1942 by a local town-college civil defense organization. Despite little if any likelihood of enemy attacks, this organization, following suggestions from a federal agency, had nineteen committees overseeing the local effort.[19] Blackouts were carried out in the evenings in order to teach residents to darken their homes and thus save lives in the event of an enemy air attack. Mary Fetter Stough remembered them well:

> We had blackouts, and you had to buy black coverings for your windows. Air raid wardens would go around, and if any light showed you had to do something. One time we were playing bridge in the library, and the cop told daddy that somebody had left the lights on in the movie theater. Daddy had to drive down the street without any lights on in his car to go to the movie and turn off the lights.[20]

Blackouts were especially inconvenient for college students, who were allowed to go to the movie theater during blackouts but (like other Davidsonians) were not permitted on the streets or sidewalks. The effort to keep Davidson students indoors during a blackout on 30 April 1942 led to "a little trouble" between students and blackout enforcers, an article in the college newspaper reported.[21]

Despite such inconveniences, life went on pretty much as usual, especially for young people. Children played on the streets and playgrounds until the town siren sounded at 5:30 p.m., signaling that it was time to hurry home to listen to the popular "Lone Ranger" radio program.[22] Black and white scout troops continued to meet regularly; high school students organized square dances, hayrides, and other social occasions; and the town's several churches continued to serve important spiritual and social functions for youths and adults alike. Book clubs remained active, and middle-class white women continued to work in their homes and gardens—or in the community garden—and visit each other informally in the afternoons.[23]

While working in his office and making public appearances, the town's most prominent resident, President Cunningham, was immaculately dressed and conveyed what Mary Beaty described as an "every-hair-in-place appearance."[24] Yet, reflecting his rural roots, he kept chickens for eggs and, in the pasture behind his home, horses to ride. Many other residents kept farm animals, including cows.[25] On the level of daily life, in short, lines continued to be blurred between the town and its rural environs.

"All the girls in town (about thirty, to be exact) have formed a Victorette Club," the *Post Exchange* reported in early 1943. "They are going to do Red Cross work, help entertain the cadets, and try to keep in touch with all the boys from the town."[26] Especially noteworthy was the dance the Victorettes sponsored for the Army Air Corps cadets in December 1943—"a huge success, complete with fifty girls from Queens [and] an orchestra."[27] For the first time ever, stoutly Presbyterian Davidson College permitted on-campus dancing—initially for the air cadets, and then in early 1945 for its own civilian students.

Perhaps the most significant wartime development for the future of the town and college was the fund-raising campaign for a new Davidson College Presbyterian Church. President Cunningham and the pastor, Carl Pritchett, believed that the existing church building was too small to meet the needs of the many white Presbyterians in the town together with the larger number of students—mainly Presbyterians—at the college. "The present structure is manifestly inadequate and suffers dreadfully by comparison with the beautiful new structures which house other departments of the college's life," Cunningham noted in early 1944, alluding to the new library that had been dedicated in 1941 and the new science building that would be dedicated later that year.[28]

After church members agreed in the fall of 1943 to permit the college to own the new building, Cunningham led an intensive fund-raising campaign that raised roughly $210,000—including $27,000 from the members of the local church—by December 1944.[29] The wartime fund-raising for the new church, together with a concurrent campaign to raise funds for a new gymnasium at the college, eventually bore fruit in impressive buildings completed several years later.

As was true throughout the nation, the ending of the war with Japan's surrender on 14 August 1945 brought exuberant joy to Davidson. "I remember there was great excitement," Patty King recalled. "We [children] were playing in the street, and somebody at Dr. Woods's house heard and I remember that moment."[30] The Woods family was even happier when Dr. Woods returned to Davidson from long service in the Pacific theater on Christmas Eve, 1945. When he came in late at the service that evening at DCPC, a close friend, Heath Whittle, stood up, walked over to him, and hugged him right in the middle of the service.[31] For the many families with loved ones in the military, and for their friends, the war did not really end until the discharged soldiers returned safely to Davidson.

The Town's Postwar Economic Engines

Economically, postwar Davidson is best described as a moderately prosperous town. As had been the case for generations, Davidson was overwhelmingly middle class, working class, and poor in the late 1940s and 1950s, with very few wealthy residents. At least at the college, where figures are available, average wages more than kept up with the inflation that saw prices rise by almost 50 percent between 1945 and 1954 and by another 10 percent between 1954 and 1960.[32]

The two keys to even a moderate prosperity were, first and foremost, money received from outside the town that provided a living for local residents, and second, Davidson residents who spent money within the town to bolster its economy. The largest generators of income from outside the town were the college and the mills. The third main center of economic activity, the downtown business district, benefited both from spending by town residents (including college students) and from the patronage of others, mostly from nearby rural areas, who came into Davidson for groceries, gasoline, haircuts, movies, and many other products and services.

A smaller but still significant source of income, especially for working-class black women, was domestic service in the homes of college professors and other middle-class families in the more affluent neighborhoods on North Main Street and, further south, largely east of Main Street. Further redistributing money within Davidson, relatively affluent whites often paid black men and teenagers of both genders to do lawn, garden, and other maintenance work. "The professors hired most anybody that wanted to work," Talmadge Connor, then a teenager living on the west side, recalled. "They'd give them something to do."[33]

A story in the *Charlotte News* in September 1948 rightly referred to the college as the town's "overwhelmingly dominant enterprise." The author estimated that, on average, each of the college's roughly 900 students "brings somewhere between $800 and $1,000 to the town every year." This money was spent, among other things, on "[s]hirts and ties and tuition and books and the magazines and note-paper at Hatley's [Brothers Soda Shop] and the theater down the street, and even the gadgets that can be found at the hardware store."[34]

In contrast to the paucity of students during the war, the college's enrollment jumped dramatically in 1946 as returning veterans used funds from the federal government's G.I. Bill of Rights program to finance their college educations. The influx of students, including some who were married with children, led to an acute housing shortage that was partly alleviated by a "cardboard village" of prefabricated structures—occupied during the war by officers on a military base in Florida—that were erected on a vacant lot across from Shearer Hall on the west side of North Main Street. "These apartments are used at present by seventeen married veterans and their wives," the *Davidsonian* reported in October 1947.[35] After peaking at 980 with veterans joining younger students, the student body stabilized in the 800s from the late 1940s through the mid-1950s, and then rose again to 920 in 1959–60.

A key indicator of the college's economic impact on the town was its budget, which rose from $491,577 in 1946–47 to $1,741,725 in 1959–60.[36] Because most of that money went to wages and benefits, and because almost all professors and top administrators—and many other employees—lived in Davidson, the impact on the town of the college's growing prosperity was profound.

The college had roughly 175 to 225 employees during these years, including 50 to 75 full-time faculty members. Except for a white female professor hired in 1956, all faculty members and top administrators were white males. Although exact figures are not available, probably as many as

50 college employees (including cooks and housekeepers at college-related fraternities) were black men and women who lived primarily on the west side of town. In 1949–50, President John Cunningham earned $9,000 (about $81,000 in 2008 dollars) plus housing and travel expenses. The best-paid full professors earned $5,000, a figure that grew to $7,500 by 1955–56.

Not surprisingly, the less educated hourly employees earned much less. In April 1950, according to Cunningham, wages for hourly employees averaged about $30 per week (roughly $1,500 per year).[37] In a letter to a prominent Presbyterian, Cunningham noted "that in colleges wages and salaries for [hourly workers] tend to be controlled by the prevailing salary level. We have a cotton mill, an asbestos mill, and some other competing agencies of that type which have had a stimulating effect upon salaries here."[38] Nancy Blackwell, a white woman who worked as a secretary, remembered the low wages she received during these years: "When I got promoted to a dollar an hour, I thought I had arrived."[39]

In addition to its modest but rapidly growing operating budget, the college's ambitious building program—based on equally ambitious fundraising efforts—added to the aura of progress in the town and, in some cases, provided jobs for local residents. Johnston Gymnasium, which cost roughly $750,000, was dedicated in October 1949. The large new Davidson College Presbyterian Church, which cost nearly $800,000 (mostly raised by Cunningham outside of Davidson), was dedicated on 1 June 1952. Other noteworthy new buildings at the college in the 1950s included Belk Dormitory, the Dana Science Building, and the several structures that form Patterson Fraternity Court. Before the end of the decade, fundraising began for the Cunningham Fine Arts building, which opened in 1961. Davidson residents frequently helped to construct these buildings, thus increasing the college's economic impact in the community.[40]

While the college provided steady employment and rising wages, the town's manufacturers offered uncertain prospects for their employees. Yet they still contributed greatly to the town's prosperity by providing a good living for managers and hundreds of jobs for working-class residents of Davidson and environs. Aileen Cantrell, who worked in a downtown restaurant, remembers workers coming in to cash their paychecks. Although the sums were relatively small—Cantrell recalls weekly paychecks ranging from $12 to $18 in 1950—local businesses welcomed the patronage. "You could buy groceries for $10" then, Cantrell noted.[41]

The postwar fate of the Davidson Cotton Mill illustrates the uncertainty facing factory workers. Although the mill had prospered during wartime, its owners sold it to McCanless Mills of Salisbury in 1945. Employment was uncertain thereafter. Operations at the mill stopped abruptly in the spring of 1947, and the mill shut down again in the summer of 1948. "It sure makes it hard on folks who depend on the mill for a living," one white resident of Delburg Street commented in August 1948.[42]

The mill closed permanently in the early 1950s, and the property was sold in 1954 to a Connecticut company that spent $500,000 to convert the space to produce fabric for zippers and for the backing for the tubing that sealed car doors. By April 1955 an associated company, Bridgeport Fabrics, with headquarters in Bridgeport, Connecticut, had received roughly 700 applications for the fewer than 100 initial jobs in the mill. The enterprise prospered, and by 1959 the plant had 140 employees. The executive who moved from Bridgeport to manage the operations in Davidson, Burl Naramore, became a respected civic leader in the 1960s and 1970s.[43]

Another enterprise that prospered was the Carolina Asbestos Mill, located in the old Linden Mill building on Depot Street just west of the railroad tracks. By early 1953 the mill had about 225 employees and, after building a $200,000 addition that year, the plant was expected to have about 300 employees. Before 1953 a wide variety of asbestos textiles, yarns, cords, and ropes were produced; the addition made possible the production of asbestos siding shingles.[44] The plant's manager, Tom Sadler, was a well-known civic leader who served the town in many capacities, including mayor. He is best known today as a key figure in the development of Sadler Square on Griffith Street.

In retrospect, the asbestos mill is a classic example of how good and bad intertwine in human affairs. According to Grover Meetze, who worked at the mill off and on for twelve years, the management treated white and black workers equally and sincerely cared about their welfare. When managers learned that some local grocery stores were overcharging poorly educated workers, for example, they started selling groceries at wholesale prices until the stores changed their policies. Meetze and Sadler also worked hard to design machines to suck up as much of the asbestos dust as possible, and cooperated with North Carolina state inspectors who came to measure dust levels in the plant.[45]

Despite the efforts of Meetze and Sadler, dust levels in the plant often were high and many workers developed serious, at times fatal illnesses from breathing air laden with lead and other toxic substances. "You'd walk into that asbestos [air]," Doodle Brown recalled, "and there was so much dust, you didn't know who you were talking to." Mabel Fearington agreed: "You couldn't even see your own hands in that stuff." Nancy Blackwell, who lived nearby, said that the door and window screens at her house were "covered" with the airborne particles coming out of the asbestos plant. "They called it asbestosis; they said [workers] died of asbestosis," Blackwell recalled. "That was a horrible place."[46] How many local people died prematurely from asbestosis is unknown. But some employees, including a black man named Sam Harris, "died pretty young of brown lung disease," Mary Fetter Stough recalled.[47]

Two other local plants—both located on South Main Street—employed far fewer people. The larger one, the Southern Cotton Oil Company, which turned cotton seeds into marketable products and also made fertilizer, burned down in a spectacular fire in 1945. It was rebuilt and prospered in the 1950s as part of the much larger Wesson Oil and Snowdrift Company.[48] The smaller one was the Davidson Ice and Fuel Company. In addition to supplying ice locally, including to eating establishments at the college, the company sold ice to the Holly Farms poultry operation in Hiddenite.[49]

Although manufacturers provided needed jobs and patrons for local businesses, the downtown business district was Davidson's heart and soul, small though it was. It stretched south along Main Street for a couple hundred yards from the intersection of Main Street and Depot Street, and west along Depot Street for roughly one hundred yards toward the railroad track. Despite its modest dimensions, the downtown contained a great variety of businesses plus the jail, the post office, the town office/volunteer fire department, the public library, and a few private residences.[50] It also was dynamic in that new businesses repeatedly popped up to replace establishments whose time had passed. "I remember the downtown as a thriving little self-contained community," John Woods recalled.[51]

How much the downtown thrived financially varied from business to business. The Bank of Davidson, which changed its name to Piedmont Bank and Trust in 1949 when it established branches in Mooresville and Mount Pleasant, was the most prosperous.[52] In contrast, a clothing store, Wrenn's Men's Shop, closed in the spring of 1950—as did many other businesses in the 1950s and 1960s.[53] The fact that most business people rented the space for their operations may have contributed to the frequent turnover.[54]

Apart from the bank, the Davidson Printing Company was probably the town's most important downtown business. Founded in 1947 by a middle-aged couple from South Carolina, Horace and Mabel Broyles, the company survived its first year by printing the college's newspaper, the

Davidsonian, and doing other printing jobs for the college.[55] The first issue of a weekly paper, the *Cornelius-Davidson Gazette*, appeared in August
1948, with Horace as publisher and Mabel as editor. Supported by both
advertising and subscriptions, the paper prospered, changing its name in
1949 to *The Gazette* (to reflect a desire for advertising and subscriptions in
Huntersville as well as Davidson and Cornelius) and, in the late 1950s, to
Mecklenburg Gazette.

With its small staff, the paper did a better job alerting local residents
of upcoming events in the town and at the college than it did in covering the events themselves. But, with a paid circulation of 1,600 by 1956,
it helped to build community in Davidson as well as in Cornelius and
Huntersville. The Broyleses also helped Davidson by insisting that, under
state law, town commissioners' meetings and minutes were open to the
public, including reporters, and by leading a successful campaign to bring
toll-free telephone service between Davidson/Cornelius and Charlotte.[56]

Like the town's bank and newspaper, grocery stores and restaurants
provided vital services to the community. Both Anderson's Grocery and
Johnston's Grocery offered delivery of groceries. "Every day you could call
up and they would deliver your groceries," Lacy Dick recalled.[57] And restaurants, including the College Restaurant and M&M Soda Shop, served
meals and snacks to town people, college people, and visitors. The two
M's in M&M were Mary Potts, famous for her orangeade, and Murray
Fleming, well-known for his fresh egg and chicken salad. The Soda Shop
eventually became a Davidson landmark, serving generations of town residents and Davidson students. "Oh, we've seen lots of changes," Murray
commented on the 25th anniversary of M&M's opening in 1951. "Everywhere but here."[58]

The three downtown businesses owned by blacks also did well during
these years. Warren McKissick, a well-liked, highly skilled shoe repair-
man, worked alone.[59] In contrast, both Johnson's Barber Shop (owned
by Ralph Johnson) and Norton and Son Barber Shop (owned by Hood
and Ken Norton) employed several black barbers to cut the hair of local
white men and boys and Davidson students, many of whom frequented
the barbershops due to the strict R.O.T.C. standard that, the *Gazette*
noted, "requires the cadets' hair to be neat and trimmed regularly."[60]
James Puckett, who grew up in the 1950s and 1960s, remembered Ralph
Johnson as "reticent and quiet . . . thoroughly professional, thoroughly
dignified."[61] Margaret Thornburg, a white woman who worked as a wait-
ress in a downtown restaurant, recalled Ken Norton's kindness in coming
to her house during the years when her husband was an invalid. "He

Mary Potts in front of the M&M Soda Shop

would help my husband out of the bed . . . cut his hair, and put him back in bed," Thornburg commented. "I loved Kenneth, and—of course—the [other] Nortons."[62]

Young people liked buying candy at the five-and-dime store at the corner of Main and Depot and picking out the bike they hoped to get for Christmas at the Western Auto store.[63] College students enjoyed browsing and buying paperback books and magazines at White's Drug Store. "Plato, Shakespeare, and Mickey Spillane meet in the magazine racks," a writer for the student newspaper exulted.[64] People of all ages enjoyed seeing the "newest appliances"—including Davidson's first television sets—at Withers Electric, located where Ben and Jerry's and adjacent stores are now.[65] People of all ages, but especially young people, also enjoyed watching movies—and eating popcorn and candy—at the Davidson Theatre, located on the east side of Main Street where CVS Pharmacy is now.

Unfortunately, the movie theater burned on Valentine's Day of 1955. The fire apparently began in the furnace room in the back of the building during the early evening showing of a Western movie, attended by about thirty people. According to a student watching the film, the auditorium

Buying tickets at
the movie theater

began to be "filled with smoke, but we thought it was from the cigar of U.S. Grant as he sat beneath a tree talking peace with Sitting Bull." The student wrote that several patrons, wishing to see the end of the movie, "stayed in their seats until the lower section of the auditorium was enveloped in flames."[66] Everyone in the theater got out safely. A tardy response from the volunteer fire department, combined with the fact that the inside of the building consisted largely of highly flammable wood, contributed to the theater's total destruction.

The owners, postmaster S.T. Stough of Davidson and Frank Stough of Cornelius, did not seriously consider rebuilding the theater. Television's popularity was growing every year, and attendance at the theater had declined since the glory days of the 1930s and 1940s.[67] Within a year, a Gulf service station was built on the site, another example of the turnover of businesses in downtown Davidson at this time.

Progress—But Also Problems

As Alexis de Tocqueville and many other commentators on American life have observed, the public as a whole has believed in progress, in the idea that the future will be better than the past and present. That certainly was the case in Davidson in the years after World War II, especially for whites but even for many blacks, despite ongoing discrimination. The belief in progress often took the form of calls to action. In initiating a clean-up drive in April 1950, members of the junior class at the white Davidson School sent a letter to the heads of eleven local organizations. "We think Davidson could be as pretty as any small town in the country, but we know that at present it is not," the students noted. "We feel ashamed for strangers to pass through here and see the paper that is thrown on our sidewalks, around our places of business and in our yards."[68]

In Davidson, progress was most obvious in construction projects, especially in new buildings and in new or improved roads and highways. We have already mentioned two of the most significant buildings, the Davidson College Presbyterian Church dedicated in 1952 and the Methodist church's new facility—across South Main Street from the old church—that opened in 1960. Getting funds for building the Methodist church was more challenging, because most of the money had to be raised within the congregation or borrowed.[69]

Other white churches also had important building projects in the 1950s. Episcopalians dedicated St. Alban's Chapel on Lorimer Road in 1957, and local Baptists—donating time after work and on Saturdays—

Unity Church and Lingle Hut on Watson Street

built a church on the west side of town that same year.[70] In 1949, Unity Church affiliated with Presbyterians and became Calvary Presbyterian Church. It dedicated a new Sunday school building in 1955.[71]

The facilities of the two local public schools were also improved substantially. The impressive new building for the white Davidson School opened in the fall of 1948, more than two years after the old classroom building burned after being hit by lightning in July 1946. And the black school received an addition, including eight classrooms and a health room, in the early 1950s.[72]

Another much appreciated public space was the new post office, which opened in May 1958.[73] Located in a new building owned by the college and facing Main Street, it replaced a much smaller facility located nearby on Depot Street. Benefiting from ample parking in the rear of the building and the leadership of Postmaster Bill Mayhew, one of Davidson's best-liked residents, the new post office quickly became the town's social center, especially for middle-class whites. "When either or both of our parents announced that they were going to the PO, we knew they would be gone awhile," James Puckett recalled. "Folks just naturally congregated

Davidson students making daily walk to post office

there."[74] Indeed, going to the post office and greeting friends and acquaintances was so popular that many residents in later decades opposed the occasional proposals to switch from picking up mail at the post office to receiving home delivery.

Some of the people who congregated at the post office lived in the new single-family homes along Concord and Grey roads outside the city limits at the time, and north and south of Concord Road inside the town. The most significant building project was a college initiative in the mid-1950s to facilitate the construction of twenty homes, mainly for faculty members, on Lorimer, Hillside, and College streets.[75]

Whites and blacks who lived on the west side of town generally had much more modest dwellings. A story in the *Gazette* in 1950 described forty-eight homes on several streets that were owned by a mill company and rented to workers. The homes, ranging in size from three to six rooms, were being bought by a Winston-Salem firm that intended to make improvements and sell them to the current residents or other people. "Plans are to connect these homes with water and sewer lines and to install a kitchen sink and additional facilities [presumably including a bathroom] in each home," the story noted.[76] Progress, albeit modest, was occurring for at least some people on the west side of town.

The town's existing housing and socio-economic patterns were reflected in Davidson's first zoning ordinance, passed unanimously by the town board in July 1957. Lots for houses east of Main Street and School Street (now South Street) had to contain at least 10,000 square feet (slightly less than one-fourth acre), whereas lots for houses west of Main and School could be much smaller: a minimum of 6,000 square feet (slightly less than one-seventh acre). Under the ordinance, the town was divided into five zones: the two residential zones, restricted business (the property owned by the college, then the largest area in the town), business, and industrial.[77] Reflecting the college's influence as well as its desire to beautify Davidson, the college's treasurer/business manager and future president, Grier Martin, chaired the committee that wrote the ordinance.

The college also played a key role in getting two roads built that substantially changed Davidson, the bypass highway west of town that opened in 1955 and the road which connected Main Street to that highway, Griffith Street, which opened in 1956. President Cunningham spoke with North Carolina Governor W. Kerr Scott about the need for a bypass road during the governor's visit to the college in December 1951, and then pressed Scott, members of the State Highway Commission, and other officials to bring his desire to fruition. As he wrote Scott in May 1952,

"[O]ur people who live on Main Street . . . are harassed day and night by the noise, particularly from heavy trucks, and by the congestion. . . . I earnestly hope that a by-pass can be worked out in our behalf."[78] By September state highway officials were doing a survey for the new road. Early in December Scott announced the release of "$260,000 for a by-pass on US #21 around Davidson College . . ."[79]

Given that the new road would bypass the towns of Huntersville, Cornelius, Davidson, and Mooresville, thus providing less in-town traffic and easier access to Charlotte for residents of several communities, it might seem strange that Scott referred only to bypassing Davidson College. But because Cunningham played the key role in getting Scott and other officials to make the project a priority, the wording in the press release was partly accurate. The new road was named U.S. 21; the road through the towns that had been U.S. 21 became N.C. 115. "I remember when Carol and I moved here," Ralph Quackenbush recalled, "we thought 21 was the greatest road in the world." Quackenbush especially remembered the highway's impressive width and the absence of traffic lights.[80]

In regard to the access road, Cunningham shrewdly judged, as he confided to Grier Martin, "that it may be best if the college does not seem to be too much alone as the promoter of the new road."[81] Thus, while college officials largely worked behind the scenes, town officials and the state highway commission were the public face of the project, which ran for 1.1 miles from Main Street through the west side of town and across three farms to U.S. 21.[82]

In 1959–60, town officials, led by Mayor Frank Jackson, took the lead in getting the State Highway Commission to widen Concord Street (now Concord Road) to 44 feet, including parking on both sides, from Main Street to the town limits.[83] In contrast to the other two major road projects, this time the college gave its approval reluctantly because it lost many beautiful trees when the road was widened.[84]

Davidson officials deserve considerable credit for whatever progress the town made during the late 1940s and 1950s. With college and church property tax exempt, the town's tax base was low, finally reaching $3 million in 1957.[85] The town's budget also was small, growing from about $59,000 in 1946–47 to about $196,000 in 1960–61—roughly 15 percent of the college's budget in both years.[86] Yet the honest, frugal town commissioners—all white men—pinched pennies in order to provide a range of services, including (among others) police protection, garbage collection, water and sewer, electricity, road and sidewalk repairs, maintenance of the white cemetery, and recreation programs for young people.

Mayor Frank Jackson and town commissioners in 1960

And town employees—notably a black Davidsonian in the maintenance department, Roosevelt Wilson—were admired for how hard and how effectively they worked on behalf of local residents. With the leadership of mayors such as Ernest Beaty and Frank Jackson, both with strong connections to the college, the town board did not hesitate to ask President Cunningham and President Martin for contributions in lieu of taxes on college-owned property and for gifts and loans for such projects as buying a new fire truck and building a modest new town hall/fire station.[87] Getting the state government to assume most of the costs for building Griffith Street and widening Concord Road—and requiring the owners of new homes to pay for paving their streets—were prime examples of the frugality and shrewdness of town officials.

Town officials dealt with many other local problems. Although comparative statistics are not readily available, Davidson appears to have had an average amount of crime and juvenile delinquency during these years. The town had a small jail on Depot Street that held suspects until they could be picked up by county or state officials. Petty crimes—especially ones involving children or teenagers—were tried in Mayor's Court, held on a weekday evening in the town hall.[88] Judged from the number of stories in local newspapers, crimes involving violence or the threat of violence—such as Margaret Thornburg's being robbed at gunpoint while sitting in her car on Depot Street near the post office—were rare.[89] Much more common were acts of vandalism and thefts from downtown stores and college dormitories.[90]

One persistent problem in the town in the 1950s was what Mayor Jackson called "dogs running loose," especially dogs that local residents described as "vicious." "Several persons have complained of having been bitten and are really afraid for the safety of themselves and their children," the *Gazette* reported in June 1951.[91] Many residents were concerned about dogs that had not been vaccinated against rabies. "There were always mad dogs that had rabies, and they would bite you," Clark Readling recalled. "And if they bit you, you'd have to go through all those shots."[92] Although Davidson required that vicious dogs be tied or muzzled at all times, this law generally was not enforced. At a time when many residents believed that their dogs should be allowed to protect their property, public support for a leash law was lacking.[93]

Another problem that persisted, despite determined public efforts to solve it, was speeding and reckless driving, especially on Concord Road and North Main Street. Spurred by a petition signed by seventy-seven concerned residents, in September 1955 the town board set up the Davidson Safety Council to recommend steps to improve public safety on the roads in the town.[94] The safety council came up with a list of recommendations, including two new stop lights and two new blinker lights.[95] The council even held a weekend pledge drive in March 1957 in which 547 residents promised to be "careful drivers."[96]

Unfortunately, drivers who liked to speed undercut these efforts: on the weekend of the pledge drive, when the town was crawling with state and county police enforcing the traffic laws, a person driving 70 miles per hour was arrested while leaving the city limits. Sixteen other drivers were cited for traffic violations that weekend.[97] Under normal conditions, when only one town police officer was on duty during each eight-hour shift, law enforcement was no match for most speeders and reckless drivers.

A problem that was somewhat alleviated during these years was downtown parking. In July 1957 the town board decided to lease a lot behind the old post office (near where the current post office is now) for a free public parking lot.[98] The lot behind the new post office, opened the following year, also offered a place to park for those who wished to make a quick purchase downtown while picking up their mail. But these two changes did not solve the parking problem, especially for those who wanted to park on Main Street. "Parking [downtown] has always been a problem," Elaine McArn observed. One reason, she thought, was that "merchants in town parked on Main Street," thus occupying spaces that shoppers could have used. "And I could never understand that."[99]

The town's biggest problem in the late 1940s and 1950s almost certainly was the dilapidated housing, often with no indoor drinking water or plumbing, in which many poor and working-class blacks lived. Davidson was small enough—and one of the areas of poor housing was close enough to Main Street—for residents of both races to know about this problem. And if anyone needed a reminder, they could read a story about it in August 1948 in the first issue of the *Cornelius Davidson Gazette*: "A five-room house occupied by a colored family collapsed Sunday morning around three o'clock. . . . The supports evidently gave way, allowing the floor to crumble in." Fortunately, the parents and their four children "escaped uninjured."[100]

In 1950 Davidson residents—led by Carl Pritchett, the pastor of DCPC —made a concerted effort to alleviate this problem. The effort began with a well-known event in Davidson's twentieth-century history, one that contemporaries remembered as "the fire that stopped the preacher."[101] While Pritchett was preaching on 19 February 1950, the siren wailed at the fire house on Main Street a couple hundred yards away. Pritchett cut short his sermon, gave a final prayer, and invited the congregation to leave and help put out the fire. The fire was on Brady's Alley, an area just west of Main Street where eighty-seven poor and working-class blacks lived in eleven small, dilapidated rental houses. Pritchett appealed successfully to townspeople and students for clothes for the families, several of which had lost almost everything they had in the fire.[102]

More important, Pritchett organized a town meeting in the high school auditorium, attended by roughly 350 residents, that led to a broad-based community effort to improve living conditions for poor and working-class blacks. At this meeting two local doctors warned that outdoor toilets raised the risk to the town of typhoid and other communicable diseases, and a local businessman offered practical ideas for improving housing. The meeting also set up a Citizen's Housing Committee, composed largely of prominent local businessmen, that worked over the next several weeks to come up with a practical plan of action.[103] The committee's work led to a new housing ordinance for Davidson that required, among other things, that all houses have bathrooms, sewer service, and electricity.[104] The town

Black and white leaders at site of Brady's Alley fire

board spent $30,000 that summer and fall to provide sewer service to Brady's Alley and other areas of town that had lacked it, thus making it possible for the ordinance to be enforced.[105]

At another well-attended town meeting on May 8, the Citizen's Housing Committee reported that Davidson College students had promised to raise $5,000 toward making new housing a reality, and urged "at least 50 citizens [to] sign surety bonds for $100 each to finance construction."[106] As a news story about the meeting noted, "the signed bonds assure credit at the bank for persons eligible for the building loans."[107] Reflecting the community's broad support, $6,000 in bonds were signed at the meeting, $1,000 more than the committee had requested.[108]

The committee purchased land for new houses in the Mock Hill area on the west side. By December ten four- and five-room homes with full bathrooms and hot water had been built there at an average cost of $2,700.[109] Moreover, the fund-raising campaign to provide money to be loaned for additional homes surpassed its goal both at the college and in the black community.[110] "The Davidson Housing Plan has been widely publicized as an instance of local initiative and civic concern . . . ," the *Gazette* observed proudly in its issue for December 21. "Hodding Carter, famed newspaperman, has referred to this whole experience as 'the best

Christmas story I know.'"[111] Thus began a long-term, sporadic effort to improve housing for the town's poor and working-class residents.

The impressive response to "the fire that stopped the preacher" happened partly because Carl Pritchett fervently believed that helping the less privileged was one's obligation as a Christian. Even more, it occurred because many of his parishioners and other residents of Davidson agreed with him, even though most whites in town did not yet share his belief in racial equality.[112]

Social and Community Life

Life in Davidson in the late 1940s and 1950s remained divided largely along lines of race and social class. White and black young people attended legally segregated schools and, with very few exceptions, whites and blacks of all ages attended segregated churches. Among whites, informal but often painful town-gown divisions existed: children with a parent employed at the college, for example, could use the gym and other recreational facilities year round, whereas "town" children were not supposed to be on campus except for designated summer programs. In these programs race came to the fore: whites and blacks had separate programs, and only the white youth were permitted to swim in the college pool.[113]

Town-gown divisions were especially painful for some middle-class "town" women who wanted "college" women to accept them socially. Aileen Cantrell, who managed the Western Auto store with her husband, recalled that "it took a long time for [college women] to be friendly with me, because I wasn't with the college." She remembered attending the college church and having "nobody" speak to her.[114] A "college" person, Adeline Ostwalt, noticed "a lot of feeling between town and gown" when she moved to Davidson in the 1950s. She said that some faculty members were "uppity" and some book club members were "snooty." But she also observed that "original sin" existed on both sides.[115] Elaine McArn recalled that her father, a "town" man, "thought that professors were not very practical."[116] Another "town" man made the same point more graphically: "them educated idiots [professors] ain't got the common sense that God gave a billy goat."[117]

Living in a close-knit community had costs as well as benefits. As columnist Belle Banks wrote in the local newspaper with her usual complement of ellipses: "small town folks are nosy . . . if there's anything going on, nine times out of ten, everyone in town knows about it . . . and talks

about it."[118] Living in Davidson had other disadvantages, Erving Mc-
Clain, a middle-class black woman who worked as a nurse in Charlotte,
recalled: "Davidson is an all right place to live if you don't set goals that
are higher than you can attain in a small town . . . you have to be willing to go out of Davidson in order to expose [your children] to the better
things that are not offered here."[119] Working-class blacks employed in
Davidson generally seemed less critical of the town, but they often complained of low wages, including at the college.[120]

Despite the social divisions and disadvantages, Davidson offered a re-
warding life for many of its residents—especially for middle-class, college-
connected whites. Tish Kimbrough described Davidson as "totally safe"
and "an idyllic place to grow up."[121] Another professor's daughter, Patty
King, recalled: "It was a wonderful place to be—such a simple life, such
a happy life . . . everybody knew everybody."[122] "At Davidson we saw the
same people at church, the grocery store, [and] the post office," Martha
Newell, the wife of the pastor who followed Carl Pritchett, remembered.
"In our other churches, we only saw them on Sundays."[123]

Despite generally modest financial circumstances, many blacks rejected the concept of racial inequality and worked to better themselves.
Garfield Carr recalled that "my parents always taught me that you're just
as good—and in some cases better—than someone else. . . . You always
strive to be better than the next person. And never let anybody tell you
that you can't do it."[124] Other parents instilled the same attitudes, Carr
noted. Evidence of the desire for betterment among both parents and
children can be found in the number of black youth attending institutions of higher learning. A news story in September 1956 noted that fifteen
local blacks recently had left for college, and that one had departed for
seminary.[125]

The churches—all Protestant—remained the most important social
institutions in Davidson. Both whites and blacks revered their churches,
and it seems likely that most residents attended at least one church service
per week. "Very few people weren't going to church," Martha Montgomery recalled.[126] Almost everyone was Protestant. One Jewish man with a
gentile wife lived in Davidson for a while, but there were "no Catholics,"
Van Lear Logan commented. "I remember when I first saw one in Charlotte, I was just amazed."[127]

Given the piety and Protestantism of most Davidsonians, it is not surprising that the speaker who attracted the largest crowds in the 1950s was
evangelist Billy Graham.[128] And it also is not surprising, in light of the
churches' condemnation of strong drink, that no alcoholic beverages could

be sold in the town legally—and none was permitted at the college—until the winds of change swept through Davidson in the 1960s. Partly because of pressure from Davidsonians who wished to keep the Christian Sabbath as a day of worship and rest, the town also had an ordinance that required gasoline stations to be closed on Sundays.[129] The town board repealed that law—and all other Sunday-closing laws—in the late 1970s.

Especially among whites, churches tended to reflect social and economic divisions. Professors and administrators at the college, plus their families, were preeminent in DCPC, whereas the Methodist church consisted largely of merchants and tradespeople. The small Episcopal church also was solidly middle-class. The white Presbyterian and Baptist churches on the west side were largely working-class. As among whites, the largest, most prestigious black church was Presbyterian, though the A.M.E. Zion and Baptist churches were important as well.[130]

In addition to performing typical religious functions, churches were seedbeds of ideas for social betterment in the town—from the improvement of housing for poor blacks, as noted above, to (among many others) sponsoring scout troops, starting day-care centers, and supporting Hungarian refugees. Equally important, churches were social centers, with potluck suppers, "circles" for adults, and Sunday evening programs for teenagers. One teenager, Clark Readling of Cornelius, had a practical reason for attending the Methodist church: his girlfriend, who lived in Davidson, went there.[131] A Davidson student, Leland Park, found his most meaningful community not at the college, but at the Episcopal Church and at lunch in the Sadlers' home after the services.[132]

Even more than for whites, churches served as social centers for blacks. Whereas many whites could participate in social activities at the college, at Erwin Lodge, or in the large auditorium in the new white school, the church provided virtually "the only recreational outlet" for blacks, Brenda Tapia recalled.[133] "All the social life was through the church or the school," Ken Norton noted.[134] Black churches were famous for their plentiful, tasty picnics that drew large crowds after church or in the late afternoon. They also had fellowship and service groups, including the Geneva Fellowship at Davidson Presbyterian Church and the Missionary Society at Reeves Temple A.M.E. Zion Church.

Apart from the churches, the leading social institution for white men was the Davidson Lions Club, founded in the mid-1940s, which had roughly sixty members in the early and mid-1950s.[135] The club brought together men from the town and faculty members in twice-monthly meetings to hear speakers and raise money for a wide variety of causes, both lo-

Ken Norton camping with his Boy Scout troop

cal and statewide. One speaker, Davidson political science professor E.O. Guerrant, presciently predicted in May 1954 that Indochina would become communist if French colonialism ended.[136]

Between 1950 and early 1956 the club distributed more than $3,500, including locally $1,141 to schools, $381 to scouts, $250 to the new Teen Canteen, $125 for Christmas baskets for the needy, and $120 for wheelchairs.[137] The Lions raised money in various ways, including well-attended talent shows and musicals plus sales of brooms, mats, and light bulbs. Many Davidsonians supported the club's work: in a door-to-door solicitation one evening in September 1951, for example, Lions sold roughly 500 brooms, a huge number for a town that did not have that many dwellings.[138]

Another impressive white civic organization was the Davidson Parent-Teachers Association, founded in 1940. Although both men and women served as P.T.A. officers, middle-class women did most of the work. Mary Lu Daggy and other women led the effort to raise funds to buy the equipment needed to ensure that the Davidson School received the highest possible accreditation in 1950.[139] The biggest fund-raising event was the annual Halloween Carnival. The 1949 carnival included pony rides for children, a dog show, a hillbilly band, a barbershop quartet, and a square dance.[140] In 1951 the P.T.A. had 257 members, with 95 percent of the 229 student homes represented.[141]

White women also played key roles in numerous fund-raising and blood-donation drives during these years, including the 1953 Mothers' March of Dimes campaign and the 1955 campaign of United Appeal, the forerunner of United Way.[142] When the Red Cross Bloodmobile was in town for two days in April 1960, all sixty-one volunteers were women.[143] White women had numerous other social outlets, including several book clubs and a garden club. White women and men also participated in bridge groups, square dances, turkey shoots, plays, and other social and cultural activities.[144]

In contrast, except for the churches and occasional intergenerational activities at school, the civic and social outlets in Davidson for black women and men were sparse. Social events—including a "moonlight frolic" in October 1951—were held in the small black community center on Graham Street.[145] The Davidson District of the Huntersville High School—a support group for the black high school whose name soon would be changed to Torrence-Lytle—"sponsored a fish fry Friday evening and a tea Sunday afternoon at the [community] center," the *Gazette* reported in November 1952. The same story reported on a business meeting and dinner of the Men of the Year Club, another black organization.[146]

The most significant social event for blacks not sponsored by churches was the annual picnic—often accompanied by a baseball game—on the last Saturday in July to raise money for the Christian Aid and Benevolent Society, whose purpose was to assist members in paying doctors' bills and burial expenses. According to Annie Norton, this event raised as much as $1,000. This special day in the town's history ended in the 1960s.[147]

For nine months each year, school was the main activity for both black and white youth. Black Davidsonians were proud of the Ada Jenkins School, which was known for high expectations and the ability to stretch limited resources. Ada Jenkins offered grades 1–8, with high school in Huntersville. "At that time I thought [Ada Jenkins] was great," Mary Archie recalled. "We all did."[148] Garfield Carr remembered his principal as "a mathematical genius [who] made sure you knew your math."[149] In 1957–58 the school had only 13 teachers for 440 students, resulting in an average class size of 34. "The principal and school secretary also teach," a newspaper article noted.[150] "When we were in eighth grade we had only two basketballs," Roosevelt Wilson observed.[151]

As shown by their support for the P.T.A., whites in Davidson were equally proud of the Davidson School. It served grades 1–12 until North Mecklenburg High School opened in September 1951, and grades 1–9 until Alexander Junior High opened in September 1960. The Davidson School was known for its excellent teachers—often well-educated, unmarried daughters of Davidson College professors who devoted much of their lives to teaching and mentoring their students. The school had "the most wonderful teachers," Lawrence Kimbrough recalled.[152] "You respected those teachers," Nancy Blackwell remembered. "They knew your family, and if anything went on in school, your family knew it."[153] Both teachers and students benefited from smaller classes than at Ada Jenkins; in 1957–58, classes averaged 27 students.[154]

For white youths, school was a place where the town-gown and other divisions among adults often could be ignored or transcended in social interactions in the halls, on the playgrounds, and in after-school activities. "We were all friends," including the mill children, Martha Montgomery recalled, "around school and around the basketball games."[155] "We had friends who lived over on Delburg Street that were really rather itinerant in their backgrounds and families," John Woods noted. "But as kids we really didn't see the difference."[156]

"College" parents often maintained distinctions, however, as John's sister Lacy Dick remembered: "I heard one mother say that we, the college children, played with the town children until a certain age, and then they weren't invited to the birthday parties anymore."[157] But "college" and "town" youth did belong to the same scout troops and sports teams into the teenage years.[158] Youth baseball was especially popular after Gene McEver led an effort beginning in 1958 to build baseball fields and bleachers on town-owned property at the end of South Street.

In general, white children who lived on the west side of town were more likely to play with black children than were whites who lived on the east side. Doodle Brown, who lived on Depot Street, had many black friends and played with them frequently. "We always had a good relationship," Brown recalled. "We used to get together all the time." Fights between working-class whites and blacks did not undermine their friendship, Brown noted: "We'd fight for a while, then go play again. Then we'd go back and fight a while, and then go play again some more."[159]

Nancy Blackwell, who lived in the mill area, had fond memories of playing with black youth on the ball field that Tom Sadler and several volunteers built on the land he owned that eventually became Sadler Square. "You ought to have seen the donkey ball game we had one time with the blacks," Blackwell recalled. "You batted the ball, and you hopped on that donkey to get to first base. . . . And you had to get off to touch the base. We had the best fun."[160]

Some white youth on the east socialized with black youth, but others did not. Sandy Carnegie, who lived on Concord Road, remembers playing with Garfield Carr and several white friends in the old medical college building across from DCPC.[161] In contrast, Jane Power Schenck, who lived on Walnut Street, "didn't mingle with [black children] at all."[162] "We didn't know many black kids," Mary Martin recalled, "because we didn't socialize with [them]."[163]

Although we will never know how many white and black children had friendships across the racial divide, the evidence is overwhelming that many black and white children enjoyed themselves while growing up in Davidson in the late 1940s and 1950s. Garfield Carr put it succinctly: "We had fun."[164] Both black and white children loved playing sports, especially baseball, football, and basketball. Boys of both races enjoyed hunting and fishing, while girls liked to play indoor and outdoor games and ride ponies. Black youth loved dancing around the maypole at their school, and white children especially enjoyed outdoor games like Kick-the-Can and building small dams in the creeks. "I felt like we had . . . an idyllic, very happy childhood in Davidson," Lacy Dick recalled. "We had a lot of freedom; we could go anywhere and ride our bikes anywhere."[165]

Some boys occasionally crossed the line separating legitimate play from juvenile delinquency. Doodle Brown recalled greasing the tracks so that trains, having stopped at the depot, would not be able to get up the small incline as they headed north toward Mooresville. "People would get off the train to put sand on the tracks," Brown recalled, "and we'd throw rocks at them. They'd cuss us."[166] John Woods, who lived on Lorimer Road, remembered that "there were seldom any street lights . . . burning in the summertime in our neighborhood, because we were proficient rock-throwers."[167]

During these years some Davidson students, typically committed Christians, worked through the campus Y.M.C.A. to make life better for black and white youth. They made their most impressive contributions among blacks, organizing scout troops and youth sports teams, supervising after-school recreation programs, teaching Sunday school classes, and showing films at the black community center—also known as the Y Hut—weekly during the school year. In 1954, after school officials requested that the community center be moved from its Ada Jenkins School location, the "Y" raised the $3,750 needed to purchase a lot on Graham Street, move the building there, and remodel it, adding two new bathrooms and a storage room.[168] By early 1955 a black teen-age group was meeting in what was now called the David McLean Community Center.[169]

White youths and adults—and a few black youth—benefited from the opening in 1947 of Erwin Lodge, located among tall pine trees on the east side of the Davidson campus near Grey Road. The stone structure, roughly 40 feet by 40 feet with a large main gathering room, was a gift from Davidson English professor Edward Erwin and his wife Mary. They wished to honor the memory of their sons who had died while serving in the armed forces during World War II. A news story in May 1947 reported that "two very lifelike portraits of Phifer and 'Little Ed' are placed one on each side of the fireplace." The story also noted that "any group is welcome to use the lodge for a party, picnic, dance, or other function regardless of whether they are connected with the college."[170]

For many years thereafter, Erwin Lodge was one of the most popular meeting places in Davidson. Between January and October 1951, for example, an average of four organizations or family groups used the inside of the lodge each week, and many others had picnics or other social activities outside on the picnic tables and benches.[171] "We had a lot of our teenage parties out there," Martha Montgomery recalled.[172] Despite "lots of chaperones," Elaine McArn remembered, much "smooching" occurred during the many dances at the lodge.[173] The Lions Club sponsored Easter egg hunts for children under twelve, and Davidson students held a Christmas party for their two black scout troops, one from Davidson and the other from Cornelius.[174]

White youth also enjoyed the Teen Canteen, located on the first floor of the Carolina Inn on Main Street. Around the beginning of 1955, members of DCPC began to discuss the need for a structured, wholesome social outlet for young people, especially ones in grades 7 through 10.[175] Soon the white Methodist church and the Lions Club became involved, and by April a delegation of six prominent Davidsonians met with the town board to request financial support to supplement funds pledged by the Lions Club and the churches.[176] The college offered free use of the Carolina Inn, and a local couple agreed to provide adult supervision. The canteen opened in June with "two ping-pong tables; one pool table (second hand); a record player with records; numerous small games; a badminton set; [and] horseshoe games."[177]

It took a couple years to get effective rules and regulations established —and also to find adults who could handle the challenges of supervising freedom-seeking, hormone-heavy young people between the ages of 12 and 18.[178] By October 1957 the canteen operated only on Wednesday afternoons and Saturday evenings—limited hours that ensured adequate attendance when the canteen was open.[179] Boys especially liked playing pool, which induced some girls to "congregate around the pool tables," a news story reported.[180] "A lot of the boys do not rock n' roll," an adult

Louise Sloan posing inside a tree trunk in 1941

supervisor commented in 1960. "But on Saturday nights the boys dress up a little and they'll slow dance."[181]

Any discussion of community life in Davidson in the 1940s and 1950s would be incomplete without mentioning that era's great eccentric, Louise Sloan. Like beauty, eccentricity is in the eyes of the beholder. Some people, for example, found it amusing that Davidson's immaculately dressed president, John Cunningham, raised chickens behind his stately college home, and that his wife would turn on her favorite television show, women's wrestling, during parties with faculty members.[182] Like many people who have lived in Davidson, the Cunninghams had modest rural backgrounds.

Louise Sloan's background was not as modest: the daughter of a Davidson businessman and mayor, James Lee Sloan, Jr., she graduated from Duke and had substantial wealth in Davidson real estate and other assets. She lived by herself in the family home on South Main Street, next to the current town hall. "She was always very dressed and had her rouge on," Elaine McArn recalled. "She wore a little black suit a lot with a black hat with a veil."[183] "She wore fifty-year-old clothes or older and walked all over town and picked things up," Mary Fetter Stough noted.[184] "Every evening she would go through the garbage cans [downtown]," Jane Power

Schenck observed. "We [children] were always afraid of her because we thought she was a witch."[185]

Louise Sloan's main eccentricity was her extreme frugality. She resisted spending money on anything, including installing indoor plumbing until the town finally insisted upon it. She filled her house with newspapers, other paper products, and twigs that she collected on her daily outings. "I don't think she ever threw anything out," Carol Quackenbush commented.[186] She loved reading the *Wall Street Journal*, but only if she could read it at the college library or retrieve copies from the trash at the post office. She also enjoyed seeing movies at the local theater; but she waited until 9:30 p.m., after the ticket attendant had gone home, before sneaking in to watch the late show.[187]

Sloan was famous for attending weddings at DCPC to which she had not been invited. During the receptions in the fellowship room, invited guests watched with amusement as she filled her purse with goodies that she presumably ate at home later.[188] After Warren McKissick cleaned and painted the property that he rented from her on Main Street, she commented, "Warren, it looks so nice, I'm going to have to raise your rent!"[189] It would be hard to dispute Carolyn Readling's observation that "Miss Sloan" was a "real character."[190]

Cracks in the Edifice of Segregation

Like the overwhelming majority of cities and towns in the South, Davidson remained highly segregated in the late 1940s and 1950s. In addition to the segregation in the public schools, the Soda Shop and other restaurants did not permit blacks to sit down at tables to eat the food they purchased, and the movie theater was not open to blacks except when they were bringing white kids to watch children's films.[191] The waiting room at the doctor's office was segregated. A town ordinance prohibited taxis from transporting white and black passengers at the same time.[192] The owners of the local newspaper strongly opposed the *Brown* decision that "forced integration" of the public schools. In September 1957 one of Davidson's leading citizens, Ernest Beaty, applauded the *Gazette*'s "stand on the integration problem."[193]

At the local level, the South's system of racial segregation required (a) whites who were largely united in enforcing it, with the majority viewing critics as misguided, isolated outsiders; and (b) blacks who generally accepted this unequal system, at least outwardly.[194] After the *Brown* decision in 1954, whites in the town remained largely united in trying to enforce segregation. But influential voices at the college—partly separate, but still a respected part of the town—challenged the system, sparking an ongoing debate that undermined the unity among whites that segregation required. And while most blacks continued to accept outwardly the unequal treatment they experienced, an African-American man in his twenties challenged local social mores in 1956. Because of these challenges from whites and blacks, and because of national and regional pro-integration developments that could not be ignored, segregation in Davidson was more fragile by the late 1950s and early 1960s than it had been a decade earlier.

President Cunningham believed that the Christian faith required church-related institutions, including Davidson College, to treat whites and blacks equally. As he wrote to a correspondent in April 1954: "One of my deep concerns is that we in the church and in church colleges do not bypass the Christian responsibilities that we have to Negro students, leaving it for the [government] to assume complete leadership in this field." Yet Cunningham acknowledged in the same letter that the college's board of trustees—not he—would decide if and when Davidson admitted black students: "For the present, at least, the college does not desire Negro applications."[195]

Despite his awareness that most trustees, faculty members, and students were not ready to admit blacks, Cunningham made a strongly pro-integration comment when the *Brown* decision was announced: "Basically, I hardly see how the court could have made any other decision on the basis of right and wrong in a free democracy."[196] Referring implicitly to the college, Cunningham wrote several months later that the Supreme Court decision "creates a climate of opinion which is going to make the church and its institutions seem very inhuman if they fall behind industry, labor, transportation, the military forces, and the state institutions in its regard for people of other races."[197]

Building on the Y.M.C.A.'s positive experiences in having meetings on campus with students from nearby black Presbyterian colleges, Cunningham obtained the trustees' approval for a four-week interracial, international seminar in the summer of 1956 sponsored by a liberal Quaker organization, the American Friends Service Committee. Twenty-two undergraduate and graduate students from nine nations attended the seminar, including two American blacks. One of the blacks was Calvin Houston, a highly intelligent, articulate Presbyterian from Davidson who was attending Union Theological Seminary in Richmond. Houston's niece, Brenda Tapia, recalled that he was "tall and good looking, with lots of charisma."[198]

Extreme white racists, probably members or supporters of the Ku Klux Klan from nearby communities, showed their anger at the fact that the interracial seminar was meeting by burning a cross on the football field on June 21, the day the participants arrived on campus. Two more crosses were burned after dark on Friday, July 13. One was in front of Duke dormitory, where the seminar was being held, and the other was in front of the Houston family home on Catawba Avenue in Davidson.

The two cross burnings on July 13 took place on the day that Houston accompanied an attractive white female participant in the seminar to see Dr. James Woods in his office on South Street. Sam Spencer, the dean of students at the time, recalled that "either or both of them were wearing shorts—very informal—and he took her down there and stayed with her until she was properly seen by a doctor."[199] Reports quickly spread that Houston and his companion were holding hands as they walked down Main Street, which if true would have challenged the town's mores regarding acceptable behavior between a black man and a white woman.[200] When they arrived at the waiting room, Brenda Tapia recalls, Houston sat in a straight chair in the black waiting area and urged his companion to sit on one of the comfortable couches in the white waiting area. Disregarding his request, she plopped down on his lap—an unmistakable assault on southern mores at the time.[201]

After the seminar ended, Cunningham wrote a letter to the *Gazette* in which he tried to justify the college's decision to host it. Cunningham defended the seminar as "an effort of Christian people [Quakers] to bring together outstanding young people from around the world." He called the cross burnings "illegal and inexcusable." Referring vaguely to participants' behavior that had angered local whites, he expressed regret for "unfortunate incidents which took place" that "caused anxiety and strain in the community."[202]

What followed was a rare, perhaps unprecedented event in Davidson's history: a rebuke of the college by town leaders. On August 6, the town's six elected officials, including Professor Beaty and former college treasurer Frank Jackson, met at town hall and drafted a letter to Cunningham. "Regardless of the intent and purpose of the seminar," the officials noted, "a belief persists that it was brought to Davidson to encourage intergration [sic] between the white and Negro races. This interpretation has developed tensions and aroused emotions which have threatened the peace and quiet of our community." The officials urged Cunningham to "consider the wisdom of not holding other interracial groups on the campus until tensions have lessened and emotions have died down."[203]

In the spirit of trust and cooperation between town and college, the town's leaders did not make the letter public. Cunningham, in turn, made sure that the college established clear guidelines for the next interracial conference, a gathering of Christian students from colleges across the South that occurred that December. The participants were to remain on campus and avoid contact with townspeople.[204] Thus, while maintaining his commitment to holding interracial meetings on campus, Cunningham also worked to prevent "any permanent breach between the town and the gown."[205]

Meanwhile discussion was increasing at the college about whether, in the wake of the *Brown* decision, Davidson should admit qualified blacks as students on the same basis as whites. Among faculty, informal conversations on the subject were the norm. Among students, casual conversations were supplemented by articles in the student newspaper on both sides of the issue. In a symposium in the *Davidsonian* in November 1954, for example, Ronald Wilson argued that the college should follow the recent pro-integration stance of the General Assembly of the southern Presbyterian Church and admit black students. "How can [any Christian] call another inferior to himself?" Wilson wrote. In contrast, Bob Jones argued that "both the white and the colored races are much better off in being segregated." In his view, integration "could only lead to miscegenation."[206]

According to an article in the student newspaper, the college invited far more integrationists than segregationists to speak at convocations, which students were required to attend. To provide balance, the article reported, the college asked economics professor C.K. Brown to elucidate the "southern position" in a lecture in March 1956.[207] In his talk Brown sharply criticized the Supreme Court's insistence "that the southern states shall no longer embody in their law the boundaries that they have considered it desirable to maintain between the races." He also argued that the Christian concept of brotherhood should not "be used to describe a condition of worldly equality." "Nowhere in the New Testament," Brown insisted, "can I find that it is the purpose of Christianity to wipe out the differences that exist among [human beings]."[208]

Brown's fervent defense of segregation exposed divisions on the issue. Sam Maloney, a young religion professor, was a committed integrationist. His memory of the day Brown spoke was vivid:

> I remember going to my class right after [Brown's lecture] and opening my class with a prayer that went something like "Forgive us our bigotry and our narrow-mindedness." Later I overheard

[Math Professor] John Kimbrough speaking to another faculty member. He said, "We've got to do something with these young Turks around here, fellows like Maloney."[209]

In April 1958, a black man from Gastonia, Frank Parker, wrote to the director of admissions asking whether his son, then a high school junior ranked number one in his class, could be considered for admission in September 1960.[210] This letter prompted discussion within the administration and, subsequently, in the board of trustees. At its meeting in February 1959, the board, in President Grier Martin's words, "decided that it was not in the best interest of the college to admit a Negro student at this time."[211] An editorial in the *Davidsonian* criticized the decision, noting that "any defenses erected to keep qualified Negro students out of Davidson must be based on such flimsy arguments that they seem to be rationally untenable."[212]

By early 1960, student views were almost evenly divided between those who wanted continued segregation and those who supported integration either immediately or in the future.[213] But faculty views, which almost certainly were more important to the trustees, were generally supportive of integration. A December 1959 poll that was shared with the trustees revealed that thirty-two faculty supported integration "at the earliest possible date," while only ten were totally opposed. Seventeen others tentatively supported integration in the future.[214] Even some who had supported segregation in the past, including Ernest Beaty and John Kimbrough, signed a statement in January 1960 saying that, if the trustees decided to "admit qualified Negroes," they would "accept such a decision."[215]

While most members of the all-white faculty finally were agreeing to support integration at the college, or at least not to engage in die-hard opposition, the virtually all-black sit-in movement, beginning in Greensboro in February 1960, led to the integration that year of many restaurants and lunch counters in numerous southern cities, including Charlotte. And the major-party candidate more favorable to civil rights for black Americans, John F. Kennedy, was elected president that November. Although both the town and the college were still segregated in 1960, any perceptive observer would have been able to conclude that the era of rigid segregation in the South—and in Davidson—was likely to end soon.

7 The Times Were Changing, 1961–1984

On a Sunday afternoon in June 1968, black and white Davidsonians met at Reeves Temple A.M.E. Zion Church to honor the Community Relations Committee, a biracial group of townspeople who had envisioned and then made possible a new housing development for upwardly mobile blacks, Lakeside Park, on Davidson's west side. The chair of the Mecklenburg County Board of Commissioners, Davidson resident Jim Martin, presented certificates of appreciation to the members of the committee. Other speakers from the town included two white males, Burl Naramore and Dan Rhodes; one white female, Pat Stinson; one black male, T.M. Powe; and one black female, Annie Mildred Lowery. After the brief talks, the townspeople toured the three-bedroom brick homes located on a hill west of the "algae pond" that had been created when Lake Norman filled with water in the early 1960s.[1]

This meeting epitomized some of the many changes that occurred in Davidson from the early 1960s through the early 1980s. Without the relatively new Lake Norman, there obviously would not have been a development named "Lakeside." Moreover, in contrast to the modest housing developed for working-class blacks in the 1950s, Lakeside Park's substantial homes symbolized middle-class status and respect. Equally important, the leadership of the town had begun to change. Whereas white males had predominated in the town's public life before 1960, white women and blacks increasingly played major roles from the 1960s forward. Finally, Jim Martin's presence as leader of a Republican majority in county government demonstrated that Mecklenburg County had a functioning two-party system for the first time since the Civil War.[2]

So many changes occurred in the town and at the college during these years that evaluating their relative importance is a daunting task. For those Davidsonians who were able to live in Lakeside Park, that change might have been the most significant. For some residents, the closing of the asbestos plant in the 1970s might have been life-saving. For local and visiting shoppers, new businesses, including the Village Store in the 1960s and the Needlecraft Center in the 1970s, were welcome additions to Main Street. The downtown became more attractive in the mid-1960s when, led by Piedmont Bank, several businesses updated store fronts to reflect what one owner called the image of "a quaint college town."[3] In 1974 the town board, responding to repeated reports of people being bitten by dogs, passed Davidson's first ordinance requiring their licensing and restraint.[4]

Many Davidsonians on both sides of town appreciated the ending of segregation in the 1960s and the growing influence of blacks and women in civic life. Many residents also appreciated the college's growing national reputation, its stellar basketball team, its shift to co-education, and the widespread acceptance of alcohol consumption both at the college and in the town. Some lifestyle changes were more controversial, especially the widespread use of marijuana at the college and the more relaxed approach to sexuality both at the college and in the town. Given the town's typically hot summers, a welcome change for many residents was the much greater presence of air conditioning in all types of buildings in 1981 than had been the case in 1961.[5]

From the perspective of the late 1970s and early 1980s, the most important change might have been the impact of Interstate 77—opened to Davidson on 31 December 1975—on the town's planning process and on its inadequate water and sewer systems.[6] Also significant was the arrival in 1982 of cable TV, which permitted subscribers to choose from many more channels than had been available via antennas.[7] Less noticed by average residents but still significant were the frequent annexations of land that increased Davidson's size, as well as the "perimeter zoning" that gave the town power over land use beyond its boundaries.[8] Also little noticed at a time when more and more college students and other residents had cars was the gradual ending of the Greyhound bus service in Davidson in the late 1970s and early 1980s.[9]

Although much of this chapter is justifiably devoted to change, continuity also characterized many areas of the town's life during these years.

Ingersoll-Rand plant near Lake Davidson

The local economy remained balanced, with the college, industry, and retail outlets continuing as the three main sources of employment. The main economic change was that, by the late 1960s, manufacturing firms—led by General Time, a large-scale manufacturer of clocks, surpassed the college in employment.[10] When General Time's production declined in the late 1970s, the Ingersoll-Rand manufacturing corporation became a major employer.

Reflecting growing prosperity in town and expanding enrollments on campus, Davidson's population grew 22 percent from 1960 to 1980, from 2,573 to 3,241. Most of that growth—491 of 668—occurred in the college's student body. With the non-student population growing modestly from 1,661 in 1960 to 1,838 in 1980, Davidson remained a small town during these years.[11] As Betty Cumming, a church and town leader, wrote in 1969:

> Davidson is still a village, thank goodness. There is still the same
> delight on returning to it from Charlotte, or New York, or Bombay,
> to find the woods and fields close and the nights country-quiet,
> with only the companionable wail of the little train. . . . People are
> building . . . farther and farther out, but the children can still race
> across cornfields in the autumn dusk and build dams in little creeks
> near home, as our boys did in the 30's.[12]

In addition to keeping its small-town feel, Davidson also maintained roughly the same proportion of whites and blacks. In 1960 the population was 76 percent white and 24 percent black, while in 1980 the comparable percentages were 78 and 22. The big change between 1960 and 1980—reflecting the college's becoming co-educational in the 1970s—was in the percentage of women in the town's population: from 34 percent in 1960 to 45.5 percent in 1980.

The most important continuity between the early 1960s and the early 1980s, as Betty Cumming's evocative words suggest, is that the town remained for most residents a good place to live, to work, to raise children, to attend school and church, and to engage in social, cultural, athletic, and service activities. With the founding of a vibrant senior center in the late 1970s, it even became a better place to grow old. Having overcome the worst features of white racism while retaining its traditional small-town friendliness and concern for others, and having welcomed capable newcomers into leadership roles, by the late 1960s or early 1970s this prosperous, forward-looking community was experiencing something like a golden age.

The Often Rocky Road to Racial Integration

The most significant changes in Davidson during the 1960s involved major steps toward racial integration, first at the college and then in the town. These changes were historic, for Davidson had been highly segregated since its earliest days. The changes also were difficult to achieve because relatively few black students enrolled at the college in the 1960s and because some individuals of both races—notably die-hard white segregationists and black barber/landlord Ralph Johnson—resisted specific changes in race relations as fervently as other whites and blacks supported them.

Integration at the college proceeded slowly. Responding to a letter from nine Davidson graduates who were serving as Presbyterian missionaries in the Congo, in February 1961 the Board of Trustees agreed to admit up to three qualified Congolese students as part of the college's foreign student program.[13] The first African student, Benjamin Nzengu, enrolled nineteen months later, in September 1962; the second, George Nzongola-Ntalaja, came in September 1963. At the time, Nzengu recalled later, "racism was everywhere"; he remembered being asked to sit separately from his white friends when they dined in local restaurants.[14]

On 17 May 1962, before either African student enrolled, the trustees, encouraged by a 53–14 faculty vote to end segregation, instructed the faculty to admit "properly qualified" students without regard to "race, nationality, creed or class."[15] Two years later, college leaders happily announced that two African Americans, Leslie Brown and Wayne Crumwell, had agreed to matriculate at Davidson in September 1964.[16]

President Grier Martin was happy partly because officials at the Ford Foundation had made it clear earlier that the college would not be considered for a grant until black Americans had enrolled.[17] Once Brown and Crumwell were on campus, the college applied to the foundation for a $2 million challenge grant, by far the largest amount that the college had sought from a foundation up to that time. When the grant was approved the following June, Martin was on course to raise the funds needed to transform Davidson from a good but needy regional institution to a more prosperous college with a national reputation.[18] Martin's ambitious fund-raising also permitted him to increase salaries and benefits for all employees, including working-class blacks and whites from the town's west side.[19]

Partly because only thirteen African Americans enrolled at the college during the six years from 1964–65 through 1969–70, being a black student at Davidson in the 1960s was highly challenging. "You'll never get a Negro to come here and enjoy it," Leslie Brown commented in December 1967, "unless you have a larger Negro student body." Wayne Crumwell's comment that was quoted in the same article was equally perceptive: "Both races have their hang-ups. The Negroes are suspicious of white people's motives and the whites have this sense of superiority that is part of their heritage." As Crumwell also observed, "What good is integrating if the feeling behind it is not real?"[20]

For some white students, feelings of equality had not yet emerged: when members of his fraternity heard the news that Martin Luther King, Jr., had been shot, William Brown recalled, a group of students came out the front door celebrating.[21] Some white townspeople reacted with similar expressions of joy.[22] More positively for black students, in September 1966 college officials decided that the Confederate flag would no longer fly atop campus buildings on football Saturdays, and that the band would not play "Dixie" during football games.[23] Moreover, the housing supervisor at the college, Scotty Nicholls, recalled that she "never had anyone refuse to have a black student as a roommate."[24]

The December 1967 story also noted that the three black students interviewed (out of the five then on campus) "agreed that life was gradually becoming easier for Davidson's Negro students, and that the college

and student body has tried to create a more natural environment for Negroes."[25] Two black students became the first African Americans to accept
bids from fraternities that fall, for example, and Calvin Murphy helped to
organize the Black Student Coalition about the same time. Conditions for
black students continued to improve gradually, most notably for the social
life of black men when African-American women were admitted as part
of co-education in the 1970s. Growing numbers also helped: in welcome
contrast to the handful of blacks at the college in the 1960s, ninety came
between the 1970–71 and 1978–79 academic years, with larger enrollments
thereafter.[26]

Integration also arrived slowly and haltingly in the town, especially in
some restaurants and in both barber shops. A bright spot was the smooth
integration of the Davidson Elementary School. Yet for many blacks the
success of this integration was balanced by the closing in 1966 of a longtime focal point and source of pride in their community, the black school.
"Ada Jenkins was like your other family," Ruby Houston recalled. "It's
like losing a family member; you lose resources, you lose your power."[27]
When the school closed, Talmadge Connor observed, older black people
"grumbled and growled"; but black children were happy because "many
had never ridden a bus before . . . , so they liked that."[28]

Integration in Davidson schools occurred over two years. In 1965–66,
Adeline Ostwalt became the first and only white to teach at the black
school, thus introducing black students to a white teacher. The kind and
caring Ostwalt was so well accepted by her students that, as the school
year progressed, at least one of them was no longer aware that she was
white. Once when her husband, Davidson College Professor Jay Ostwalt,
came to the school, one of her students asked her, "Is that your boyfriend?"
"No," Adeline responded, "that's my husband." The boy replied, "Are you
married to a white man?"[29]

Beginning in October 1965, shortly after Ostwalt began teaching at
Ada Jenkins, two classes of the school's second graders and their teachers
were bused to the Davidson School to have all their classes there, thus
starting integration of students in the town. In 1966–67 full integration
arrived in north Mecklenburg: all the black schools were closed, and the
racial balance at the schools attended by Davidson youth was Davidson
Elementary, 193 white and 127 black; Alexander Middle School, 655 white
and 248 black; and North Mecklenburg High School, 1,059 white and 299
black.[30]

Black and white parents agreed that integration worked well at Davidson Elementary and that the calm, resourceful principal, Wayne Roberts,

deserved much credit. "To my knowledge, everything went well," Mary Archie recalled.[31] Another black parent, Evelyn Carr, noted Roberts's leadership and said that the school "helped our children a lot."[32] A white parent, Jane Avinger, commented that Roberts "deserved tremendous credit for running a wonderfully integrated school and having . . . a great understanding of how to handle little things [between white and black students] that could have blown up into a huge thing."[33] Not surprisingly, the modest Roberts praised the teachers and volunteers—especially parents and Davidson College students—for students' gains in "academic achievement" and in "self-assurance and social relationships."[34] To Adeline Ostwalt, there was another reason why integration generally went well in Davidson: "they [blacks] knew us, and we knew them."[35]

Overall, the early years of integration at North Mecklenburg High School did not go as smoothly. White students, including Shaw Smith and John Woods, enjoyed playing football with blacks and getting to know them better.[36] They and other white students from Davidson, including Bill Strong, had largely positive memories.[37] In contrast, Brenda Tapia and other blacks who transferred to North Meck in 1965 found their experience there, in Tapia's words, "very trying."[38] Ruby Houston found it "challenging in that we were accepted by some and not accepted by many."[39]

Garfield Carr agreed. He characterized his three years at the largely white school as "uncomfortable," partly because the athletic teams were the Rebels and "Dixie" was the school's fight song. Carr's reflections in a 2001 interview are similar to some of the opinions, discussed earlier, of the first group of African-American students at the college:

> It was tough going from an all-black school [Torrence-Lytle High School] to North Mecklenburg. You always had to prove yourself and you also had to break down the stereotypes that [fellow students and teachers] had already placed on you. . . . But . . . it seemed like each year got a little better.[40]

A definite boost for integration were the day-care and other pre-school programs that often brought together black and white children across lines of social class as well as race. These programs would not have been possible without the determined efforts of two remarkable women, Pat Sailstad and Betty Cumming. Both were well-educated, egalitarian northerners who had come to Davidson when their husbands had taken positions at the college. Both were active members of DCPC who inspired their co-religionists and others in town. And both believed strongly in the value of early childhood education. Cumming and Sailstad "were a wonderful team," John Kelton recalled. "Betty could speak for a cause and it was just compelling. And Pat was a go-getter who would grab folks and tell them what we wanted to do."[41]

In early 1966, Sailstad recalled, "there was a real need for a pre-school for the black children so that they would be ready to go to first grade, because we had no kindergartens in the state at that time."[42] When Sailstad asked whether DCPC or the Methodist church could provide facilities for a black pre-school, both declined. Fortunately, Brown Patterson and others in the Episcopal church, located on Lorimer Street close to the Sailstads' home, agreed to let the black youth use its play area. Pat recalled telling Patterson that "he not only saved the school but he saved my religion," which had been sorely tested by her church's refusal to provide facilities.[43] Thus, in February 1966 Sailstad, assisted by several other local women, began a pre-school in her basement and in the Episcopal church's play area for twenty-seven black children aged four and five.

Twelve months later, again at Sailstad's instigation, a pilot kindergarten opened in the recently closed black school for 166 five-year-olds from Davidson and other communities in northern Mecklenburg County. Pat, assisted by her husband, Robert, started this initiative by applying for funding from the United Way. They soon learned that funds intended to help children from low-income families might be available through Title I of the federal Elementary and Secondary Education Act of 1965, a program administered locally by the Charlotte-Mecklenburg school system. Thus the well-funded, integrated North Mecklenburg Child Development Center—made possible by one of President Lyndon Johnson's Great Society programs—opened in February 1967 in the refurbished Ada Jenkins building with a staff led by Adeline Ostwalt that included eight teachers, eight assistant teachers, and support personnel.[44] The Child Development Center continued until federal funds declined and school board priorities changed in 1973, after which DCPC carried forward some of the center's activities in an integrated pre-school program.

Like many leaders in Davidson over the years, Pat Sailstad did not rest on her laurels. Instead, she, Betty Cumming, and other white and black leaders in Davidson, recognizing the need for day-care facilities for working-class parents, formed the North Mecklenburg Child Development Association in early 1968 to build and supervise a day-care center to serve Davidson and Cornelius. Having received a donation to purchase a lot on Gamble Street next to the Child Development Center, the group launched a campaign in July 1968 to raise $50,000—later increased to $60,000—to construct a facility on this land.[45]

Adeline Ostwalt greets students at the Child Development Center

Betty Cumming led this campaign, shrewdly recognizing that sub-stantial gifts from local industries and out-of-town foundations would be needed to complement the smaller donations from townspeople. She also understood that money had to be raised among both whites and blacks, so that both communities could claim ownership and thus nurture the new facility.[46] With $42,000 raised by spring 1969, construction began on a building in Davidson while the association offered a day-care program in a temporary facility in Cornelius.[47]

The new building was dedicated on 24 May 1970. It was the tangible expression of a vision articulated by Cumming and Sailstad—and held by many other whites and blacks in town—that all families should have adequate day care for their children regardless of their ability to pay, and that black and white children needed to attend pre-school together if the society were to become truly integrated.[48] Jane Avinger, a long-time board member, summed up the significance of the Davidson-Cornelius Day Care Center for local children in the 1970s: "I can remember the teachers at the Davidson Elementary School saying they could look at their first graders—this was before kindergarten—and they could tell who had been to the day-care center and who hadn't."[49]

The white men who did the most to improve race relations in the town in the 1960s were Burl Naramore and Dan Rhodes. Both had come to Davidson recently, Naramore to manage the Bridgeport Fabrics plant and

Rhodes to teach religion and humanities at the college. And both became widely respected members—and then chairs—of the Community Relations Committee, a biracial group appointed by Mayor Frank Jackson in October 1963 to "pinpoint places where [racial and other] inequities exist and to determine the best methods, apart from outside influence, for making needed changes."[50]

The reference to averting "outside influence" was significant because a more militant biracial group, inspired by a field worker for the Congress on Racial Equality (CORE) and led by liberal Davidson College students, also began meeting that same month.[51] The mayor and other moderate-to-conservative town leaders saw the Community Relations Committee, modeled after a similar group in Charlotte, as a better choice to oversee the inevitable process of racial integration in town than the CORE-inspired Davidson Civil Rights Committee. The latter group was active in 1964 in supporting the Civil Rights Act and in encouraging President Johnson's election to a full term, but faded quickly thereafter.[52] The most "radical" action for racial equality that liberal Davidson students undertook in 1964 was inviting young people from Davidson Presbyterian Church and Johnson C. Smith University to accompany them to regular Sunday services at DCPC and the Methodist church.[53]

The major achievement of the Community Relations Committee in the 1960s was planning the Lakeside Park housing development, mentioned at the start of the chapter. Soon after its founding in late 1963, the committee recognized that better housing, especially for the working class and the poor, was one of the town's most pressing needs. The problem was how to move forward given the fact that the town government had little money to devote to this purpose.

In 1966 the committee, led by Naramore, came up with a workable solution. At the committee's urging, Naramore and Mayor Jackson spoke with a representative of the Duke Power Company about the possibility of purchasing a 32-acre tract of land the company owned west of the "algae pond." When the company offered to sell the land for the very reasonable price of $19,000, the committee set up the non-profit Davidson Community Development Corporation (DCDC) to oversee the project. With Duke Power's generous offer, Naramore persuaded his associates at Bridgeport Fabric to lend the needed $19,000 to DCDC interest-free so that it could complete the purchase and keep the land-development costs low. The committee also learned that, because Davidson's population was less than 5,500, the Farmers' Home Administration would be able to make long-term loans at reasonable rates to finance the houses in the proposed development.[54]

Lakeside Park neighborhood

Many other individuals and institutions, white and black, helped to make Lakeside Park a reality. To provide working capital for DCDC and to support black employees who wanted better housing, the college purchased ten lots early on and another ten later.[55] A retired math professor and experienced surveyor, W.N. Mebane, divided the property into lots.[56] The town government provided services while extending the time for payment until a sufficient number of lots could be sold.[57] Perhaps most important, Dan Rhodes and members of a recently established black organization, the Piedmont Area Development Association of Davidson (PADA), encouraged local blacks to assume the responsibilities of home ownership and then assisted them in the countless tasks involved, including choosing a lot, picking a house plan, and planning for maintenance and taxes. "Many times the people who were going to build would bring their plans over and sit at our dining room table," Ethel Rhodes recalled. "They and Dan would go over the plans and talk about what you needed to do."[58] Of the white committee members, the patient, soft-spoken Rhodes was most effective in bridging the racial divide.[59]

Lakeside Park was a huge success. Construction began in 1967, and by December 1968 twenty-three homes had been completed. "It's wonderful, just wonderful," James Raeford exclaimed. "I never thought I could have a house this nice."[60] By February 1972, a story in the *Charlotte Observer* noted, "45 families own their own brick homes there" and "not one default on a payment" had occurred.[61] Moreover, Lakeside Park provided a model for how other small towns could improve their housing, and even prompted a change in federal law that permitted the Farmers' Home Administration to make loans that included the lot as well as the house.[62] Although greatly pleased with the town's accomplishment, Burl Naramore observed that Lakeside Park was only "a first step in solving the housing problem in Davidson. . . . Anyone who drives around will see that more needs to be done."[63]

The Community Relations Committee was less successful in convincing downtown businesses to integrate, even after the Civil Rights Act of 1964 required restaurants and other public facilities—but not barber shops—to treat all customers equally. Ralph Quackenbush, the owner of the Hub, did not need to be persuaded: his quick-order restaurant on Main Street served blacks and whites equally when it opened in 1962, though virtually all of his customers for the next several years were white college students.[64]

The Coffee Cup on Depot Street had a largely working-class clientele, white and black. It had two entrances, one customarily used by whites and the other by blacks, with service areas separated by a large coat rack. The owner was willing to serve black college students in the "white" section, the *Davidsonian* reported in September 1963, "when they come in with white students on Saturday night." But she was reluctant to integrate fully because "she lost some business last year when a Negro student came into the ["white" side] alone."[65]

The Coffee Cup's failure to integrate fully resulted in one of the most talked-about incidents in Davidson in the 1960s. During the 1965–66 academic year, the college's highly successful basketball coach, Charles "Lefty" Driesell, was recruiting Charlie Scott, a black player from New York City who told people in Davidson that he intended to enroll at the college.[66] The lightning-quick Scott "plays basketball like he invented the game," a local journalist noted.[67]

Having attended Lefty's basketball camp the previous summer, Scott appeared to be committed to playing for the college. When Scott visited the campus in early 1966, the co-owner/waitress at the Coffee Cup told him and his party to leave the "white" section and request service on the "colored" side.[68] Reports of this incident spread quickly, and many Davidsonians blamed the restaurant's owners when Scott broke Lefty's heart—and the town's—by announcing that he would be attending the University of North Carolina at Chapel Hill. Scott said that he was impressed with the "cosmopolitan atmosphere" there.[69]

In the late 1960s, members of the Community Relations Committee

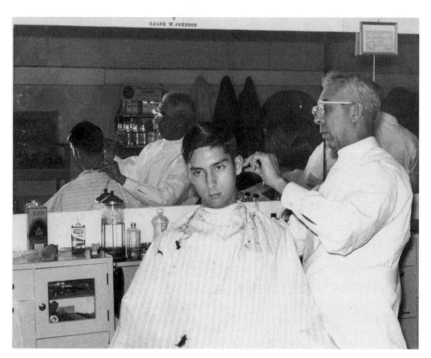

Ralph Johnson at work in his barbershop

conducted a low-key but persistent campaign to integrate the Coffee Cup fully. Annie Mildred Lowery, a black member of the committee, remembers being refused service while sitting for hours on the "white" side.[70] James Raeford, Lawrence Kimbrough, Betty Cumming, and Tony Abbott also made repeated efforts to persuade the owners to remove the coat rack and serve all customers equally. "They kept insisting that they just didn't have any other place to put [it]," Abbott recalled. The committee "didn't get rid of the coat rack," Abbott observed, referring to the owners' determination to resist the committee's entreaties; "it just kind of disappeared one day."[71]

The town's most famous episode involving efforts to achieve full integration centered on another proud owner of a downtown business, Ralph Johnson, a light-skinned, intelligent, suspicious African American who never felt comfortable with—or trusted—most of the town's whites or most of its blacks. Many local blacks, Johnson wrote later, had an attitude of "resentment" toward him, partly due to his family's "industry and resourcefulness."[72] Johnson's practice of attending services at the Methodist church, not at one of the black churches, may have heightened the perception that he considered himself superior to most local blacks.[73]

Student protest outside Johnson's barbershop

A longtime Davidson barber, Johnson moved his shop in early 1966 to the desirable property that he bought at the corner of Main and Depot streets. Johnson's purchase made him the first black owner of a downtown property in the town's history. Before the property changed hands, Johnson recalled, "blood-red paint was splotched and thrown on my large plate glass windows on the front of the building. This I interpreted as a threat that my blood would be spilled if the transaction were carried through and I became owner of the property."[74] To Johnson, this incident and several acts of vandalism against his property in late summer were fresh examples of the white racism he had experienced throughout his life.[75]

Others in town, including some blacks and many Davidson students and faculty, saw Johnson himself as prejudiced in his own way because, while he and and the several other barbers in his shop cut the hair of the few black college students, Johnson's shop—like Hood Norton's farther south on Main Street—did not serve local blacks during regular business hours. After Annie Mildred Lowery complained about Johnson's policy to Davidson student Robert Pyeatt in the spring of 1968, Pyeatt and twelve other students, with the encouragement of several faculty members, organized a boycott aimed at forcing Johnson to cut the hair of all who requested service on an equal basis. The boycott, including picketing in front of Johnson's shop, began on 2 April 1968, less than an hour after Johnson refused service to two local blacks whom the organizers had sent to test his policy. The students wrote the next day that the boycott was justified because Johnson's policy was "unfair, unjust, and immoral."[76]

As it unfolded over the next several weeks, the boycott involved a mix of nonviolent direct action, intimidation, and efforts to persuade Johnson and Hood Norton to change their policies. The picketing was generally nonviolent and dignified, though one student was arrested and charged with disorderly conduct.[77] Working-class whites from nearby communities shouted epithets at the picketers from passing cars, and a rock shattered a window in the shop.[78] Johnson was especially concerned about black demonstrators demanding an end to his policy. "The [barbers] who worked near the front of the building," Johnson wrote later, "began to express anxiety for their safety as more Negroes assembled," especially in the aftermath of Martin Luther King's assassination. "And I, in this mountain of trouble that had been caused me by the people of Davidson College, was caught helplessly in a whirlwind of hate."[79]

As the boycott continued, its supporters at the college worked hard to persuade Johnson to change his policy. Recognizing the validity of Johnson's concern that he would lose white customers if he chose to integrate, students and faculty at the college and members of the Methodist Church raised funds to cover losses.[80] That approach did not work: Johnson and Hood Norton refused all offers of money. Conversations between well-meaning whites and Johnson also were ineffective. Dan Rhodes and a student, John Spratt, spent an hour talking with Johnson in Rhodes's car across the street from the barbershop, but to no avail.[81] "Ralph, you're wrong on this," Sam Maloney recalled telling Johnson. "You've got to take a chance."[82] Max Polley's recollection of his conversation with Johnson is poignant:

> When I talked to him, I said, "You know, now it's time. Why don't you go ahead and cut the hair of the little whites and blacks. It's coming." And he said, "Dr. Polley, when I started this shop, the white people said you are only going to cut white people's hair, and that's what I did. Now the white people say we want you to cut black people's hair also. When do I get to make a decision? I just have to do what the white people say."[83]

On May 7, five weeks after the boycott started, Johnson decided to begin serving white and black customers on an equal basis. Why did this proud man decide to change course? At the time, and for many years afterward, Johnson refused to comment. In his memoirs, published in 2000, however, he noted that the barbers who worked for him virtually forced the change. As the boycott continued, the barbers "were coming . . . under the influence of the college people and Negro associates and taking sides against me. . . . The stark fact was that if they refused to work for me, as they were being urged by some to do, I would have to close the business, for it would be impossible to replace them."[84]

A comment by James Raeford after the policy changed lends support to Johnson's analysis: "It's something that had to be done, and I'm glad he did it. It takes a lot of pressure off us, the employees, and I think we will profit by it."[85] Hood Norton also fully integrated his shop five months later, thus ending racial segregation on Main Street in Davidson.[86]

As Johnson had feared, the boycott hurt his business. He lost many working-class white customers while gaining relatively few black ones. Perhaps even more important, the number of college students seeking haircuts declined sharply during the next few years. This was due both to the ending of the required two years of military training at the college, during which students had been required to get haircuts every two weeks, and to the longer hairstyles for young men that became fashionable in the late 1960s and early 1970s. By 1971 only one other barber worked with Johnson in the shop, down from seven a few years earlier. On 15 November 1971 Johnson, aged 67, closed his shop and retired from barbering after more than fifty years.[87]

During the boycott in 1968, large numbers of Davidsonians took sides: "college" whites and local blacks typically supported it, while most "town" whites probably opposed it.[88] Some "college" whites criticized the boycott in the years around Johnson's death in 2001,[89] but continuing to choose one side or the other may impede understanding.

In retrospect, it is clear that both the boycott's supporters and its critics were right in some ways and wrong in others. Racial segregation was wrong and needed to be challenged, but so was what one anti-boycott student later called "asking [Johnson] to destroy his own business."[90] Like the white owners of the Coffee Cup who also feared losing their livelihood, Johnson was caught between the slow-moving tectonic plate of segregation on one side and the fast-moving one of integration on the other. Of all the episodes in Davidson's history thus far, the story of the boycott of Ralph Johnson's barbershop is most deserving of being turned into a tragic movie or play.

Basketball Unites, Vietnam Unifies and Divides

The biggest surprise in Davidson in the 1960s—a pleasant one indeed for most residents—was Lefty Driesell's tranformation of the college's basketball team from an also-ran in the Southern Conference to one of the top ten squads in the nation. No one in town expected great accomplishments when the college hired the twenty-seven-year-old high school coach with no college-level experience in the spring of 1960. And yet the hard-driving, charismatic Driesell foreshadowed future accomplishments when his team, short on talent but long on effort and desire, defeated third-ranked Wake Forest, 65–59, on 3 December 1960 in Lefty's first game as coach. At the end of the game, James Puckett recalled, Johnston Gym "went berserk." As happened many times after victories in the 1960s, the celebrating spread quickly:

> After the game I ran over to the Teen Canteen and announced
> that Davidson had stuck it to Wake. My friends laughed and asked
> me to tell them the real score. When the Davidson fight song . . .
> blared out over the loud speakers in the dome of Chambers Build-
> ing, they became believers, and that place went berserk. We all
> were literally dancing in the streets.[91]

Driesell spent much of that first winter recruiting highly skilled players for future teams, a strategy that paid off when a young but talented squad defeated second-ranked Duke at the Charlotte Coliseum on 18 December 1962. "In grocery stores, snack shops, on the sidewalks," the *Charlotte News* reported, "people were talking about the greatest athletic victory in Davidson's history."[92] By then the town, or at least the "college" and "town" whites and the local newspaper, were unabashed enthusiasts for Driesell and his team. "[The players] ran up and down the floor like crazy and beat those Yankees from Duke, 72–69," columnist Belle Banks exulted. "Davidson, hotter than a two-dollar pistol, was not to be denied."[93]

While unexpected, Davidson's victory was no fluke: it won twenty games for the first time ever that year, an accomplishment repeated in each of the remaining six seasons of Driesell's tenure in Davidson. By the middle of the 1963–64 season, undefeated Davidson was the third-ranked team in the nation, the highest ranking ever achieved by any sports team at the college.[94] From then until Driesell left in the spring of 1969 to coach at the University of Maryland, the team typically was ranked in the top ten and received extensive coverage in *Sports Illustrated* and other national media. Its three trips to the NCAA tournament were capped by two close

Charles "Lefty" Driesell

losses in the regional finals—now called the Elite Eight—to University of North Carolina teams led by Charlie Scott, the All-American player who thrice broke the town's heart. Despite these disappointing season-ending losses, Ava Spencer recalled that "people were all excited about the basketball team" when she and Sam, the college's new president, returned to live in Davidson in 1968.[95]

Davidson had three All-Americans during the Driesell years: Fred Hetzel from Washington, D.C., and Dick Snyder from Ohio in the early to mid 1960s, and in the late 1960s Mike Maloy from New York City, the only African-American star on a Driesell-coached squad. Belle Banks notwithstanding, Duke obviously was not the only southern school that recruited "Yankee" players. In view of the fact that Driesell was recruiting for a small, all-male, academically challenging, and overwhelmingly white college in a still largely rural and small-town region of North Carolina, and given the college's modest budget for athletic scholarships and recruiting, Driesell's accomplishments at Davidson may be unparalleled in the history of college basketball.[96]

Certainly Lefty was an exceptional recruiter: among other things, he stretched his tight budgets by sleeping in his Chevy station wagon so that he could offer potential recruits steak dinners, and he used all his folksy southern charm on the recruits and especially on the mothers who often influenced their sons' difficult final choices.[97] If Lefty had been able to combine Scott's ball-handling and shooting skills with Maloy's stellar inside game, Davidson almost certainly would have made the Final Four at least once or twice between 1968 and 1970. Even without Scott, Maloy and a fine group of supporting players kept Davidson in the national rankings. Moreover, Maloy's warm, modest personality won him many friends on campus and in the town, thus contributing to greater acceptance of racial integration among both whites and blacks.

During the Driesell years, Sam Spencer observed, "the college became nationally known as it had not been."[98] Tony Abbott, a new professor at Davidson in the 1960s, agreed: "I think the basketball [program] really helped get Davidson moved from being a regional school to a national school."[99] While President Grier Martin and many faculty members wished that the college's improving academic programs could have received as much favorable publicity as the basketball team, Lefty's successes helped the college by increasing the number of applicants for admission, thus making the college more selective, and by enhancing alumni interest and financial contributions.[100] Perhaps most important, Lefty's highly successful teams—and the excitement and unity they engendered both at the college and in the town—helped Davidson weather the controversies that developed at the same time over issues such as racial integration and the Vietnam War.

Unlike integration, which affected both blacks and whites, the Vietnam War largely affected local whites. The only Davidson resident who died in Vietnam was Jimmy Woods, the son of the town's main doctor, James Woods, and his well-known wife, Elizabeth. Jimmy's death in February 1966 shook the white community not only because of his parents' prominence, but also because he had many friends in town, both at DCPC and in local schools and the college, where he graduated in 1962. Woods's death also was poignant because Jimmy's older brother, Dan, had also died young—in his case, from encephalitis—and because Jimmy's death was from friendly fire.[101]

At the time of Jimmy's death, Davidsonians believed that he was the second resident of Lorimer Street and graduate of the college to die in Vietnam. The previous October, the Defense Department reported that Porter Halyburton, a Navy pilot shot down over North Vietnam, had been killed in action. St. Albans Episcopal Church held a memorial service for Porter on 21 October 1965.[102] Fortunately, the reports of Porter's death were incorrect: in early 1967 the Defense Department informed relatives that he was alive and being held as a prisoner of war in North Vietnam.[103]

The good news led to a heartfelt, persistent campaign—initially led by Ernest Patterson, Charles Lloyd, and other Davidson professors—to try to find a way to persuade North Vietnamese officials to release Porter. "He is a local boy and a former student of mine at Davidson College," Patterson wrote the famous British mathematician and activist Bertrand Russell. "His mother is seriously ill with cancer and his return before her death would be a humanitarian act that would add stature to the government of [North Vietnam] even among its critics."

Other Davidson professors contacted Secretary of State Dean Rusk, a Davidson graduate, and Senator J. William Fulbright, a prominent critic of the war. President Martin wrote a Catholic bishop to inquire whether the Pope could intervene.[104] None of these efforts bore fruit, nor did a letter-writing campaign in the town in the fall of 1970 that sent at least one hundred letters pleading for Porter's release to North Vietnam's government.[105]

Although his friends and neighbors in Davidson could not shorten Porter's seven-year imprisonment, they could honor him after prisoners of war were released at the end of America's direct military involvement in the war in January 1973. With Lorimer Street blocked off to traffic, a festive celebration was held on the street and in the lawns near the old family home on 17 March 1973. A large crowd, including North Carolina Governor Jim Holshouser, gathered for a picnic lunch, several short speeches, and a chance to say hello and thanks to Porter. The *Mecklenburg Gazette* captured a key moment in the celebration:

> Charles Lloyd, [Porter's] favorite teacher, perhaps spoke for all. "I never knew how much I loved you, until I thought you were dead, Porter." "You would have loved your funeral," he added, "but thank God you missed it."[106]

Despite all the heartbreak and divisiveness that the Vietnam War engendered, at times it could pull together a significant portion of a community.

At other times the war deeply divided town residents. This was especially true in the Methodist church where Parks Todd, the pastor from 1967 to 1969, angered a large percentage of the congregation by repeatedly condemning U.S. policy in Vietnam.[107] Todd alienated so many people that he told one member, Randy Kincaid, that the church would have to close if he did not agree to serve as treasurer. Todd's fearless preaching contributed to a substantial decline in contributions, Kincaid recalled, and the bitter divisions led to Kincaid's leaving the church when his term as treasurer ended.[108]

At DCPC, members of a men's Sunday school class that James Woods attended had to be careful not to criticize the war because the doctor,

Davidson students and professors protest the Vietnam War

who strongly supported U.S. policy in Vietnam, viewed any criticism as an insult to the sacrifice that Jimmy had made there. "I talked about the war in very careful terms," Will Terry, DCPC's pastor at the time, recalled, "because we had people like the Woods who had been so tragically scarred by it."[109] Angered by what he saw as efforts to undermine the war effort, in November 1967 Woods complained to Grier Martin about the college's allowing "extremely biased" liberal activists to speak and to pass out anti-draft materials on campus.[110]

As during the picketing of Ralph Johnson's barbershop, many town residents disliked the antiwar vigils and other protests, typically held either on campus or in front of the post office on Main Street and involving Davidson students, professors, and other "college" people. These protests occurred repeatedly between 1967 and 1972, culminating in May 1970 after President Richard Nixon's controversial decision to invade Cambodia and the subsequent killing of four students during antiwar protests at Kent State University.

After Taylor Blackwell, the owner of the local newspaper, published an editorial that criticized "our young people" because they "find a ruckus all too attractive," a non-college white man, long on passion but short on skills in capitalization, praised Blackwell "for your Firm stand taken in Connection with the Cambodia affair." "Wars are fought to win," he insisted. The writer especially criticized "Young Egotistic Adults [who] urge the Long

Haired Hippies to act like FOOLS or Revolutionists."[111] He apparently was referring to young, committed antiwar professors—notably Fred Gaige, Bill Jackson, and Dave Kaylor—who often led antiwar efforts among the faculty and stood shoulder-to-shoulder with students in demonstrations.[112]

Only once, when student anger about the war and the Nixon administration peaked in the aftermath of the Kent State shootings on 4 May 1970, does the word "revolutionists" come within a country mile of applying to the generally peaceful, well-conceived antiwar protests that occurred at the college and along Main Street. On the afternoon of May 5, between 40 and 70 students blocked access to the ROTC offices and then, with their ranks swelled to roughly 100, taunted the cadets and surged onto the field during the drill, thus inducing the cadet commander to end the exercises early.[113]

President Spencer wrote in July that "the ROTC incident was the nearest thing we came during this troubled spring to any kind of disruption. We had many discussions and some demonstrations, but they remained rational and non-violent."[114] What Spencer called a "potentially explosive situation" developed on the evening of May 7 between demonstrators, primarily from the college, and pro-war local whites. But this confrontation, which local police skillfully contained, clearly did not result from the actions of "revolutionists."[115]

Before the invasion of Cambodia, Davidson senior William Brown recalled, only a small number of students took part in antiwar protests. After the killings at Kent State, more than six hundred students signed a petition against the war, and many also participated in demonstrations.[116] "The war used to be out there," one student told Brown at the time. "Now it's right here," he said, pointing at his heart.[117] Even the normally discreet Spencer publicly criticized the Cambodian invasion, thus alienating some pro-war alumni.[118]

Brown recalled that "roughly half" of the graduating seniors, himself included, wore black armbands at graduation that June to protest the ongoing war. Even after Kent State, however, many Davidson students remained relatively conservative, as shown not only by the half who chose not to wear the armbands, but also by the similar percentage of graduates who, having completed four years of ROTC training, accepted commissions as second lieutenants in the U.S. Army Reserve.[119] As in the town, students and faculty were divided on whether to support U.S. policy in Vietnam and, if opposed, on how to express their opposition. As in the nation as a whole, in Davidson the Vietnam War was a much greater source of division than of unity.

Davidson Flourishes in the Late 1960s and 1970s

Despite the divisions over the Vietnam War, the town as a whole flourished from the late 1960s through the 1970s. Davidson at its best has always combined small-town friendliness and concern for others with numerous concrete actions reflecting a strong sense of community spirit. It also has been forward-looking while seeking to retain the best of the past and present. In the late 1960s and the 1970s, the town and the college, despite continuing problems, exhibited all of these qualities.

A landmark in Davidson history was the election of the town's first black commissioner, Joe McClain, in November 1969. Together with blacks who served on the Community Relations Committee and other town committees, McClain helped to bring the concerns of black residents to the rest of the board and to the mayor. After being re-elected three times, McClain decided to retire from the board when his fourth term ended in 1977.[120] Because whites cast roughly 80 percent of the votes in town elections, this symbol of changing race relations—and the election of other blacks in subsequent decades—occurred only because large numbers of voters of both races believed that it was important to have at least one African American on the town board.

In regard to the acceptability of consuming alcohol, the college was more forward-looking than the town. In the fall of 1968, the college, with trustee approval, ended the ban on consuming alcoholic beverages on campus—a major change for an institution where even the discovery of alcoholic beverages in the trunk of a student's car could lead to expulsion.

That same fall, Coleen Norket, the owner of the Davidson Grocery on Depot Street, applied to the state of North Carolina for a license to sell beer and wine in closed containers. In contrast to college officials, who readily acceded to student requests to permit consumption of alcoholic beverages on campus, town commissioners unanimously passed a resolution in November 1968 opposing her request for a license.[121] Yet the result was the same as at the college: in February 1969 the State Board of Alcoholic Control approved Norket's request, permitting her to sell beverages with up to 20 percent alcohol content.[122] A story in the local newspaper explained the decision's significance: "Beer and wine . . . can now be bought and consumed legally within the town limits," thus ending a prohibition that dated to the college's founding in 1837.[123]

The new era in regard to alcoholic beverages lessened hypocrisy in the town, where shades often had been lowered before alcohol was consumed socially.[124] It also decreased the extent of rule-breaking at the college, where the consumption of alcoholic beverages in dorm rooms with doors closed—or elsewhere away from campus police—had long been common. Perhaps more negatively for young children observing their parents' behavior, Lacy Dick recalled, the new era meant that much more alcohol "was suddenly being served around town."[125]

An undeniably positive change in Davidson was the college's decision in the early 1970s to gradually become coeducational. President Spencer deserves much credit for both the timing of this decision and the gradualness and smoothness with which it was implemented. But he also benefited greatly from the support of most students and faculty members in overcoming objections from some faculty and staff—notably librarian Chalmers Davidson—and from many alumni. The change was indeed gradual: the percentage of women in the student body grew slowly, from 17 percent in 1973–74 to 34 percent in 1979–80. Roughly equal numbers of men and women in the student body were not seen until the mid-1990s.[126]

Coeducation resulted in greater numbers—and a higher overall quality—of applicants for admission; it improved social life on campus, partly by lessening the importance of fraternities to male students; and it allowed for a level of friendship and mutual respect between young men and women that had not been possible when the student body was all male and large numbers of female students from other colleges had come to campus for pressure-packed, often socially awkward party weekends.[127] Ralph Quackenbush, who took the town's pulse from behind the counter at The Hub on Main Street, said in December 1973 that coeducation was "the best thing that ever happened to Davidson, both the college and the town."[128] Even many opponents, including Chalmers Davidson, soon acknowledged that they had been wrong on this issue.[129]

The other big change at the college in the 1970s was the trustees' decision in May 1977 to eliminate the requirement that only faculty who belonged to a Christian church could receive tenure.[130] This change, long sought by many faculty members and students, was precipitated by a series of events earlier that spring. After Ronald Linden, a Jewish candidate for a position in political science whom the college wanted to hire, denounced the policy as "morally repugnant, socially anachronistic and scholastically unwise," students and faculty pressed the trustees to change the policy.[131] Although Davidson remained a church-related college after 1977, this change—added to such changes in the 1960s as ending required attendance at weekday chapel and Sunday church services—meant that, for most students and faculty, Davidson had become more similar to a secular college than to the intentionally religious institution that it had been until the mid-1960s.[132]

Although the town's white and black Protestant churches remained strong in the 1960s and 1970s, there was much less coverage of church programs in the local newspaper than there had been in the late 1940s and 1950s. Moreover, there was less social pressure to attend church services, at least among whites, or, to take two other examples, to abstain from drinking alcohol or to view premarital sex as morally wrong. An important change at DCPC was the ordination of women as elders, starting with Marjorie McCutchan in January 1972. Twenty-two more women were ordained as elders between 1974 and 1984, thus greatly increasing women's role in governing the church.[133]

In line with national trends that celebrated self-expression, some white students and married couples challenged traditional religious values. By "streaking" naked across campus and, more frequently, by holding loud, "wild" parties in houses along north Main Street and elsewhere in town, students openly celebrated their new freedoms, including those engendered by the legal right to consume alcohol at age eighteen and the presumed right to use marijuana and other illegal drugs.[134] Combining obvious exaggeration with stereotyping, a local journalist in September 1978 described Davidson students as "barbarians" who were "hirsute, weirdly patched, modishly dirty" and who enjoyed listening to "the cacophonous howls in the night they misname music."[135] Challenging religious teachings that criticized adultery, several couples—typically ones with young children—engaged in "open marriage" in the 1970s.[136] Given these social developments and the fact that longer hair styles were more common for male students in the 1970s than earlier, one could argue that the cultural changes typically associated with the 1960s became evident in Davidson mainly in the 1970s.

Reflecting the importance of religion in the black community, impressive building projects occurred at all three black churches in the 1960s and 1970s. Davidson Presbyterian Church constructed an educational building in 1962; Reeves Temple A.M.E. Zion Church moved into a new building in 1966, as did Gethsemane Baptist Church in the late 1970s. Laura Grosch, a prominent local artist, remembers being "very inspired by Grandma Rosa Potts as she asked people in the 1970s to save their Cashion's [grocery store] tapes as her congregation struggled to raise the funds to build Gethsemane Baptist Church."[137] When the collected receipts were taken to the store in Cornelius, a small but still significant

Babysitting class at West Davidson Teen Canteen

percentage of the total was donated to the designated charity. An important social outlet for black young people, especially in the 1960s, was the West Davidson Teen Canteen, which often met at Davidson Presbyterian Church's educational building and benefited from the leadership of John Brandon, Evelyn Carr, James Howard, Esther Johnson, and other well-known blacks and whites.[138]

Among whites, what was most noticeable in the town's flourishing in the 1970s was the growing public role of "college" women, many of whom were busy parents who often had flexibility in their schedules because they did not have paying jobs. The most extraordinary of these women was Nancy MacCormac, a Pennsylvanian who had come to Davidson when her husband, Earl, accepted a teaching position at the college in 1961. Upon arriving in Davidson, Nancy lacked knowledge about the lingo of racial segregation. When she went to wash her clothes at a laundromat in Cornelius that said "white only" on the door, she thought to herself, "Well, I can't do my dark wash."[139] That experience soon became one of the most frequently told stories in town, illustrating both the ironies of white racism and the cultural gap between northerners and southerners.

By the time MacCormac was elected to the town board in 1973, becoming the first woman on the board in the town's history, she had been

Nancy MacCormac
at town gathering

a mover and shaker on the Parks and Recreation Committee, she had
served as president of the PTA at the Davidson Elementary School and as
a member of the executive board of the Charlotte League of Women Voters, and she had been a Sunday School teacher and served on the action
committee of DCPC.[140] Indeed, taking action herself—and getting others
to act on behalf of good causes—were her trademarks. She was a "very
bright and smart and savvy woman," Susan Abbott recalled. And when
she phoned with "a wonderful idea, you couldn't say no, because it was *so*
important."[141]

Because MacCormac was the most energetic and determined member of the board, it is not surprising that the other members chose her as
mayor after the incumbent, Tom Sadler, died suddenly of a heart attack
in October 1978.[142] MacCormac brought her usual high level of commitment and shrewdness to this office, winning reelection three times before
resigning in the summer of 1984 to pursue graduate study at Harvard. In
her eleven years in town government, she epitomized the steadily growing

role of the public sector—often including grants to the town from state and federal agencies—in the town's life.

The town's flourishing in the 1970s resulted at least as much from private initiatives as from government programs. Davidson residents benefited greatly, for example, from the privately funded recreational opportunities at the new North Mecklenburg YMCA that opened in June 1975 on a 17.5 acre property on Lake Cornelius. Although the facility was in Cornelius, the planning and fund-raising occurred primarily in Davidson, starting in 1969. Bob Stone, an inspiring, persistent Davidsonian who sold insurance on Main Street, deserved much of the credit. Other Davidson businessmen and professors—notably Lawrence Kimbrough, Burl Naramore, Jack Tate, and Richie King—helped Stone turn his dream into a reality, as did Mayor Wesley G. Rood and grocer Robert Cashion of Cornelius.[143]

An ongoing private effort that also enriched life in Davidson and surrounding communities, one led by Gene McEver since the late 1950s, involved the countless Pony League youth baseball games played at McEver Field on South Street. The fact that the teams were integrated, with black and white parents sitting side by side in the stands cheering for Davidson or for other area teams, helped to build friendships and understanding between whites and blacks.[144]

An impressive example of the town's flourishing during these years was an annual event that also resulted from private initiatives. This event began as a six-day "clean-up campaign" in April 1970 led by Anne White of DCPC and Annie Mildred Lowery of DPC. In a news story the leaders stressed "cleaning up personal property around town, cutting weeds, picking up cans and bottles and disposing of old refrigerators and washing machines that pose potential hazards to the community."[145] Eleven local organizations, mostly Scout troops, participated in the clean-up campaign, which ended on April 25 with a short parade followed by presentations of awards to participants in the clean-up.[146]

Although clean-up efforts continued in subsequent years, the emphasis gradually shifted to "Town Day," with leadership coming from local whites and blacks and from Davidson College students. The mayor announced the date each year, beginning in 1971.[147] Although the ostensible purpose of the clean-up week culminating in Town Day was to make the town cleaner and more attractive and then to celebrate what had been done, the deeper goal, Nancy MacCormac recalled, was to "build a sense of community" between the town's "different neighborhoods."[148] At least in terms of involvement, the deeper goal was achieved in the 1970s: large

Early Town Day parade on Main Street

numbers of "town" and "college" whites, blacks, and college students participated in the first Town Day on 15 May 1971 and, with continuing enthusiasm among many event planners and participants, in future Town Days as well.

Town Day succeeded in 1971 and in subsequent years mainly because there were many ways to have fun. There were rides, games, and contests for children; street dances and music shows for teenagers and adults; and a magic show for all ages by Shaw Smith, Sr., and his family. In the early years, the town's main black activist organization, the Piedmont Area Development Association, sold fried fish or hot dogs with Cokes for supper.[149] Scotty Nicholls enjoyed seeing Ellen Winkler dressed up as Lady Liberty on a float in the parade.[150] Ever civic-minded, Ralph Quackenbush agreed to occupy a dunking booth during the first Town Day. "I got dunked lots of times and the weather was 50-something," Quackenbush recalled. "I have never been so cold in my life."[151]

After some disputes over leadership in the early years, the town board decided in 1974 that the town's Parks and Recreation Committee would "act as coordinators."[152] Adaptability—as in the decision in 1978 to emphasize environmental concerns—helped to keep Town Day alive and moving forward. No motorized vehicles were permitted in the 1978 parade; instead, prizes were given for "best bicycle float, most original cycle theme, historic cycling, and bicycle safety."[153] Even this more specialized environmental theme attracted "hundreds of people," the local newspaper reported; this Town Day "packed bike races, a parade, raffles, dunking, music, good food, and bargains galore into a long beautiful spring Saturday."[154] Whatever its shortcomings may have been, including a feeling among some blacks that whites "took [control of] it from us," Town Day was a positive experience for many Davidsonians in the 1970s.[155]

Perhaps the most impressive manifestation of the town's flourishing at the time—one that required the active involvement of governmental entities as well as private individuals and groups—was the Davidson Community Center, which took shape in 1974 when the county board of education agreed to lease the vacant Ada Jenkins School building to the town for a dollar a year. In the fall of 1973, blacks on the town's west side vehemently opposed a proposal by a Charlotte group to use the facility as a drug-treatment center for people mainly from Charlotte.[156] As an alternative, a local newspaper reported, "members of the community which surrounds the school may be very interested in coverting the school into a community center."[157]

This idea had originated the previous spring in a loosely organized interracial coalition that at times sought to encourage more fundamental social and political change in Davidson than the members of the town board and most other prominent Davidsonians were willing to accept.[158] This coalition spawned several short-lived organizations in 1973 and 1974. A news story in December 1973 credited one of these, the Davidson Community Development Association, with coming up with the idea for the community center.[159] James Bright, Jr., the leader of what was probably the same group with a new name, emerged that fall as the most prominent black advocate for the community center.[160] Because of his involvement, Bright became a member of the newly revamped Parks and Recreation Committee, which gained official recognition as an advisory committee and managed the center for the town government.

Although black leaders including Bright and Annie Mildred Lowery helped to set up the community center, the majority-white town board ensured that the outgoing chair of the Parks and Recreation Committee, Nancy MacCormac, and the new chair, Davidson economics professor Randy Kincaid, had greater influence. Newly elected to the town board, MacCormac helped to ensure that most of the federal-revenue sharing funds that Davidson received would go toward funding the new center, and Kincaid chaired the committee that hired the center's first full-time director, Sauni Wood. Thus, even though the Davidson Community Center had black staff and programs that attracted blacks, as well as white leaders like MacCormac, Kincaid, and Wood who cared deeply about racial equality, the predominant power in this institution, as in Town Day and most other community activities beyond the black churches and all-black civic groups, remained in the hands of college-educated whites.[161]

That whites had the final say on most issues relating to the community center does not detract from its many impressive programs and services between its opening in April 1974 and the gradual diminution of its activities in the early 1980s. Perhaps most appreciated was Senior Citizen Meals, a government-supported program that attracted roughly seventy seniors from Davidson and nearby areas each weekday for singing, games, conversation, and a no-cost lunch. In addition, roughly thirty no-cost lunches were taken to the homes of elderly who were unable to come to the center.[162] Attracting both whites and blacks, including many widows and widowers, the lunches offered opportunities for socializing for people who often acknowledged being "lonely" when they were at home. One staff member made a comment that epitomized the lunches' joyful spirit: "Have you ever seen people so happy?"[163] Apart from the public schools, the senior meals program also was one of the most racially integrated programs in Mecklenburg County—and perhaps in the entire state.

Many other programs attracted hundreds of additional local residents during a typical week. Informal and planned recreational activities after school and in the evenings attracted a sizable number of mainly black youth to the center, and fine-arts courses offered by volunteers working for the New Schoolhouse of the Arts attracted mostly white young people. A Mecklenburg County extension agent, sometimes working with teachers from Central Piedmont Community College, offered a wide variety of courses and services for adults. And, to take another example, Davidson College students and townspeople volunteered to ensure that less advantaged local residents were able to receive advice on legal and financial matters through the Legal Aid Society of Charlotte.[164] "The Community Center builds bridges in the community and this end of the county," Sauni Wood commented in March 1975. "Besides the services that we offer, I've seen it build stronger human relationships."[165]

While the town paid for the administrator and utilities, many of the programs were made possible through county and state agencies and through contributions from local churches. A few programs, including courses offered by the New Schoolhouse of the Arts (NSA), were staffed by women who basically volunteered their time in the belief that young people should have a chance to experience the fine arts. NSA offered courses in music appreciation, piano, painting, dance, and theater. Its tireless director —who also taught theater at the center—was Connie Welsh, one of the most admired Davidsonians at the time.[166] Before heading NSA, Welsh had formed the Children's Drama Workshop and the Davidson Community Players. She also enhanced theater in the public schools with Theater in Education and the Taradiddle Players. During her years in Davidson, she attracted hundreds of young people and adults to act in the plays she directed and to volunteer to help stage them. One of Welsh's few regrets— one shared by another NSA teacher, Laura Grosch—was the unwillingness of black youth to sign up for her courses and workshops.[167]

Another example of the town's flourishing in the 1970s was the use of the recently refurbished railroad depot on Depot Street as both a meeting place for the Senior Citizens Club and as the location for a program that offered services to the elderly, Davidson Senior Services. After gaining a dollar-a-year lease from the Southern Railway, the college YMCA spent $12,500 in 1973 to refurbish the depot for use as a community center. But partly because of the success of the community center in the much larger Ada Jenkins facility, the depot was little used until local senior citizens, aided by grants from foundations, made it the meeting place of the Senior Citizens Club and a services center for older people who sought help in remaining in their homes as long as possible before moving to a nursing home or retirement facility.[168] The Senior Citizens Club brought together about thirty to fifty whites and and a small number of blacks for both recreational and educational activities.[169]

Perhaps above all else, numerous community-wide celebrations in the 1970s epitomized the town's flourishing. These included the Town Day activities discussed earlier, as well as a parade and watermelon-cutting on July 4 and the annual Christmas parade. The parade to celebrate the nation's bicentennial—4 July 1976—was larger and more elaborate than usual, and was followed by a talent show, a watermelon cutting, and a square dance in the community center.[170]

In some ways the most impressive celebration, one that reflected the concern for others and service to neighbors that characterizes Davidson at its best, was the Dr. James B. Woods Jr. Day that took place on the grounds of the Davidson Elementary School (formerly the Davidson School) on Saturday, 19 May 1973. Annamarie Burts, who chaired the planning committee, said that she had "never worked on anything for which there was such total community support."[171]

Large numbers of Davidsonians and people from surrounding areas—

Nurse Selinda Mayhew and Dr. James Woods

white and black, young and old, poor and affluent—came to the school grounds to thank the 75-year-old Woods for his roughly thirty years of selfless, tireless service to the community, often as the town's only physician. The doctor, who planned to continue his practice "as long as mind and body hold together," was known for his quick, accurate diagnoses; his availability seven days and nights each week, except for one afternoon of golf; his inexpensive $5.00 charge per visit; and his service to everyone, regardless of ability to pay.[172] One speaker offered simple but fitting praise: Dr. Woods was "an example of the Christian life."[173]

On the weekend of 5–6 May 1979, the *Charlotte Observer* reported, Davidsonians celebrated the town's centennial, beginning "with parades, speeches, yard sales and disco dancing" on Saturday and ending with a community worship service on the village green on Sunday afternoon. Vendors raising money for local churches and civic groups set up stalls on the village green.[174] Providing advance publicity, a local newspaper noted that, among many planned events, the Lions Club would hold its annual auction and the Davidson Bicycle Co-Op would offer "numerous activities." Reflecting the growing importance of arts and crafts in the town's life, the Copeland House Galleries and the Glass Emporium had "special craft and art displays" and the Davidson College Wind Ensemble gave "its annual spring concert on the plaza in front of Chambers building on the campus."[175] Once again, many of those who greeted friends, neighbors, and new acquaintances while participating in that weekend's activities must have thought to themselves that Davidson was indeed a good place to live.

More Changes—And Some Criticisms— in the Late 1970s and Early 1980s

Davidson experienced many physical changes in the late 1970s and early 1980s, especially in the downtown area and, spurred by the completion of I-77 and the desire of town leaders to provide better housing for low-income residents and better shopping for everyone, on the west side. The changes that had occurred in Davidson from World War II through the mid-1970s generally had received little if any criticism in public meetings or in comments or letters that appeared in local newspapers. In the late 1970s and early 1980s, in contrast, publicly expressed criticisms—offered largely by lower-income whites and blacks living on the west side and by a few affluent whites living on the east side—became fairly normal. Although these criticisms did not prevent the changes from occurring, they reminded town leaders that residents had the right to speak up and to use their votes to try to change town policies.

To most town leaders, including Mayor Tom Sadler, Davidson College President Sam Spencer, and the black and white members of the Community Relations Committee, the lack of quality, affordable housing for low-income residents was the town's most serious problem in the mid-1970s. After a series of *Davidsonian* articles on the town's substandard housing embarrassed college and town officials, Sadler acknowledged in October 1974 that a large number of houses, especially on Griffith Street, "are definitely substandard," but the town "can't destroy them until we have a place to put the people."[176]

The town was "faced with a stark reality," Sadler wrote the regional director of a federal housing agency in early 1975. "The moderate income people who can . . . maintain a single family residence have built living quarters [at Lakeside Park], but the low income group who must be subsidized remain without acceptable housing."[177] While political moderates like Sadler viewed high-quality, affordable apartments for the poor as "a modest attempt to make our town a better place to live," liberals like Charlie Ratliff and Daisy Raeford, the successive chairs of the Community Relations Committee, believed that providing quality housing was a Christian obligation to make possible a "life of dignity" for everyone in the community.[178]

President Spencer played a pivotal role in the long process that led to the town board's approval of building rent-subsidized Lakeside Apartments near Beaty and Armour Steets in May 1978, and to their occupancy the following winter and spring. A committed Christian, Spencer shared the liberals' conviction that the affluent had a moral obligation to help the less fortunate. But he also was under pressure from alumni to remove the dilapidated houses on Griffith Street that, in their view, lessened the attractiveness of the mile-long "gateway" to the college between I-77 and Main Street.

Spencer thus worked hard to ensure that an established, college-connected firm agreed to undertake the project when the original developer was unable to secure financing, and that the college's Board of Trustees approve a $40,000 guarantee to ensure that the firm, the John Crosland Company, did not lose money during the apartments' first six years of operation.[179] When Nancy MacCormac became mayor after Sadler's death, Spencer wrote her that Sadler had "assured" him during the planning process "that the town would either raze any sub-standard housing vacated by tenants moving into the new project, or require the owners to bring such dwellings up to standard. I hope very much that this is still the town's position."[180]

Town leaders expected little if any opposition to the project. They apparently assumed that people would support it because Lakeside Apartments met a town need and was supported by both black and white leaders, because the rent subsidies were being funded by the federal Department of Housing and Urban Development (HUD) and not by local taxes, because the 50-apartment complex was well designed and located on 5.1 acres near the General Time clock factory on Armour Street, and because the developer promised that illegal activities would not be tolerated at the apartments. Proponents were surprised by the defeat in the November 1977 election of Grover Meetze, the commissioner who had worked the hardest to bring the project to fruition. Even then, however, town leaders sought public input only after the local building inspector noted in March 1978 that the new land-use ordinance required both a public hearing by the planning committee on all proposed multi-family projects and a special-use permit approved by the town board.[181]

In April 1978 the generally working-class whites who lived near the proposed apartments made known their deeply felt and nearly unanimous opposition to the project. On April 3, about twenty residents of Watson, Delburg, and Armour streets attended a joint meeting of the planning commission and the town board and presented a petition opposing the project.

The petition was signed by sixty-four residents, representing roughly 95 percent of the people living in that area. Sixty-three residents signed another petition that was presented at another joint meeting of the planning commission and the town board on April 24.[182] This petition cited the town's "neglect of this neighborhood's needs" and "the enormous amount of existing traffic in the area," mainly involving employees of General Time. At this meeting, local residents raised concerns about the additional traffic that the apartment complex would generate and complained that they had received no letters from the town informing them about the proposed project. According to a news story, they also feared that "property values would drop and vandalism would increase."[183]

Despite the opposition from nearby residents and from a General Time executive, the town approved Lakeside Apartments with only one dissenting vote on the planning committee (cast by the iconoclastic Ralph Johnson) and then unanimously on the Town Board, thus confirming the feeling of powerlessness in town affairs that many white residents in the Delburg area experienced. "We're on the wrong side of the tracks for the college," Selinda Mayhew, a much loved and admired nurse who worked with Dr. Woods, commented in 1980. "I think that's the way people feel."[184]

From the viewpoint of the town as a whole, Lakeside Apartments was a success, at least in its early years. With well-known community leader Julia Maulden as resident director, the racially integrated apartments were

Lakeside Apartments under construction

fully booked by May 1979. The complex, including tennis and basketball courts, was attractive, a news story reported, as was the view "across the Davidson side of Lake Norman and I-77 onto the expanse of the main body of the lake."[185] Residents appreciated the rent subsidies that made it possible for them to live there on low incomes, and Maulden liked the "chance to be of service among people whose lives have never been easy."[186] Mayor MacCormac noted that nearly two-thirds of Lakeside's residents in May 1979—78 of 122—were from Davidson.[187] As town leaders had hoped, the apartments seemed to meet a local need.

While many working-class whites who lived north of Griffith Street were unhappy about changes in their neighborhood, a good number of the largely working-class blacks who lived on or south of Griffith Street were complaining about developments in that part of town. Indeed, a remarkable feature of life in Davidson in the late 1970s and early 1980s was the high level of public criticism by blacks of the town's white-led institutions, especially the college and the town government. Open expressions of black anger and resentment that made national headlines in the 1960s and early 1970s arrived in Davidson in the mid-to-late 1970s.[188]

As chair and then as a member of the Community Relations Committee, Charlie Ratliff often attended meetings in black neighborhoods on the west side. Local blacks "accepted me as somebody they could talk in front of," Ratliff recalled. "The things they said about Davidson College were not printable."[189] Although news stories at the time contained no profanity, they did include many negative comments by blacks about white institutions and individuals who, they believed, were mistreating local black people.

Black anger surfaced unmistakably at a meeting organized by Annie Mildred Lowery at the community center in February 1976 to discuss the proposed town park next to the Algae Pond. White leaders who served on the Parks and Recreation Committee, including Nancy MacCormac and Randy Kincaid, believed that local blacks would welcome this park. Challenging this perception, several speakers commented that the park was being planned because local whites wanted it, and expressed the fear that blacks would be forced to move from their homes when the park was built. "The reason that the park is being built is because the college wants to make its entrances look better," one resident commented. "Let them build their park by the interstate. That lot is empty." Another speaker noted that "everyone knows that this town is run by Davidson College. Nothing else matters but what the college says."[190]

Many blacks were resentful and angry about other developments along

Griffith Street. When Tom Sadler sold his property to developers who built the town's first shopping center, Sadler Square, in the late 1970s, local blacks lost the baseball field that had meant so much not only to them, but also to black teams from throughout the region who had played on the field in front of enthusiastic crowds. Although local residents petitioned the town board in December 1978 to "Save Our Ballfield," plans for the shopping center moved forward, and it opened in January 1980 with a supermarket and a drug store as the two main tenants.[191]

Many local blacks resented the efforts by a group of affluent alumni in the 1980s to purchase and tear down the modest homes on Griffith Street that black families lived in, especially between Watson and Sloan streets, even when the alumni did not try to force anyone to sell and helped the displaced families find affordable houses that complied with current building codes. As Esther Johnson commented in 1984, many local blacks believed that the college people "want to uproot us, to move us out." Nancy MacCormac noted that the acquisitions were "a very hot, emotional issue within the [black] community."[192]

With backing from the Community Relations Committee, the town in 1979 received a $500,000 grant from the federal Department of Housing and Urban Development to be used to rehabilitate substandard housing, mainly in a largely black neighborhood just west of the railroad tracks. Because the grant paid for the repairs, and because the town's building inspector, William Potts, supervised the contractors, town officials expected that there would be only minor complaints about repairs made with the federal funds. In an interview in August 1981, Potts noted that, with "about 45 to 50" projects completed, "we have received [only] three or four complaints."[193]

A different picture emerged from a meeting of about forty blacks that the Community Relations Committee held at Gethsemane Baptist Church a few days earlier. Local residents complained about shoddy workmanship and accused Potts of approving "anything those [home repair] workers do." They also insisted that the project administrator, Marshall Case, "won't listen to what we have to say." Evelyn Carr, a member of the Community Relations Committee, told the gathering that "we've got two Davidsons—a white Davidson and a black Davidson. We pay our taxes and . . . all we get is garbage pick-up and police protection."[194] Even when public employees like Potts and Case and the town's elected leaders thought that they were helping lower-income blacks, they found themselves subjected to sharp public criticisms from a black community that, while by no means united, clearly was willing to speak up.

The generally more affluent whites who lived on the east side were less inclined to voice their criticisms publicly. Yet Burl Naramore did so when, in an action unprecedented in recent memory, he resigned from the town board in July 1979 because of "philosophical differences" with Mayor MacCormac and other elected officials.[195] In an "Open Letter to the Citizens of Davidson" explaining his decision to resign, Naramore criticized town officials' "hastily contrived" application for the HUD grant to repair run-down housing. "I believe the Davidson town government should attempt to provide solutions for local problems from within its own resources," Naramore wrote. "Our citizens must decide whether the often-expressed wish to maintain a small town atmosphere is compatible with the enlargement of government functions."[196]

That Naramore's thinking was outside the mainstream is suggested by the fact that the other fiscal conservative on the town board, Bill Mayhew, did not resign with him to protest what Naramore called "big government" approaches. While both Naramore and Mayhew reflected local sentiment against raising Davidson's tax rate, Mayhew—like MacCormac and the other town officials—did not hesitate to solicit federal and state funds for improvements in the town. Narramore's go-slow mindset also was outside the mainstream because the town board, with the voters' implicit approval, moved forward with ambitious plans to transform the downtown area behind Main Street and to approve unprecedented residential projects on the lake on both sides of I-77.

With leadership from Jack Tate, the head of the local Piedmont Bank, a committee came up with a plan in the early 1970s to transform the downtown. The plan included connecting Railroad Avenue from Depot Street to south Main Street and encouraging new businesses to locate between Railroad Street and the backs of the properties facing onto Main Street. This "downtown plan" lay dormant until 1980, when the need to build a new, larger post office prompted efforts by Tate, MacCormac, and others to update and implement it. By enhancing the vitality of the downtown and by refusing to permit retail outlets near I-77, town leaders hoped to maintain what several merchants and other speakers at meetings in March 1980 called Davidson's "village character" or "village atmosphere."[197]

To town officials, the new post office was the key to the plan, because without it there would not be enough people using the area east of Railroad Street to entice new businesses to locate there.[198] In May 1982 several property owners, including among others Piedmont Bank, the college, and Town Commissioner Russell Knox, agreed to combine their small parcels east of Railroad Street into a 1.1 acre lot to sell to the U.S. Postal Service.[199] Piedmont Bank employee Don Howie, representing these land-holders and the non-profit Davidson Community Properties, handled the lengthy, complicated negotiations with the Postal Service.[200] The town and private entities also cooperated to assemble the property needed to create a wide walkway and a small parking lot between Main Street and the post office.

After the Town Board promised to upgrade and extend Railroad Street to South Main, the Postal Service bought the lot in late 1982 and began to build the new facility in 1983. Meanwhile the town used local and state funds to upgrade and extend Railroad Street, renamed Jackson Street in honor of former mayor Frank Jackson. In September 1984 the town board voted to close Brady Alley to traffic and convert it to a public sidewalk linking Main Street and Jackson Street.[201]

Although much of the plan for the space between Main Street businesses and Jackson Street would come to fruition only in later years, an impressive start occurred in the early 1980s. Clearly, town leaders in that era helped to ensure that the downtown would become more vibrant, attractive, and accessible than it had been earlier.

With town officials focusing on the downtown plan, Tom Clark, a former professor at the college who had started a local company that made and sold large numbers of small collectible statues called gnomes, told the town board in December 1983 that he wished to build a bed-and-breakfast inn with roughly twenty rooms on property that he owned along and behind Main Street south of Depot Street. Clark requested that the town's zoning ordinance be changed to permit hotels and motels at this location.[202] "The inn will be a place of character with a superior restaurant which will draw people from all areas around Davidson," Clark told a reporter in January 1984. Interviewed for the same story, Nancy MacCormac said that the town board "will decide whether [Clark's proposal] is compatible with the town's plan."[203]

In discussions with the local officials that winter, Clark and his deputy, Joe Poteat, were unable to reach a mutually acceptable agreement with the town that would permit them to move forward with their project. According to Randy Kincaid, a town commissioner at the time, a key issue was parking: the spaces needed for patrons and employees of the proposed inn versus the spaces needed by the town for customers at downtown businesses and the post office.[204] After what MacCormac later called an "unfortunate impasse" developed, the town board decided in March 1984 to

Tom Clark with
his gnomes

offer Clark $39,500 for a parcel of land between Main Street and the new post office needed to implement the downtown plan and, if Clark refused the offer, to begin procedures to condemn the property for public use.[205]

Another town commissioner, Sandy Carnegie, recalled that "we really labored hard about condemning somebody's property, but when we looked at what was best for the town . . . that's what we did. [It led to a] lot of hard feelings."[206] Although the town condemned the small parcel of land and Clark's inn was not built, the Davidson Village Inn was constructed later on Depot Street near the post office.

Another debate concerning what was best for the town occurred in the fall of 1980 over a proposed housing development on the western side of Lake Davidson just north of Griffith Street. SYNCO Properties, a Charlotte developer with close ties to the college, sought town approval for the project, the first of several that it hoped to build in west Davidson.

Among others, Leland Park, the well-known director of the college library, strongly opposed it.

Park pointed out that SYNCO hoped to eventually build 900 apartments, duplexes, patio homes, and condominiums, and that having so many new people living in Davidson would change the town's "ambiance." "People speak on the street," Park noted, and "[d]emocracy and representative government really exist here."[207] Park wrote that he supported development based on "one house, one lot," but not the "condominium/garden apartment . . . approach," whose "high density . . . can be devastating to a small town."[208]

The editor of the local newspaper, Tom Williams, supported the project with equal conviction, praising the financial stake in SYNCO of the college and several of its graduates who "love the community" and arguing that the developer's "plans show nothing but the greatest concern to protect the character and quality of the town." Moreover, the development was "a very good . . . use of the land" and would "create new tax revenues, new customers for our craftsmen and shopkeepers, [and] new jobs for our citizens."[209]

Town leaders did not join the public debate. But they made it clear by their actions—and by their stated desire that the main retail sector remain downtown—that they supported the well-designed, upscale housing projects that SYNCO proposed to develop on both sides of I-77. On 10 November 1980 the town board approved the construction of twenty single-family homes on the property fronting on Lake Davidson, with multi-family units to follow as soon as the capacity could be increased on the Griffith Street sewer line.

Definitive proof that the town board supported upscale multifamily housing on the west side arrived with a 4–1 vote in January 1983 approving the construction of 150 condominiums on the lake west of I-77 by the Lake Norman Company, an affiliate of SYNCO.[210] The dissenter, Commissioner J. Rutledge Withers, said he voted against the proposal because he feared that it would "double the historic growth rate of the town."[211]

On 24 July 1984 the town board passed an ordinance transferring ownership of its water and sewer systems to the Charlotte/Mecklenburg Utilities Department (CMUD). This transfer had come gradually, with the town ceding control of the sewer system in January and voters approving the more controversial sale of the water system in May by a vote of 267 to 188.[212] Because the water and sewer systems had long been symbols of Davidson's autonomy, the town board had resisted selling them even after greatly increased local demand for water, especially from industries, and much tighter environmental regulations on sewage treatment made the town's ownership highly problematic by the late 1970s. Negotiations to sell the systems in the early 1980s stalled when Charlotte officials insisted on charging higher rates to customers in Davidson and other towns in the county than city residents were paying.[213] Agreement was finally reached in early 1984 on the basis of equal rates for all customers, thus freeing the town board from recurrent worries about how to pay for upgrades to its systems.

As with the growth of upscale housing on the west side oriented toward people who worked in Charlotte, the transfer of the water and sewer systems—like the non-controversial sale of the town's electric service to the Duke Power Company in 1975—increased Davidson's connections to the broader Charlotte metropolitan area. The town also became more tied to the region when First Union Bank of Charlotte bought the locally owned Piedmont Bank in 1983, thus ending Jack Tate's long tenure as a pivotal figure in the town's life.[214] As had been true during most years from 1961 forward, Davidson clearly changed in important ways in 1983 and 1984.

A final change linking Davidson to the broader area during the late 1970s and early 1980s was the college's decision—one that many students opposed—to transform its 10-watt student-oriented radio station, WDAV, into a professionally managed, 18,500-watt station focusing on classical music that could be heard throughout the region.[215] Sam Spencer recalled that the revamped WDAV, which began operating in 1978, was created to "give us more of a presence in Charlotte," where many alumni and other supporters of the college lived.[216] Funded mainly by listeners and by the federal government through the Corporation for Public Broadcasting, the new WDAV quickly emerged as a revered institution not only in the town/college that was Davidson, but also among lovers of classical music in the entire region. It thus became a hallmark of Davidson's flourishing.

More than most years in Davidson, 1984 witnessed major transitions in the town and at the college. One could debate which was the more important change for the town: the transfer of the sewer and water systems to CMUD or the resignation of the dynamic, change-oriented Nancy Mac-Cormac as mayor and her replacement by the more low-key Russell Knox, the respected co-owner of Knox Realty on Main Street.

At the college, the visionary, goal-oriented Sam Spencer resigned as president in 1983 after fifteen years of service. He was succeeded in 1984 by another alumnus, John Kuykendall, an exemplary listener and consensus-builder who became known for raising the funds to build the Baker Sports

Complex, for working with Herb Jackson of the art department and Laura Foxx of the development office to raise the money for the Visual Arts Center, and especially for nurturing the college's many strengths. Kuykendall recalled that the $150 million fund-raising campaign was the largest at a liberal arts college up to that time.[217] This campaign, combined with ever-higher tuition and other charges for students, permitted the college to expand the student body and the faculty, and to increase faculty and staff compensation substantially.

Remarkably, Kuykendall's successor, Bobby Vagt (1997–2007), was able to raise even more funds—and do at least as much to upgrade the physical plant—at the nationally renowned college. After a second consecutive non-academic alumnus, Tom Ross, replaced Vagt and served during the economic downturn between 2007 and 2010, the college appointed its first female president, historian/administrator Carol Quillan, in May 2011. Quillan also was the first president who was not a graduate of the college since John Cunningham stepped down in 1957.

In the midst of the transition from Spencer to Kuykendall in the spring of 1984, the basic continuity of values was epitomized when, at the gathering of students and faculty in Chambers auditorium to learn who would be the college's next president, the chair of the college's board of trustees requested that the assembled gathering sing the doxology. "The [college's] founders would have been pleased," local historian Mary Beaty observed.[218] Similarly, it is likely that, despite all the changes that had taken place in the interim, Davidson residents in 1961 generally would have been pleased with the town that Nancy MacCormac left to her successors in local government.

Epilogue Growing Smartly and Compassionately, 1985–2011

On Sunday, 21 October 2001, roughly 100 members of St. Alban's Episcopal Church walked from their small, 55-seat chapel on Lorimer Road to their impressive new sanctuary with seating for 300 located on six acres about half a mile east of the intersection of Concord Road and Grey Road. The Episcopal Bishop of North Carolina, Michael Curry, joined the rector, Gary Steber, in officiating at the dedication of the church and the adjacent memorial garden.[1] During the next ten years, the congregation grew to more than 500 members.[2]

The other two Protestant churches on the town's east side, Davidson College Presbyterian and Davidson United Methodist, also had major building projects and grew rapidly in membership in the generally prosperous, optimistic years after 1984. In 2008 Elizabeth McGregor Simmons became the first female senior pastor in DCPC's long history.

The building of a new home for St. Alban's is especially important for the town's history because it was the anchor of developer Doug Boone's ambitious plan to build 260 houses and town-homes on 80 acres located east of Grey Road and north of Concord Road. When Boone first approached the town several years earlier, he envisioned a traditional development of roughly half as many single-family homes on good-sized lots, as specified in the town's 1977 zoning ordinance. But after the town approved a new planning document in 1995 that reflected "new urbanist" thinking, Boone adjusted his plans. "The development, as drawn," the *Charlotte Observer* reported just before the town board approved the project in June 1998, "is a testament to new urbanism, a style of design that incorporates traditional small-town touches such as interconnecting streets rather than cul-de-sacs, ample sidewalks and park space, alleys and backyard parking instead of garages pointed toward the street."[3]

Davidson town planner Tim Keane praised Boone's development as "a planned community that fits into the town—that isn't traditional suburbia."[4] Keane, a new urbanist, almost certainly would not have had as positive an opinion of River Run, a development well to the southeast of traditional Davidson with single-family homes for the affluent. In a deal announced in April 1989, town leaders agreed to help River Run's developer obtain public water and sewer service, and the developer accepted eventual annexation by the town. From the perspective of officials in the late 1980s, annexing River Run, with 712 lots on 858 acres, "significantly increas[ed] the town's size and its tax base and allow[ed] Davidson to control development."[5] While many residents considered River Run an excellent place to live, most town officials in the mid-1990s saw it as the kind of income-segregated development that the town should no longer approve.

The big issue for the town government in the 1990s and early 2000s was how to manage and plan for population growth, which was occurring rapidly throughout northern Mecklenburg and southern Iredell counties. Because property owners have the right to develop their land, town leaders faced a choice: they could either continue with traditional zoning, which would lead in the eastern part of town—and in the adjacent rural areas whose zoning the town board controlled—to suburban-style single-family homes on large lots, like those in River Run and in other parts of town; or they could insist on zoning according to new urbanist, "smart growth" principles that would require that living units be closer together, with a percentage of them affordable to lower-income residents, and with strict requirements for providing small parks and retaining undeveloped land as a significant percentage of each development.

With guidance from a town-appointed planning group that solicited public input, local officials, including long-serving commissioner Margo Williams and commissioners (later mayors) Randy Kincaid and John Woods, chose the latter approach. They combined it with the "smart growth" model of an even greater density and variety of housing and commercial spaces near the town center, which, it was hoped, would be served in the future by commuter rail into Charlotte. The development of greenways and bike lanes enabled residents living in River Run, McConnell, and other developments away from the town center to use bicycles for safe transportation and exercise.

Town leaders insisted that, insofar as possible, all housing and commercial buildings had to be designed to enhance the town's livability and attractiveness. Indeed, members of the town planning board and the design review board, working long hours as unpaid volunteers, succeeded in maintaining, and at times even enhancing, the town's beauty at a time of rapid population growth and the construction of hundreds of new buildings.

In addition to volunteers, town employees—led by the capable, unflappable Leamon Brice, who began working for the town in 1990—deserve credit for helping to steer the town through the transformative years of the late 1990s and early 2000s. Responding to the rapid growth of the town and its increasingly complex governance, the commissioners adopted the town manager form of government in April 1997. It took full effect on July 1 of that year, with Brice as town manager.

Reflecting in early 2007 on what the town had been able to accomplish with its "smart growth" philosophy, Mayor Kincaid noted, among other things, "neighborhoods designed to bring people together rather than separate them" and "a permanent set-aside of huge amounts of open space," especially in the area east of the traditional town limits. He also took pride in "notable absences," including "no four-lane streets that make it difficult for walkers; no drive-through restaurants; no big-box stores; and no gated communities."[6] Mayor Woods observed in 2008 that, beginning in the early 1990s, "our brand of planning has attempted to get ahead of the curve."[7] Impressed with Davidson's planning, the federal Environmental Protection Agency honored the town with a smart-growth award in 2004.

As might have been expected given the novelty and ambitious scope of the town's approach, some residents offered criticisms as specific proposals worked their way through the planning process. In the late 1990s, an ad hoc organization that included about fifty residents, Preserve Small Town Davidson, questioned whether the neighborly quality of life could be maintained if large numbers of new housing units were added in the older parts of town as well as in the Boone development and in other new projects to the east. This group also raised concerns about whether the town's approach would lead to traffic jams and shortages of downtown parking spaces. "We think Davidson is awfully nice the way it is—single-family homes, lots of trees," PSTD member Lynn Burris commented.[8]

A more serious challenge occurred two years later, when angry landowners in the town's extraterritorial jurisdiction (ETJ) threatened to sue if town officials insisted on maintaining up to 50 percent of undeveloped land in that area as open space. In addition to the threat of lawsuits, in

As Davidson moves into the 21st century and its population surpasses 10,000, residents continue to hold on to a strong sense of community and civic commitment. Photos in this section were taken and supplied by Bill Giduz, the college's director of media relations, unless otherwise noted.

Local business owners host town-wide celebrations and concerts

Children dance with band at a Concert on the Green

Students performing on the town green

Volunteers turned a local school into a vital community center

The Ada Jenkins Center at a quiet moment

Residents actively participate in planning meetings

Planning charette with attentive audience

Volunteers contribute many hours to keep the fire department going

Davidson College students participate in training exercises

Others make sure that children have safe places to play

Baseball at McEver Field

Caring for neighbors includes creating award-winning rental housing

The Bungalows managed by the Davidson Housing Coalition. Photo courtesy of the DHC.

Town and college worked together to create a retirement community

Residents of the Pines retirement community are active participants in town events.

Town commissioners step out of town hall to hold neighborhood meetings

Tim Dreffer, Brian Jenest, Margo Williams, Connie Wessner,
Mayor John Woods, Laurie Venzon, 2011

Police officers know people by name

Traditional 4th of July parade with children on bikes

Public art can be whimsical and new buildings are a focus of public interest

The Stowe Building designed to blend and enhance Main Street

Andrew Dunnill sculpture under construction in front of the post office

Main Street continues to welcome everyone to stroll and take time to greet friends

the spring of 2001 landowners protested at the Town Hall with signs that read "STOP! THE LAND GRAB."[9] At least some of the anger subsided after a committee composed of landowners and town board members embraced a creative solution, proposed by landowner Hugh Barger, that the town agree to purchase at the fair market price any property that developers had refused to buy because of the town's zoning restrictions. The town could either keep the land as open space or sell it to developers who agreed to abide by Davidson's zoning ordinances. After the committee supported this plan, the town board approved it in the summer of 2001.[10] The $10 million that the town board had set aside to protect undeveloped land made this solution possible.

As had happened in the early 1980s but with less of a sense of grievance two decades later, some blacks expressed concerns about the rapid pace of development on the west side and about blacks' perceived lack of influence in the town's planning process. The Davidson African American Coalition, chaired by the Reverend Dora DuBose, frequently discussed these issues, expressing concern about "gentrification" in that part of town and the need for better "communication with all groups."[11] The situation was exacerbated when Garfield Carr, the only black on the town board, retired in 2005 after twenty years of service, thus leaving Davidson with no black elected officials at a time when the percentage of blacks in the town's rapidly growing population had dropped below 10 percent.[12]

In early 2006 a member of the town planning staff, Lauren Blackburn, and the chair of the planning board, Bill McCoy, met with black residents to try to address the community's concerns.[13] But, as Mayor Kincaid commented, the situation was complicated by the fact that blacks in the area were free to sell their properties to any buyers, thus potentially reducing the stock of housing available to lower-income black residents.[14]

Despite criticisms and concerns expressed by some blacks and whites, it seems fair to conclude that town leaders did a commendable job of managing growth in the town and ETJ in the 1990s and early 2000s. Instead of basically agreeing to whatever developers and commercial interests wanted to do, as happened especially near I-77 exit 28 in Cornelius and I-77 exit 36 in Mooresville, Davidson's leaders insisted that developers and commercial interests either follow the town's strict rules or work with more compliant town officials elsewhere. Moreover, by insisting on a wide variety of housing options including affordable units within high-cost developments, local leaders kept the town more economically diverse than it otherwise would have been. The town government also encouraged citizens to walk, bike, and use the town-subsidized buses that travel to nearby towns and to

Charlotte in an effort to reduce the number of cars on the streets and the amount of pollutants in the air.

Although the town's population grew at a moderate pace from 3,241 in 1980 to 4,046 in 1990, and then much more rapidly to 7,139 in 2000 and 10,944 in 2010, Davidson retained a strong sense of community. This was especially true for residents living within particular neighborhoods (including the well-planned, non-profit retirement community, the Pines at Davidson, which opened in 1988), for those with children in the same schools or extracurricular programs, for those who participated in social, recreational, educational, religious, civic, and arts groups, and for those who just hung out at Summit Coffee, the Brickhouse Tavern, or other local hot spots. Many longtime residents lamented the fact that, when they went downtown to shop or attended church, they did not know the people they encountered on Main Street or in the post office or the ones sitting beside them in the pews. "It is certainly a different place," Scotty Nicholls observed. "It is not as intimate as it was when you knew everybody in town."[15] But, as relative newcomer Loretta Wertheimer commented in 2007, "There still exists a sense of identity and history that makes [Davidson] more than just a place to live."[16]

One way in which the town changed in the 1990s and early 2000s was that its residents generally were much more affluent. With developments such as River Run and Cabin Creek and the stately homes on Avinger Lane leading the way, the median value of an owner-occupied home in Davidson rose to $270,000 in 2000 and to an estimated $420,000 in 2009, more than double the national average of $185,000.[17] Moreover, median family income grew to $101,000 by 2000—again more than double the national average of $50,000—and to $116,000 in 2007, dropping only slightly to $115,000 during the recession two years later.[18]

A random survey conducted by the National Research Center in Boulder, Colorado, in September 2007 showed that, even after all the growth during the preceding decade, many residents considered Davidson an excellent place to live. The town ranked first among 154 places surveyed in "sense of community"; it ranked fourth among 194 communities as a place to raise children, and fifth among 232 communities in overall quality of life. While scoring above average in most categories, the town ranked below average in ease of car travel, in street repairs, and in job and shopping opportunities. Moreover, 70 percent of the 480 respondents said that growth was happening too fast—an unsurprising opinion given how fast the population had grown in recent years and how at the time Griffith Street near I-77 was being transformed by the construction of two roundabouts and by large building projects, including a hotel, a commercial building, upscale housing, and a new campus for Davidson Day School. It also is not surprising that 93 percent responded that managing growth was either "essential" or "very important" to the town.[19]

Although widespread concern about the town's rapid growth was understandable, many residents also appreciated the "big-town amenities" that Rosie Molinary mentioned in a 2009 article.[20] Among the amenities that the town had in 2009 but lacked in the much smaller Davidson of 1985 were numerous public parks, including the upgraded Roosevelt Wilson Park on Lake Davidson, the historic Beaver Dam property near River Run, and the 200-acre Fisher Farm Park in the ETJ to the east; a non-profit organization—the Davidson Lands Conservancy, founded in 2000—dedicated to preserving and facilitating public use of undeveloped land; the Bungalows, an attractive affordable-housing project on Jetton Street nurtured by the Davidson Housing Coalition, founded in 1996;[21] two upscale grocery stores, Harris Teeter and Healthy Home Market; two public schools on South Street instead of one; a public charter school, the Community School of Davidson, and the private Davidson Day School, on Griffith Street; many new religious congregations, examples of which are Davidson Friends (Quaker) Meeting, River's Edge Community Church, and the Lake Norman Jewish groups that frequently held services at the college or on the town green; talented bands including Davidson Local; the Masterworks School of the Arts on South Main Street; buildings for Dance Davidson and the Davidson Community Theater on the west side; two impressive new buildings on the Davidson College campus, the Visual Arts Center and the Baker Sports Complex (most famous for the nationally-ranked, Elite Eight team led by All-American Stephen Curry, which for longtime residents brought back memories of the glory days of men's basketball in the 1960s), and an imaginatively updated and expanded structure based on the old Johnston Gym, the Alvarez Student Center, which included a new theater; a successful farmer's market downtown; town-funded Downtown Davidson's highly successful Concerts on the Green, with performers using the large front porch/stage of the impressive new public library; a greatly expanded Christmas in Davidson, which has become a regional event; an internet-based source of news and information, *DavidsonNews.net*, that began in 2006; a community garden project at the corner of Catawba and Potts Streets financed by the Davidson United Methodist Church; and at least twice as many high-quality restaurants and outlets for artists and craftspeople than existed in 1985.

"If you need an egg," Ralph Johnson remarked wryly in 1990, "you must either go out of town or lay it yourself."[22] As often was the case, Johnson was right: the Food Lion that had been in Sadler Square during most of the 1980s had moved to Cornelius, and no supermarket had replaced it. But in the much larger, more dynamic town of 2009, one could buy eggs at grocery stores and, on many Saturdays each year, at the Davidson Farmers Market. Beginning on Christmas Day of 2009, one could even attend first-run movies in Davidson—at the four-screen Our Towns Cinema in Sadler Square—for the first time since fire destroyed the old movie theater on Main Street in 1955. In many but not in all ways, the more prosperous, more diverse, and more cosmopolitan Davidson of the early 2000s was an improvement on the relatively isolated but more neighborly Davidson of a half-century before.

One thing that had not changed since the early 1950s was the willingness of many Davidsonians to care about their neighbors, to do things to try to help make the town a better place to live for everyone. Especially laudable was the willingness of honest, intelligent, and public-spirited residents to run for mayor and commissioner and, if elected, to work long hours at very low pay to serve the community. As of February 2011, the mayor earned $9,014 per year, and the commissioners were paid $2,923.56.[23]

As noted earlier, the many residents who have served conscientiously and without pay on town committees also deserve recognition. For example, John and Missy Kuykendall, while serving on town committees in the early 1990s, helped to envision and then to build community support for the seminal town-planning ordinance approved in 1995.

There is space here to discuss only two of the non-governmental groups and three of the ad hoc causes that community-minded residents organized between 1985 and 2011 to make Davidson a better community or, in the case of aid to victims of Hurricane Katrina, to put the community's values into practice. And when one or a few individuals are named, it is important to remember that the organization or cause succeeded only because many other people shared the vision and contributed time and resources to bring it to fruition.

The Davidson chapter of Habitat for Humanity began in 1987 as HOOT (Housing Opportunities for Our Town). The first board, composed of eight whites and three blacks, was chaired by the dynamic pastor of Davidson Presbyterian Church, Mark Lomax.[24] The next summer, after Dave Kaylor and Ken Wood participated in a large Habitat building project in Charlotte led by former president Jimmy Carter, the group changed its name to Davidson Habitat for Humanity and began to build two homes on 3.5 acres that it had purchased on Potts Street.[25] In the spring of 1989, the first Habitat homeowner in the entire North Meck–South Iredell area, Brenda McCain, moved into a house with her two children that she and more than 100 volunteers had helped to build.[26] "Habitat seeks not just to build houses," an annual report noted, "but to build community."[27]

The group, which built an average of two houses per year, grew in strength, raising $25,000 in donations in 1990 and $42,000 in 1992. It also opened a Habitat Store on South Main Street staffed by volunteers that netted $7,400 during its first six months and inspired other Habitat chapters to set up their own stores.[28]

In late 1994, recognizing the need for a unified presence in the North Meck–South Iredell area, the Habitat groups in Davidson and Mooresville joined with interested residents of Cornelius and Huntersville to form Our Towns of North Mecklenburg/South Iredell Habitat for Humanity, later shortened to Our Towns Habitat for Humanity.[29] By July 2005 the organization, which had started in conversations among a small number of Davidson residents in 1987, had built 100 houses in the Lake Norman area that served 369 people, and had helped to build 300 houses in Guatemala for an estimated 2100 people and 14 houses in Sri Lanka for 98 people.[30]

The revitalization of the Ada Jenkins Center in the 1990s was another example of Davidson's commitment to building a community that included those who faced social and economic challenges as well as those who fit comfortably into the town's largely educated, affluent milieu. Even more than in Habitat, blacks as well as whites participated in this revitalization, with leadership coming (among many others) from blacks including Robert Shirley and Nannie Potts and whites including Ralph Gable and Gordon Peck. In the mid-1990s, the town government and local churches provided most of the funds—and volunteers from the white and black churches provided most of the labor—for fixing up the rundown building.[31]

Bonnie Brown, the center's energetic executive director from 1996 to 2001, helped to turn vision into reality. "Bonnie has been a gift to our community," Board Chair Clarence Fox commented in 2001. "Her compassion and her faith in Ada Jenkins' mission helped make this miracle possible."[32] Anyone who doubts that capable, determined individuals can shape events in significant ways never saw Bonnie Brown make reports and request support at town board meetings. She also was effective in meetings with program officers at foundations and at agencies that provided services at the center.

In providing a wide range of services to the less affluent in Davidson and surrounding communities on a modest budget that gradually grew to $479,000 in 2002–03, the revitalized Ada Jenkins Center was indeed a miracle.[33] Under the leadership of Bill Johnson, Brown's able successor, by 2006–07 the center was offering "more than 19 programs" in four main areas: "medical/dental, youth education, crisis assistance, and economic independence."[34] Because the high costs of medical and dental care often made it hard for low-income people to obtain needed treatment, the center became known for its services in these areas, including its free medical clinic, its mobile community dental clinic, its Red Cross transportation program, and its parish nurse program, started and funded largely by local churches. "I prayed for a nurse and God sent me one," Davidson resident Martha Braxton commented after receiving urgently needed nursing care. "I don't know how else to explain it."[35]

The center also became known in the early 2000s for its assistance to Latinos who lived throughout the region, providing services "from obtaining healthcare, employment, transportation and education [including teaching English and computer skills] to meeting legal requirements . . . to 1,881 Latino clients" during 2006–07.[36] That fiscal year the center "helped 5,711 neighbors in need, providing 19,407 total units of service." Latinos thus comprised 1,881 of 5,711—31 percent—of all clients. With only 16 percent of clients living in Davidson, the Ada Jenkins Center had become a regional beacon of caring and compassion.[37]

Caring and compassion across ethnic lines was the theme of a gathering on the Davidson College campus on Saturday, 26 April 1986. Exercising their legal rights, regional leaders of the Ku Klux Klan had obtained a permit to march on Main Street in Davidson at 2 p.m. that afternoon. Deciding to respond with what student government president Mark Sandy called "a positive approach," roughly two hundred students with administration approval organized a Solidarity Day celebration behind the main dining hall on the northern side of the campus, out of earshot of the Klan marchers, beginning an hour before the start of the march.[38]

The lead sentence in the *Charlotte Observer* story the next day captured the contrast between the success of Solidarity Day and the failure of the Klan march: "Blacks and whites frolicked in friendly celebration on the Davidson College campus Saturday as a Ku Klux Klan contingent marched barely noticed on the town's Main Street." The story noted that "hundreds" of people of all ages "romped, listened to folk songs, filled balloons with helium, flung Frisbees and played volleyball or table tennis on the lawn and brick plaza." Rob Ellison, the president of the Black Student

Coalition, commented that the large turnout of whites created "a very good feeling." Dean of Students Will Terry called it a "grand occasion."[39]

In contrast, only ten to fifteen people watched as the thirty-seven members of the Klan marched down Main Street, spouting their white-supremacist views mainly to themselves.[40] Reflecting the opinion of many residents, whether white or black or town or gown, Davidson police chief Hank McKiernan commented afterward that he was "proud to . . . live in a town that responded the way it did."[41]

Because of the town's rapid growth after 1990, the normal cycle of births and deaths, and the ongoing turnover in college students and other residents, fewer than 25 percent of Davidsonians in 2010 had lived in the town when Hurricane Hugo swept through the Charlotte region with winds exceeding 100 miles per hour in September 1989. Town residents and college students worked together to help the community recover, including (among other things) removing fallen trees from streets and sidewalks and assisting elderly neighbors who found it difficult to cope with the loss of electricity. The college's canopy of stately old trees was especially hard hit. "Dozens of trees were amputated or completely cut up and removed on campus during the next couple of weeks," Bill Giduz recalled.[42]

The main ad hoc cause in Davidson in 1989 and the early 1990s was the effort to keep a branch of the Charlotte-Mecklenburg Public Library in the town. Alarm bells sounded when, in August 1989, a consultant to the library system recommended replacing the small, outdated libraries in Davidson, Cornelius, and Huntersville with a much larger regional library near Exit 28 in Cornelius.[43] The reaction in Davidson, which had the highest per capita circulation of any library in the system, was strongly negative. Former commissioner Bill Mayhew doubted that "anybody around here is in favor of it," and commissioner Sandy Carnegie commented that "it would be ridiculous to take out the neighborhood libraries." College librarian Leland Park noted that a public library, along with "a post office [and] little stores . . . make people feel a part of something, and they're going to care." "You'll hear from this community" on the issue, Mayor Russell Knox predicted.[44]

In a town meeting in 1990 and in communications with members of the library board and the county commissioners, Davidson residents insisted that the town had to have a public library. At a public meeting in Cornelius in the fall of 1991, Randy Kincaid recalled, "[s]everal dozen people had signed up to speak, and all but one would tell the county commissioners and the library board that they must spare the Davidson

Public Library from the budget axe." One eloquent speaker, Betty Cumming, noted that Davidson had had a public library when "we had no supermarket or shopping center," when "we had no permanent building for our grade school," and even during the Great Depression, when "we had no money for life's frills."[45] In short, a public library was an essential expression of the community's values. Even though the county's library director strongly supported regional libraries, the library board and county commissioners clearly were looking for ways to maintain a public library in Davidson.

Serious questions remained, including where a new library would be built and how it would be paid for. The college answered the first question by agreeing to a fifty-year lease at $1 a year on land it owned on the village green as a site for the new building. The college also agreed to oversee construction at no cost. Local residents, the town board, and the library board answered the second question. A fund-raising committee chaired by John Kelton established a goal of $136,000 toward the building, while the town government borrowed $725,000 to cover most of the cost. The library board, backed by the county commissioners, agreed to make rental payments on the building to help the town repay the loan and, more important, to cover the operating costs. Perhaps most impressive, the fund-raising committee exceeded its goal by $100,000, thus allowing it to set up an endowment to provide continuing support for the library.[46]

A five-year community/college effort thus permitted the town not only to maintain a public library, but also to replace the cramped 1,500 square-foot storefront facility on South Main with a spacious, well-designed 6,100 square-foot structure on the town green. "I have never been prouder to be a citizen of the town of Davidson," Mayor Russell Knox told the crowd at the dedication of the new library on 5 November 1995. Inspired by Davidson's achievement, town leaders in Cornelius, with community support, similarly insisted on keeping a branch library and constructing an impressive new building near the town center to replace the old one.

A final example of an ad hoc cause is the town's and college's response to the devastation of hurricane Katrina in New Orleans and along the Gulf Coast in late August 2005. A story posted on *Charlotte.com* on 18 September 2005 cited many examples of the generosity and compassion that Davidson residents exhibited. Among the examples: Dr. Craig Corey spent the first two weeks after the hurricane providing medical services in Mississippi; residents of the McConnell neighborhood "furnished a home in Mooresville for a displaced family of four providing furniture, dental, medical and veterinarian services"; Davidson Elementary School raised $14,000 to be matched by Lowe's, Inc.; Davidson IB Middle School raised $2,263 in coins for the Red Cross; the college's music department sponsored a twelve-hour concert that "involved 150 volunteers and raised $12,400 for the . . . Red Cross"; and Summit Coffee "provided an 11-hour musical experience on September 10 [that] had 2,500 visitors and raised $5,018." As Summit Coffee owner Tim Helfrich commented, "This day was testament to the Red Cross motto: Together we can make a difference. Today the community pulled together in a very special way and for a very important cause."[47]

In a talk in November 2005 honoring Bernice Houston and Bill Mayhew, the first two recipients of the town's G. Jackson Burney Community Service Award, Mayor Kincaid, reflecting on his own experience as a thirty-eight-year resident, praised Davidson as "a community . . . where we know each other, support each other in times of adversity, and help to raise each other's children. It is a place that beckons us to public service. It is a place that brings out the best in us, and allows us to have civil discourse about difficult issues." But he also warned that "the concept of community is threatened. It would be easy for us to withdraw, to drive home alone to our enclave homes and close the garage door behind us. With all the new people, it is difficult for us to know even a few of our neighbors, let alone all."[48]

Mayor Kincaid, a model of the self-sacrificing public service that he mentioned, offered a cogent reflection on some of the positive values that have sustained Davidson, despite its shortcomings, as a largely caring and public-spirited community since its modest beginnings in 1837. The challenge for current and future residents, as conditions continue to change, is to honor and live up to those values.

Notes

Preface

1. Carter Lindberg, *The European Reformations*, 2nd ed. (New York: Wiley-Blackwell, 2010), 2.

2. Julie Holding, "History of Davidson to be Published," *Mecklenburg Gazette*, 27 September 1979.

Prologue: Implementing a Community's Vision

1. McGeachy, *Confronted by Challenge*, 106. (*Note:* The Bibliography contains full references.)

2. Beaty, *History of Davidson College*, 8–9.

3. McGeachy, *Confronted by Challenge*, 106.

4. "Birth of Davidson."

5. Shaw, *Davidson College*, 22. Had this effort been successful, Davidson College would not have been built and there would not have been a reason for the town of Davidson to exist.

6. In valuing education, American leaders were following in the footsteps of the great leader of the Reformed tradition in Christianity, John Calvin, and the founder of Presbyterianism in Scotland, John Knox. Two useful books are Leith, *An Introduction to the Reformed Tradition*, and Lingle, *Presbyterians*.

7. Karl A. Plank, "The Changing Context of Church-Related Higher Education," comments for the Davidson College Board of Trustees, 5 February 2004, copy of talk in authors' possession.

8. Beaty, *History of Davidson College*, 6.

9. Ibid., 3, 5.

10. Shaw, *Davidson College*, 20.

11. Ibid., 6.

12. Davidson, *Piedmont Partisan,* 134.

13. Ibid., 132–33.

14. Beaty, *History of Davidson College,* 10.

15. Quoted in Shaw, *Davidson College,* 23.

Chapter 1. College Begets Town, 1837–1860

1. James Morrow, Letter to Sarah Bull, 26 August 1839, James Morrow Papers, South Caroliniana Library, University of South Carolina, Columbia, SC (hereafter USC Library).

2. Murdock M. McLaughlin, Letter to Cousin, 27 February 1857, Typescript, Student Letters, Davidson College Archives, Davidson, NC (hereafter DC Archives).

3. Jethro Rumple, "Reminiscences of the Forties," in *Quips and Cranks,* vol. 1 (Davidson: Davidson College, 1895), 121.

4. Lease, Board of Trustees to John Johnston, 1 April 1876, Records of the Board of Trustees, DC Archives.

5. *Catalogue of the Trustees, Faculty and Students of Davidson College,* 1842, 2; "Manual Labor School of the Concord Presbytery," *Western Carolinian,* 30 May 1835.

6. "Report of the Board of Trustees of Davidson College," *Charlotte Journal,* 12 February 1839; Jennifer McMillan, "A Question of Honor: Changes in the Culture of Davidson College and the Philanthropic Literary Society as a Result of Civil Rights Movements," Unpublished essay, 1997, Philanthropic Society Papers, 1995–97, Davidsoniana File, DC Archives.

7. Hanchett, *Sorting Out the New South City,* 18–19; Tompkins, *History of Mecklenburg County,* 1:119; DC Trustees, Minutes, 27 March 1851, RG 1/1, DC Archives.

8. DC Trustees, Minutes—Report of Faculty, 10 August 1854, RG 1/1, DC Archives.

9. DC Faculty, Minutes, 5 May 1855, RG 2/3.2, DC Archives.

10. DC Faculty, Minutes, 5 July 1858 and 12 July 1858, RG 2/3.2, DC Archives.

11. Duncan Buie, Letter to Kate, 10 November 1859, Catherine Jane McGeachy Buie Papers, 1819 (1861–65) 1899, Special Collections, Perkins Library, Duke University, Durham, NC; David Gordon, Letter to Friend, 6 March 1851, Typescript, Student Letters, DC Archives; DC Trustees, Minutes, 21 February 1854 and 8 August 1849, RG 1/1, DC Archives.

12. Hanchett, *Sorting Out the New South City,* 16; Tompkins, *History of Mecklenburg County,* 2:89–90.

13. "Temperance Society of Davidson College, NC," *Charlotte Journal,* 12 January 1838; Letter to Editor, *Watchman of the South,* 15 August 1839.

14. A.M. Bogle, Letter to Editor, *Charlotte Journal,* 20 October 1842; DC Faculty, Minutes, 17 September 1845, RG 2/3.2, DC Archives; Stringfellow, "Memories of the Fifties," 295.

15. DC Trustees, Minutes, 30 July 1845 and 11 August 1848, RG 1/1, DC Archives.

16. DC Trustees, Minutes—Report of Faculty, 10 August 1854; Minutes, 25 June 1856, 13 July 1858, and 12 July 1859; both in RG 1/1, DC Archives.

17. The first known reference to Sparrow's store is in a student letter dated 8 October 1839. Beaty cites an advertisement for Brown and Sparrow Mercantile Business in *Davidson*, 11.

18. Only a portion of the original foundation of the Steward's Hall still exists. The building was located near the president's house. A portion of the original wall is visible from the front steps of the Guest House.

19. David E. Gordon, Letter to Thomas Britton, 6 March 1851, USC Library. For more information about planter families living in the area, see Davidson's *Plantation World*. According to Davidson, "The majority of the people [in the piedmont region] were non slave-owners and the majority of slave-owners owned but a few. A man who worked his own land, however praiseworthy his enterprise, and even though assisted by eight or ten 'hands,' was a farmer and not a planter. The dividing line is considered to be something around 25 or 30 slaves as the ownership of so large a number customarily required the services of an overseer. The land owner who employed an overseer was a planter" (19). J.J. Stringfellow, class of 1860, later recalled the Stinson home as "a place of pleasant but dangerous resort. He was the father of three beautiful and accomplished daughters and *there* many a boy learned for the first time *he had a heart*." "Memories of the Fifties," 295.

20. Bureau of the Census, 1850 Census (Washington, DC: GPO, 1850).

21. R.G. Dun & Company is the predecessor of Dun and Bradstreet. The company hired local representatives to send credit reports. The records of the company are now housed in the Harvard Business School Library and contain references to 1856 to 1880.

22. Mary Rice Lacy, Letter to Bess Lacy Dewey, 15 December 1858, DC0147s, Lacy Family Papers, 1851–60, DC Archives.

23. James Morrow, Letter to Pa and Mother, 8 October 1839, DC0122s, James Morrow Letters, DC Archives; William Robinson, Letter to Pa, 17 October 1857, DCC0123s, DC Archives; Beaty, *History of Davidson College*, 180; David R. Goldfield, "History," in *The North Carolina Atlas: Portrait for a New Century*, ed. Douglas Orr and Alfred Stuart (Chapel Hill: University of North Carolina Press, 2000), 57; Hanchett, *Sorting Out the New South City*, 16–17.

24. DC Trustees, Minutes, 16 July 1857, RG 1/1, DC Archives.

25. DC Trustees, Minutes, 11 April 1848 and 15 July 1857, RG 1/1, DC Archives; Mary Rice Lacy, Letter to Bess Lacy Dewey, [February 1859], DC0147s, Lacy Family Papers, 1851–60, DC Archives.

26. Beaty, *Davidson*, 12, 27; "Survey and Research Report on The Helper Hotel," Carolina Inn, Davidsoniana File, DC Archives.

27. Stringfellow, "Memories of the 50s," 295.

28. George Laurence Petrie, Letter to Father, 6 July 1857, George Petrie Papers, RG 192, Auburn University Special Collections & Archives, Auburn, AL.

29. Clement Daniel Fishburne, Letter and Recollection, 1903, Southern Historical Collection, University of North Carolina at Chapel Hill, Collection 01937-z, Chapel Hill, NC.

30. James McCombs, Letter to Brother, 22 May 1855, DC0117s, James McCombs Letters, DC Archives.

31. William Bynum, Letter to Father, 28 October 1837, Typescript, Student Letters, DC Archives.

32. Harper, "Davidson 'Befo' de War," 301–2; DC Trustees, Minutes, 3 September 1844, 21 February 1854, 8 August 1854, 28 February 1855, and 25 June 1856, RG 1/1, DC Archives.

33. "The Ball in Motion," *Charlotte Journal*, 21 March 1845, 2.

34. Hanchett, *Sorting Out the New South City*, 21–22; Goldfield, "History," 55; DC Trustees, Minutes, Treasurer reports, 1856–59, RG 1/1, DC Archives; James Logan Greenlee, Letter to Pa, 19 December 1860, DC0115s, James Greenlee Letters, 1859–62, DC Archives; Robert A. Davidson, Letter to Brother, 9 October 1859, DC1025s, DC Archives. Robert Davidson's hope of traveling to Charlotte almost every other Saturday was unlikely, given restrictions on students. Unfortunately, before the railroad could make much difference to the town's economy or population, the tracks were pulled up by the Confederate government for use on other, more critical lines.

35. Mary Rice Lacy, Letter to Bess Lacy Dewey, [February 1859], DC0147s, Lacy Family Papers, 1851–60, DC Archives. While the college's charter declares the school's purpose to be "to educate youth of all classes without any regard to the distinction of religious denominations," students of all denominations were required to attend the college church. Still, there is evidence of religious tolerance as one trustee, William Lee Davidson, campaigned for Catholic suffrage while running as a delegate to the state's constitutional convention in 1835. Davidson lost the election to the Rev. Isaac Grier, who did not share Davidson's ecumenical sensibilities. Tompkins, *History of Mecklenburg County*, 1:119.

36. Beaty, *History of the Davidson College Presbyterian Church*, 1–2.

37. J.T.K. Belk, Letter to Parents, 6 January 1845, DC0008s, James T.K. Belk Collection, 1845–47, DC Archives.

38. DC Trustees, Minutes, 18 February 1855 and 7 August 1855, RG 1/1, DC Archives.

39. Nancy Woloch, *Women and the American Experience* (New York: Knopf, 1984), 167–68.

40. Beaty, *History of Davidson College Presbyterian Church*, 2. Unfortunately, the location and staff of the "School House" are not known.

41. "Dr. Morrison's Colored Family." Typescript, Lincoln County Historical Society, NC; Pinckney B. Chambers, Letter to John Sample, 9 December 1837, DC0111s, Pinckney Brown Chambers Letters, 1837, DC Archives; Thomas Hamilton, Letter to John W. Hamilton, 5 September 1838, DC0116s, Thomas H. Hamilton Letters, 1835–39, DC Archives.

42. Mary Rice Lacy, Letters to Bess Lacy Dewey, 6 August 1856 and 2 January 1857, DC0147s, Lacy Family Papers, DC Archives.

43. Lacy's letters show her busy caring for children, nursing sick neighbors,

worrying about her garden, and serving as hostess to visiting trustees. In July 1859, she matter-of-factly notes that "we began to have company on Monday, had five gentlemen to dinner & so on from that time at every meal until this morning."

44. DC Trustees, Minutes, 27 December 1853, RG 1/1, DC Archives; DC Faculty, Minutes, 3 April 1863, RG 2/3.2, DC Archives.

45. Mary Rice Lacy, Letter to Bess Lacy Dewey, [February 1859], DC0147s, Lacy Family Papers, DC Archives.

46. S.S. Satchwell, "Obstacles to Medical Progress: Annual Address Delivered Before the Medical Society of the State of North Carolina, Edenton, NC," April 1857, http://docsouth.unc.edu/nc/satchw57/menu.html; Sarah McCulloh Lemmon, "The Decline of the Church, 1776–1816," in *The Episcopal Church in North Carolina, 1701–1959*, ed. Lawrence London and Sarah McCulloh Lemmon (Raleigh: Episcopal Diocese of North Carolina, 1987), 92.

47. Kathy Herran, *They Married Confederate Officers* (Davidson: Warren Publishing, 1997), 6; Lester, comp., "Census of the Davidson College Cemetery," 48; Donald R. Wright, "African Americans," in *A Companion to 19th-Century America*, ed. William L. Barney (Oxford: Blackwell, 2001), 198. One recorded slave death is that of Samuel Williamson's cook, who was struck with a violent headache while preparing dinner. She died as the food was being sent to the house. The smallness of the Davidson community is evident in the fact that an account of her death is recorded in a student letter with the preface "Since I have commenced writing this Dr. Williamson has lost his cook." David E. Gordon, Letter to Thomas Britton, 6 March 1851, USC Library.

48. William M. Wilson, Letter to Cousin, 30 December 1850, USC Library; John M. Cooper, Letter to Britton, USC Library; DC Faculty, Minutes, 6 February 1854, RG 2/3.2, DC Archives; Clement Daniel Fishburne, Letter and Recollection, 1903, Southern Historical Collection, University of North Carolina at Chapel Hill, Collection 01937-z, Chapel Hill, NC.

49. Powell, *North Carolina*, 307.

50. Tompkins, *History of Mecklenburg County*, 1:113.

51. John Cooper, Letter to Thomas Britton, 26 June 1851, USC Library; Powell, *Higher Education in North Carolina*, 48; William E. Drake, *Higher Education in North Carolina before 1860* (New York: Carleton Press, 1964), 248; Herran, *They Married Confederate Officers*, 11. Miss Henderson may have met Anna and Eugenia Morrison while a student. The Morrisons were living in Lincoln County at this time.

52. Mary Rice Lacy, Letter to Bess Lacy Dewey, 15 December [1858] and [February 1859], DC0147s, DC Archives.

53. W.M. Wilson, Letter to Thomas Britton, 29 May 1851, and David Gordon, Letter to Thomas Britton, 23 December 1850; both in USC Library; Mary Rice Lacy to Bess Lacy Dewey, 15 December 1858, DC0147s, DC Archives.

54. James Morrow, Letter to Pa and Mother, 28 May 1840, DC0122s, DC Ar-

chives; Junius L. Gaither, Letter to Brother, 20 June 1846, Typescript, Student Letters, DC Archives; Tompkins, *History of Mecklenburg County*, 1:122; James McCombs, Letter to Brother, 11 July 1855, DC0117s, DC Archives.

55. DC Faculty, Minutes, 5 May 1855, RG 2/3.2, DC Archives; DC Trustees, Minutes, 9 July 1861, RG 1/1, DC Archives.

Chapter 2. New Challenges in the 1860s and 1870s

1. DC Trustees, Minutes, 22 June 1869, RG 1/1, DC Archives.

2. Bureau of the Census, 1860 Census (Washington, DC: GPO, 1860). *Note:* The census in 1860 was taken in June after college students had left for the summer.

3. James Logan Greenlee, Letter to Pa, 3 October 1860, DC0115s, James Logan Greenlee Letters, 1859–62, DC Archives.

4. "Helper's Hotel," Advertisement, *North Carolina Presbyterian,* 23 June 1860; "At Davidson College, N.C.," Advertisement, *North Carolina Presbyterian,* 17 November 1860. This notice ran through 22 December 1860.

5. DC Trustees, Minutes, 11 July 1860, RG 1/1, DC Archives.

6. *North Carolina Presbyterian,* 10 November 1860.

7. Henry Chambers, Reminiscences, DC0141s, Henry Chambers Reminiscences, 1918, DC Archives; James Logan Greenlee, Letter to Brother, 18 October 1860, DC0115s, James Logan Greenlee Letters, 1859–62, DC Archives.

8. A Bell and Everett Student, "Davidson College O.K.," *Iredell Express,* 2 November 1860.

9. Duncan Buie, Letter to Kate, 29 November 1860, Catherine McGeachy Buie Papers, 1819–99, Special Collections, Perkins Library, Duke University, Durham, NC; James Logan Greenlee, Letter to Pa, 18 March 1861, DC0115s, James Logan Greenlee Letters, 1859–62, DC Archives.

10. William Dickey, Letter to Joe Thompson, 18 February 1861, Joseph Thompson Papers, DC0090s, DC Archives; James Logan Greenlee, Letter to Pa, 18 March 1861, DC0115s, James Logan Greenlee Letters, 1859–62, DC Archives; William A. Smith, Reminiscences, 1920, DC1054s, DC Archives.

11. Lefler, *North Carolina,* 486.

12. DC Trustees, Minutes, Faculty Report, 1860–61, RG 1/1, DC Archives.

13. Hugh Lefler and Albert Newsome observe that "The drastic Confederate Conscription Acts of 1862 and later were extremely unpopular in North Carolina. The soldiers considered them unethical and discriminatory; many lawyers, including Chief Justice Pearson, thought they were unconstitutional; many newspapers condemned them in strong language; the people seemed to think that they were unnecessary, undemocratic, and unjust. Especially unpopular was the provision in the 1862 law which exempted from military service all those who owned as many as twenty slaves." Lefler, *North Carolina,* 470.

14. Shaw, *Davidson College,* 104; DC Trustees, Minutes, Faculty Report, 1861–62, RG 1/1, DC Archives.

15. Franklin McNeill, Letter to Father, 9 March 1863, Hector H. McNeill Collection, Special Collections, Perkins Library, Duke University, Durham, NC.

16. Franklin McDowell, "Reminiscences of the Sixties," *Davidson College Magazine*, May 1912, 306; Dandridge Burwell, Letter to Cornelia Shaw, 9 March 1918, DC0168s, Dandridge Burwell Reminiscences, 1918, DC Archives. Burwell also recalls having taken his meals with President and Mrs. Kirkpatrick, in yet another variation on boarding house arrangements.

17. Rebecca Neal Lynch, Reminiscences, 1920, DC0161s, DC Archives.

18. "Leavenworth Letter," 12 September 1864, Typescript in DC Archives, original in private possession.

19. Quoted in Shaw, *Davidson College*, 116.

20. DC Faculty, Minutes, 14 July 1865, RG 2/3.2, DC Archives; George Willcox McIver, *Memoirs of George Willcox McIver, A Native of North Carolina*, Typescript in DC Archives, original in possession of family members.

21. McIver, *Memoirs*.

22. DC Trustees, Minutes, 18 July 1865, RG 1/1, DC Archives. The college trustees appointed a series of committees over the next seven years to seek compensation, but none of the committees was ever successful—whether from lack of action on the part of the committee or the government is not clear.

23. Ibid.

24. See Powell's *North Carolina Through Four Centuries*, 361–69; Lefler, *History of a Southern State*, 474–77; and Goldfield "History," 59, for more background on the popular sentiment during the war years.

25. McDowell, "Reminiscences of the Sixties," 307. A.J. Morrison graduated from Davidson College, class of 1869, becoming both a lawyer and a pastor before his death in 1876. There were at least five students from Alabama attending Davidson in 1865. The soldier mentioned may have been T.W. Howard, a student from Mississippi who only attended for one year, 1864–65.

26. McIver, *Memoirs, 6.*

27. McDowell, "Reminiscences of the Sixties," 303; Shaw, *Davidson College*, 133–34; DC Trustees, Minutes, 12 September 1866, RG 1/1, DC Archives.

28. Russell, *Rare Pattern*, 63.

29. Anne Sampson, Letter to Cornelia Shaw, 8 July 1920, DC0156s, DC Archives.

30. DC Trustees, Minutes, 17 July 1866, RG 1/1, DC Archives.

31. Alexander McIver, Letter to Cornelia Phillips Spencer, Collection: 468, Southern Historical Collection, University of North Carolina at Chapel Hill. Quoted in Beaty, *History of Davidson College,* 112–13. Given that Davidson students appealed to the Board of Trustees to retain McIver, McPhail's claim about students staying away was probably unfounded. See DC Trustees, Minutes, 22 June 1868, RG 1/1, DC Archives.

32. DC Trustees, Minutes, 27 June 1876, 27 June 1877, 25 June 1874, and 23 June 1875, RG 1/1, DC Archives.

33. Paul Winn, "Davidson from 1867 to 1869," *Davidson College Magazine*, May 1912, 299.

34. "Wilson's Days at Davidson," *Davidsonian*, 8 May 1918, 5.

35. DC Faculty, Minutes, 8 October 1874; William Banks Withers, Letter to Mollie, 1 July 1875 and 1 January 1876, Letters in private possession.

36. Lucy Phillips Russell, Reminiscences, 5, DC0157s, Lucy Phillips Russell, Reminiscences, undated, DC Archives.

37. Anne Sampson, Letter to Cornelia Shaw, 8 July 1920, DC0156s, Anne E. Sampson Reminiscences, 1920, DC Archives.

38. William Banks Withers, Letter to Mollie, 14 April 1873, Letters in private possession.

39. Anne Sampson, Letter to Cornelia Shaw, 8 July 1920, DC0156s, Anne E. Sampson Reminiscences, 1920, DC Archives.

40. H.E. Fries, Letter to Mother, 23 January 1876, DC0029s, Henry Elias Fries Papers, 1874–77, DC Archives; Clifton Hunter, Letter to Mother, 2 October 1874 and 30 March 1875, Lemuel C. Wheat & Thomas C. Hunter Papers, 1837–97, Special Collections, Perkins Library, Duke University, Durham, NC; DC Trustees, Minutes, 26 June 1873, RG 1/1, DC Archives. Mr. Helper, while coming to the aid of the college, did not do so totally out of charity, as the Minutes note that he was charging 10% interest.

41. DC Trustees, Minutes, 9 February 1866, 28 June 1870, 25 June 1872, 15 January 1875, 29 January 1875, and 11 June 1879, RG 1/1, DC Archives; "Thomas W. Sparrow v. The Trustees of Davidson College," *North Carolina Reports* (Raleigh: State Printing, 1916), vol. 77, 41.

42. DC Trustees, Minutes, 28 June 1870 and 30 June 1870, RG 1/1, DC Archives.

43. William Withers, Letter to Mollie, 5 October 1875, Letters in private possession.

44. Alex. R. Banks, "Administration of Prof. J.R. Blake, Chairman," in *Semi-Centenary Addresses* (Raleigh: E.M. Uzzell, 1888); Colin Munroe, Letter to Mr. Chris, 28 September 1869, Typescript in DC Archives, original in private possession.

45. William Waller Carson, Knoxville, Tenn., Letter to Cornelia Shaw, 19 July 1918, DC0166s, William W. Carson, Reminiscences, 1918, DC Archives.

46. Ibid.; DC Trustees, Minutes, 10 October 1873 and 8 January 1875, RG 1/1, DC Archives.

47. DC Trustees, Minutes, 27 June 1871, RG 1/1, DC Archives; William Withers, Letter to Mollie, 13 January 1875, Letters in private possession.

48. John Kirkpatrick, Letter, April 1866, Typescript, DC0252s, Kirkpatrick Family Papers, 1864–66, DC Archives.

49. McDowell, "Reminiscences of the Sixties," 307. In his account, McDowell says that "an insolent and offensive negro rudely pushed a student from the sidewalk, and in the altercation that ensued the freedman was badly punished." It is not surprising that his account would be sympathetic to his classmates, and

even fifty years later, the beating of one man by four men could still be seen as appropriate punishment.

50. Tompkins, *History of Mecklenburg County,* 1:145; Shaw, *Davidson College,* 118.

51. DC Faculty, Minutes, 8 January 1875 and 22 January 1875, RG 2/3.2, DC Archives.

52. DC Trustees, Minutes, 17 July 1866, 18 July 1867, and 22 June 1869, RG 1/1, DC Archives.

53. Anne Sampson, Letter to Cornelia Shaw, 8 July 1920, DC0156s, Anne E. Sampson Reminiscences, 1920, DC Archives.

54. Ibid.

55. Margaret Hunter, "Rev. W.P. Williams, Davidson's First Mayor," *Mecklenburg Gazette,* 21 August 1980.

56. *Torrence Chapel A.M.E. Zion Church 115th Anniversary, 1869–1984*; DC Trustees, Minutes, 17 July 1866 and 22 June 1869, RG1/1, DC Archives.

57. Dan Morrill, "Jim Crow Comes to Mecklenburg County," http://www.cmhpf.org/educationjimcrow.htm; William Withers, Letters to Mollie, 21 October 1875 and 26 August 1879, Letters in private possession.

58. Duncan Buie, Letter to Kate, 29 November 1860, Catherine McGeachy Buie Papers, 1819–99, Special Collections, Perkins Library, Duke University, Durham, NC.

59. DC Trustees, Minutes, 17 July 1866, 18 July 1867, and 22 June 1879, RG 1/1, DC Archives; William Withers, Letters to Mollie, 19 March 1875, 29 May 1875, and 5 October 1875, Letters in private possession.

60. Dandridge Burwell, Letter to Cornelia Shaw, 9 March 1918, DC0168s, Dandridge Burwell Reminiscences, 1918, DC Archives.

61. Tompkins, *History of Mecklenburg County,* 1:166; Jeffrey Crow, Paul Escott, and Flora Hatley, *A History of African Americans in North Carolina* (Raleigh: North Carolina Division of Archives and History, 1992), 153–54. The authors recount that "when Charles W. Chestnutt, the black novelist, arrived in Mecklenburg County in 1874 to teach summer school, he learned that local officials had expended all available school funds to erect a school house for blacks and had no money left to pay a teacher. Chesnutt found another black school located in a church, which 'was a very dilapidated log structure, without a window.'"

62. Alexander McIver, Letter to Cornelia Phillips Spencer, Collection: 468, Southern Historical Collection, University of North Carolina at Chapel Hill, 5; Shaw, *Davidson College,* 117.

63. Lucy Phillips Russell, Reminiscences, 5, DC0157s, Lucy Phillips Russell, Reminiscences, undated, DC Archives.

64. Ibid.; DC Faculty, Minutes, 16 October 1863 and 27 October 1865, RG 2/3.2, DC Archives.

65. Mary Scofield, Letter to Cornelia Shaw, 28 May 1920, DC0190s, Schofield Family Collection, 1883–1962, DC Archives.

66. Lucy Phillips Russell, Reminiscences, 5, DC0157s, Lucy Phillips Russell, Reminiscences, undated, DC Archives.

67. Anne Sampson, Letter to Cornelia Shaw, 8 July 1920, DC0156s, Anne E. Sampson Reminiscences, 1920, DC Archives.

68. DC Faculty, Minutes, 1 May 1871, RG 2/3.2, DC Archives; McIver, "Reminiscences"; Clifton Hunter, Letter to Mother, 20 December 1874, Lemuel C. Wheat & Thomas C. Hunter Papers, 1837–97, Special Collections, Perkins Library, Duke University, Durham, NC; Winn, "Davidson from 1867 to 1869," 299.

69. Clifton Hunter, Letter to Mother, 25 May 1875, Lemuel C. Wheat & Thomas C. Hunter Papers, 1837–97, Special Collections, Perkins Library, Duke University, Durham, NC

70. DC Trustees, Minutes, 9 July 1861, RG 1/1, DC Archives; Duncan Buie, Letter to Miss Kate, 7 January 1860, Catherine McGeachy Buie Papers, 1819–99, Special Collections, Perkins Library, Duke University, Durham, NC; James Logan Greenlee, Letter to Pa, 22 January 1860, DC0115s. James Logan Greenlee Letters, 1859–62, DC Archives.

71. Powell, *North Carolina*, 388; Joseph K. Rankin, Letter to Friend, 5 January 1869, William Dickson Papers, Southern Historical Collection, University of North Carolina at Chapel Hill; William Withers, Letter to Mollie, 13 January 1875, Letter in private possession.

72. H.E. Fries, Letter to Mother, 12 November 1876, DC0029s, Henry Elias Fries Papers, 1874–77, DC Archives.

Chapter 3. The Town Incorporates and Grows, 1879–1900

1. North Carolina, *Laws and Statutes of the State of North Carolina Passed by the General Assembly at Its Session 1878–79* (Raleigh, 1879).

2. Advertisements, *Davidson College Enterprise*, 22 June 1883, 3–4.

3. Town of Davidson, Minutes, 17 February 1879 and 1 April 1879, DC074, DC Archives.

4. Town of Davidson, Minutes, 17 February 1879, DC074, DC Archives.

5. Town of Davidson, Minutes, 4 May 1894, DC074, DC Archives.

6. R.L. McConnell, "Recollections of Some Forty Years Ago," Clipping, DC0190s, DC Archives; *Davidson Monthly*, November 1886, 2; October 1892, 44; December 1892, 165; November 1898, 107.

7. *Davidson Monthly*, January 1888, 22.

8. Town of Davidson, Minutes, 19 January 1891, DC074, DC Archives.

9. Town of Davidson, Minutes, 7 February 1891 and 11 April 1891, DC074, DC Archives; "Report from the General Assembly," *Landmark* (Statesville), 5 March 1891, 2; Journal of the House of Representatives of the General Assembly of the State of North Carolina at its Session of 1891 (Raleigh: Josephus Daniels, State Printer and Binder, 1891).

10. Powell, *North Carolina*, 440. Powell states, "A Mecklenburg County legislator, Sydenham B. Alexander in the late 1870s sponsored a good roads law in the

house of representatives, but when it finally passed it applied only to three counties including his own."

11. Town of Davidson, Minutes, 1 April 1879 and 5 May 1881, DC074, DC Archives. The changes to Main Street were to move it "so as to run on the East side of the R. Road from the R. Road crossing at the Irwin Lot to Mrs. Johnston's" (Town of Davidson, Minutes, 1 April 1879) and "straightened to a stake near R.J. Stough's store" (Town of Davidson, Minutes, 5 May 1881). The rock crosswalks were the same ones that Anne Sampson recalled with such trepidation.

12. R.G. Sparrow, "Waking Up," *The Weekly Enterprise*, 8 June 1883. Sparrow, grandson of both Thomas Sparrow and John Kirkpatrick, began the newspaper when he was fifteen years old. The Town Board was variously called Town Commissioners, Aldermen, and Board of Commissioners in the Minutes and in newspaper accounts.

13. Town of Davidson, Minute Book, "An Act Entitled 'An Act to Amend the Charter of the Town of Davidson College,'" 7 May 1877, 81, DC074, DC Archives. The revision provided for arbitration if the land owners and town could not agree on the price. *Davidson College Magazine*, February 1887, 31.

14. Town of Davidson, Minutes, 21 May 1887, 7 August 1887, 3 October 1887, 4 November 1887, 24 November 1887, and 3 April 1894, DC074, DC Archives. S.R. Neel was delegated to visit with the parties "opposing the charter or certain sections of it and find out on what grounds they will withdraw their opposition." He reported at the next meeting that "there was no extended objections except to certain portions of some sections of the new charter. The principle was that the college property had not been exempted from condemnation." Once the college had been accommodated, the charter moved forward.

15. *Davidson College Magazine*, April 1897, 286.

16. *Davidson Monthly*, November 1899, 89.

17. *Davidson Monthly*, October 1902, 42.

18. Town of Davidson, Minutes, 13 June 1886, DC074, DC Archives.

19. DC Faculty, Minutes, 26 September 1889, RG 2/3.2, DC Archives; Town of Davidson, Minutes, 12 March 1895 and 4 June 1895, DC074, DC Archives; Johnson, *David Played a Harp*, 24. The college had not necessarily been much ahead of the town in sanitary matters. The Trustee Minutes of 1883 record that work on a college privy had been delayed more than a year, and that Professors Hepburn and Martin did not have privies built for their homes until 1882 and 1883.

20. DC Faculty, Minutes, 25 February 1890 and 13 March 1890, RG 2/2.3, DC Archives; Town of Davidson, Minutes, 12 March 1890, DC074, DC Archives. The ordinance required that "each privy in town be furnished with boxes, according to the foll. specifications at the expense of the owner, 14 inches high, 14 inches square at top, 10 inches square at bottom, on base 14 inches square, the upper corners bound with hoop iron, and the box furnished with two strong handles." These boxes were to be emptied each week by the town with a tax of five cents per week from April to October for each privy.

21. Town of Davidson, Minutes, 7 May 1895, 15 June 1898, 7 July 1898, and 12 June 1899, DC074, DC Archives; *Davidson Monthly,* November 1898, 108; December 1898, 160; January 1899, 206; February 1899, 225.

22. Lingle, *Memories,* 67–68; DC Faculty, Minutes, 6 September 1898, RG 2/3.2, DC074, DC Archives.

23. Town of Davidson, Minutes, 5 July 1883, 14 April 1896, and 10 January 1899, DC 074, DC Archives.

24. "For Parts Unknown," *Weekly Enterprise,* 8 June 1883; "Two Colored Men in Trouble," *Weekly Enterprise,* 18 January 1884.

25. Town of Davidson, Minutes, 1 April 1879, DC074, DC Archives; David N. Laband and Deborah Hendry Heinbuch, *Blue Laws: The History, Economics, and Politics of Sunday-Closing Laws* (Lexington: D.D. Heath, 1987), 35–36.

26. Blythe, *Hornet's Nest,* 420.

27. Tompkins, *History of Mecklenburg County,* 1:181–83; Goldfield, "History," 62–63.

28. Beaty, *Davidson,* 69. Beaty records that J.G. Hood and J.W. Summers were brothers-in-law of one another and of Mr. Shelton. H.L. Smith would become J.J. Dupuy's son-in-law in 1897.

29. *Davidson College Magazine,* November 1891, 61; February 1892, 218.

30. *Davidson College Magazine,* January 1897, 163; December 1898, 160; October 1899, 43; Beaty, *History of Davidson College,* 69.

31. Tompkins, *History of Mecklenburg County,* 1:160. Tompkins notes that in 1900 "It is noticeable that as Mecklenburg has grown richer and more populous, the farms have increased in number and decreased in size. The average number of acres in a farm in the county is seventy-five. . . . There are 227,999 acres of land, and the 4,190 farms are occupied by 1,226 owners, 290 part owners, 22 owners and tenants, 55 managers, 631 cash paying tenants and 1,966 share tenants. Sixty percent of the farms are occupied by white people, and 40 percent, by colored people."

32. *Davidson College Magazine,* January 1890, 26; September 1890, 23; October 1892, 25; October 1892, 38; January 1895, 179; October 1896, 48; December 1898, 206; October 1899, 42.

33. *Davidson College Magazine,* January 1889, 23; October 1895, 21; November 1896, 91. For references to the post office, see *Davidson College Magazine,* October 1889, 33; November 1889, 28–29; December 1889, 27; January 1894, 165; November 1895, 64; November 1897, 107; January 1898, 230.

34. Dan L. Morrill, "Jim Crow Comes to Mecklenburg County," Charlotte-Mecklenburg Historic Landmarks Commission, http://www.cmhpf.org/education jimcrow.htm, 11 February 2003.

35. DC Trustees, Minutes, 19 June 1889, RG 1/1, DC Archives; "Locals," *Davidson College Magazine,* October 1892, 41.

36. Lingle, *Memories,* 43–44.

37. Tompkins, *History of Mecklenburg County,* 1:162–64.

38. DC Trustees, Minutes, 15 June 1881, RG 1/1, DC Archives; Beaty, *History of the Davidson College Presbyterian Church,* 4.

39. "About Heating the Church," *Davidson College Enterprise,* 18 January 1884, 1; *Davidson College Magazine,* December 1892, 162; Lingle, *Memories,* 135.

40. *Davidson College Magazine,* April 1887, 33; November 1887, 26; October 1888, 22; February 1889, 25; May 1891, 247.

41. "Separate Church: Colored Presbyterians Want One of Their Own," *Charlotte Democrat,* 27 May 1897, 1. The article reports that committee chair Dr. J.W. Bachman told the General Assembly that he believed that "the Presbyterian church, more than all others, should carry the Gospel to the negroes, not because the negro was inclined to Presbyterianism, but because he needed it on account of his natural superstition."

42. *Davidson College Magazine,* January 1892, 141.

43. Crow, Escott, and Hatley, *History of African Americans in North Carolina,* 97–98. On page 98 they note that "Between one third and one half of all black North Carolinians during this period belonged to churches." Reeves Temple Anniversary Book, DC0298s, Reeves Temple A.M.E. Zion Church Collection, 1993–94, DC Archives.

44. *Hopewell Baptist Church, 1879–1979* (Davidson: Briarpatch Press, 1979); *Davidson Monthly,* January 1889, 23; March 1890, 40; January 1891, 110.

45. *Davidson College Magazine,* November 1888, 24; May 1890, 35; May-June 1893, 402, December 1893, 120.

46. "Woman Question," *Charlotte Observer,* 27 May 1897, 1.

47. *Davidson College Magazine,* June 1889, 20; November 1898, 107; April 1892, 252.

48. Hanchett, *Sorting Out the New South City,* 76.

49. *Davidson College Magazine,* December 1893, 118–19; March 1894, 259–60; January 1893, 212.

50. *Davidson College Magazine,* December 1893, 118–19; November 1894, 83–84; January 1896, 149.

51. Ibid.

52. Ibid.

53. Lafferty, *North Carolina Medical College,* 5.

54. "Doors of the College Open," *Charlotte Democrat,* 1 April 1897, 1.

55. *Davidson College Magazine,* November 1899, 93; December 1899, 157.

56. "Octogenarian Recalls Grave-Robbing Past," *Davidsonian,* 18 November 1960, 4; DC Trustees, Minutes, 19 June 1899, RG 1/1, DC Archives.

57. They are Nora Little (18 years), Monroe Little (19 years), Margaret Howard (12 years), Nina Howard (10 years), Albert Caldwell (18 years), Mary Caldwell (14 years), Ann Caldwell (12 years), Damon Houston (18 years), James Cassius (16 years), and Aaron Henderson (14 years).

58. Flyer for Jurney School, 1880, Davidson, NC, Schools, DC0219s, DC Archives; *Davidson College Magazine,* May 1888, 27–28; October 1888, 21–22; Octo-

ber 1889, 33; December 1889, 26; January 1893, 210; January 1894, 164. There are several years missing for the Scotia College catalogs, so the list of students from Davidson is not complete.

59. Flyer for Jurney School, 1880, Davidson, NC, Schools, DC0219s, DC Archives; Beaty, *Davidson,* 63–64; *Davidson College Magazine*, December 1892, 163; October 1893, 34; March 1895, 284; February 1898, 312; January 1899, 206.

60. *Davidson College Magazine*, January 1893, 212.

61. *Davidson College Magazine*, April 1893, 353.

62. The Papers included "The Outline of the Story of Prometheus" by Hattie Thompson, "Mr. Browning's Translation" by Julia Dupuy, "Shelley's Prometheus Unbound" by Mary Martin, "Bryant's Prometheus" by Anna South, "An Outline of Longfellow's Pandora's Box" by Mamie Withers, and another on Longfellow's version of Prometheus by Emma Potts. *Davidson College Magazine,* November 1895, 69; March 1893, 297; January 1899, 207–8. Annie and Jennie Martin were not related. Annie's mother, Mrs. Murchinson, moved to Davidson when her son Hugh entered the class of 1893. See Theodora Penny Martin, *The Sound of Our Own Voices: Women's Study Club, 1860–1910* (Boston: Beacon Press, 1987), for more information on women's literary societies.

63. *Davidson College Magazine*, January 1890, 26; Knights of Pythias, Papers, DC0189s, DC Archives; "Notes from Alliances," *Progressive Farmer*, 5 June 1888; DC Faculty, Minutes, 6 October 1891, DC Archives.

64. Janette Thomas Greenwood, *Bittersweet Legacy: The Black and White "Better Classes" in Charlotte, 1850–1910* (Chapel Hill: University of North Carolina Press, 1994), 124–25.

65. For example, the December 1897 issue of the college magazine reported that "Dr. J.P. Munroe gave another one of his delightful entertainments on the evening of the 2nd., this time complimentary to the visiting ladies, Misses Brown, of Washington, and Montgomery, of Concord. Dr. Munroe's entertainments are always highly enjoyed, and this one proved proved no exception. Miss Brown was attired in yellow silk and pearls, while pink satin and diamonds graced Miss Montgomery. During the evening interesting geographical and musical games were introduced, after which the guests partook of a dainty repast" and that four days later "the gymnasium was the scene of a very profitable entertainment, at least from the King's Daughters' point of view. It was what is known as 'The Bazaar,' at which one could purchase things both useful and ornamental. The booths which were placed around the hall were made very attractive by the decorations and drapings of some of our talented young ladies. As one entered the door the lovely crimson and white candy booth was the first to attract. Miss Marshall Dupuy presided over this and found no difficulty in disposing of her confectionaries. Next was the blue and white baby booth with Misses Flowe, Sparrow, and Martin as the salesladies. Mrs. W.J. Martin and Miss Thompson occupied the corner, where they displayed all kinds of fancy

trinkets in a pink and white nook. Mrs. Smith and Miss Holt, under their green and white canopy exhibited their stock of household furnishings. Miss Mamie Withers, in her very becoming Japanese costume, served hot drinks. She was assisted by Miss Merle Dupuy, who was also dressed appropriately. The amount realized was much beyond expectation, and we think that this entertainment was one of the most satisfactory that the King's Daughters have devised in quite a while" (174–75).

66. *Davidson College Magazine*, February 1890, 26.

67. *Davidson College Magazine*, March 1890, 40. The next report of two events in one month did not occur until November 1892.

68. Ibid.

69. *Davidson College Magazine*, December 1892, 162; November 1896, 92; March 1893, 297; April 1897, 294; May 1898, 452.

70. *Davidson College Magazine*, March 1890, 41; May 1891, 247.

71. *Davidson College Magazine*, February 1893, 246; September 1895, 382; November 1896, 93; March 1897, 253.

72. *Davidson College Magazine,* May-June 1893, 403; March 1894, 263–64.

73. Lingle, *Memories*, 48; *Davidson College Magazine*, March 1889, 22; February 1892, 219; December 1893, 122.

74. *Davidson College Magazine*, September 1890, 25; October 1895, 20; January 1897, 164; March 1894, 263. By February 1898, the *Magazine* counted "ten or twelve of our town ladies who ride wheels," with Miss Minnie Scofield as the latest to acquire a bicycle (312).

75. "She Set the Town on It's Ear and Lived to be 103," undated clipping, Letitia Currie—Book Club Papers, Currie-Johnston Families Papers, dc076, dc Archives.

76. *Davidson College Magazine*, October 1887, 25–26; March 1890, 38; April 1890; 21 February 1887, 31; dc Faculty, Minutes, 21 October 1889 and 12 November 1886, dc Archives; Crow, *History of African Americans in North Carolina*, 106.

77. Davidson College, Catalogue, 1880, 16; *Davidson College Magazine*, February 1886, 30; Tompkins, *History of Mecklenburg County*, 2:195–96.

Chapter 4. Modern Conveniences, Traditional Social Patterns, 1901–1920

1. Examples of reports of women's travel include *Davidson Monthly,* December 1900, 132; April 1901, 45; May 1901, 115; October 1902, 43; *Davidsonian*, 25 November 1914, 1; 9 December 1914, 1; 23 August 1915, 4; 25 April 1917, 1.

2. H. Smith Richardson, Letter to Mamma, 23 February 1903, Transcript, Freshman Revolt of 1903, Davidsoniana File, dc Archives.

3. Ibid.

4. "Freshmen on Rampage: Serious Trouble at Davidson," *Charlotte Observer*, 14 February 1903, 3.

5. *Davidson College Magazine*, February 1901, 46.

6. Town of Davidson, *Minutes,* 29 August 1901, 12 August 1912, 31 August 1915, 10 August 1914, 12 August 1918, and 25 November 1920, DC074, DC Archives.

7. *Davidson College Magazine,* October 1901, 39; October 1911, 48; October 1902, 42; Town of Davidson, *Minutes,* 10 October 1911, DC074, DC Archives.

8. Town of Davidson, *Minutes,* 12 February 1912, DC074, DC Archives.

9. Town of Davidson, *Minutes,* 1–3 November 1909, DC074, DC Archives.

10. Town of Davidson, Minutes, 24 September 1917, DC074, DC Archives; *Davidsonian,* 3 October 1917, 4; George Rosen, *A History of Public Health* (Baltimore: Johns Hopkins University Press, 1993), 225, 439–40.

11. Town of Davidson, *Minutes,* 20 October 1915, DC074, DC Archives.

12. Town of Davidson, *Minutes,* 8 January 1904 and 1 July 1904, DC074, DC Archives; *Davidson College Magazine,* May 1904, 344; April 1908, 466. The Southern Power Company merged with Duke Power in 1935. DC Trustees, *Minutes,* 24 May 1906 and 27 May 1908, RG 1/1, DC Archives.

13. Town of Davidson, *Minutes,* 14 May 1917, DC074, DC Archives; *Davidsonian,* 25 October 1916, 1; 3 October 1917, 5.

14. "Store and Depot Robbed," *Davidsonian,* 19 May 1915, 6; "Testimony Taken in Jetton Case," *Charlotte Observer,* 21 February, 1914, 1; "Jetton Found Not Guilty of Murder," *Charlotte Observer,* 22 February 1914, 1.

15. "Serenity of Davidson is Rudely Disturbed," *Davidsonian,* 17 April 1918, 6; "Murder of Colored Man Occurs Near Campus," *Davidsonian,* 24 September 1919, 1.

16. "The Recent Growth & Development of Davidson," *Davidson College Bulletin*, October 1906, 5.

17. DC Trustees, Minutes, 31 May 1905 and 26 May 1909, RG 1/1, DC Archives; *Davidsonian,* 8 April 1914; Davidson Civic Club History, 23 February 1923, DC025, Davidson Civic Club Records, DC Archives.

18. According to the 1900 census, fifty-two women worked as washerwomen; in 1910, fifty women were either washerwomen or laundresses; and in 1920, the number dropped to forty-four. Judy Graham was the only woman listed as working in the laundry; the remaining women were listed as working at home.

19. "Shall We Adopt Hoover's Meatless Day?" *Davidsonian,* 17 October 1917, 3.

20. *Davidson College Magazine,* May 1904, 344; February 1907, 223; "Dr. Smith Speaks to Leaders of Town," *Davidson Observer (Davidsonian),* 8 March 1923, 1.

21. *Davidson College Magazine,* October 1908, 50; *Davidsonian,* 7 October 1914, 3; 28 February 1917, 1.

22. Town of Davidson, *Minutes,* 21 February 1912 and 20 October 1915, DC074, DC Archives; *Davidsonian,* 23 August 1915, 1; Advertisement for Flyless Restaurant, 15 September 1915, 4; Advertisement for Davidson Kandy Kitchen, 10 September 1919, 3. Ads ran for both the Flyless and Elliott cafés until September 1916. In October 1916, Smiley Washam opened the Red and Black Café, which also offered "motor service." The last advertisement for the Red and Black Café appeared in the 15 November 1916 *Davidsonian*. No further ads appeared for any cafés or

restaurants for the remainder of the school year. It is not clear whether the cafés closed or simply did not purchase advertisements.

23. "Movies, Saturday Night," *Davidsonian,* 29 March 1916, 2; *Davidsonian,* 16 April 1916, 4; 10 May 1916, 6.

24. "Movies Galore," *Davidsonian,* 4 December 1919, 3, 8.

25. "Town News," *Davidsonian,* 6 May 1914, 1; "Interesting Town News of the Week," *Davidsonian,* 25 November 1914, 1.

26. "'Colonel' Scofield to Discontinue Business," *Davidsonian,* 8 December 1915, 1; "Colonel Scofield Passes to His Reward," *Davidsonian,* 9 May 1917; *Davidsonian,* 15 January 1919, 2; 5 February 1919, 3.

27. *Davidson Monthly,* May 1901, 115; *Davidsonian, 13* October 1915, 4.

28. *Davidson Monthly,* December 1907, 202; DC Trustees, Minutes, 21 May 1908, RG 1/1, DC Archives; "Cotton Mill Builds New Addition to Plant," *Davidsonian,* 26 September 1917, 1; 11 November 1914, 1.

29. Powell, *North Carolina,* 457–58.

30. *Davidson Monthly,* November 1901, 54–55.

31. Quoted in Hanchett, *Sorting Out the New South,* 120.

32. Johnson, *David Played a Harp,* 5.

33. "Uncle Hiram," *Davidsonian,* 31 January 1917, 4; "Uncle Hiram's Grave Soon to Be Marked," *Davidsonian,* 7 March 1917, 2.

34. "Illustrated lecture on Negro Problem," *Davidsonian,* 13 February 1918, 1.

35. "A Need, An Opportunity, A Privilege" Flyer, 8 February 1953, Calvary Presbyterian Church in Davidson, Davidsoniana File, DC Archives; Mrs. J.W. Brown, "Calvary Presbyterian Church, Davidson, North Carolina History," Unpublished ms., Calvary Presbyterian Church in Davidson, Davidsoniana File, DC Archives.

36. "Davidson Vital Statistics," *Davidsonian,* 15 January 1915, 1; 26 January 1916, 3; 31 January 1917, 4.

37. "Davidson to Have Clean-Up Day Tuesday," *Davidsonian,* 4 April 1917, 3.

38. *Davidsonian,* 3 October 1917, 4; "Mass Meeting Hears Address on 'Health,'" *Davidsonian,* 3 October 1917, 6; Z.K. Justice Papers, 1914–32, DC0307s, DC Archives.

39. "Flue Has Vanished from Davidson Campus," *Davidsonian,* 23 October 1918, 1.

40. "Miss Rose Stevenson," *Davidsonian,* 23 October 1918, 2.

41. "'Flu' Situation In Town Continues to Improve," *Davidsonian,* 6 November 1918, 1.

42. "Town News," *Davidsonian,* 29 January 1920, 2; "Flu Cancels," *Davidsonian,* 12 February 1920, 1; "Town News," *Davidsonian,* 12 February 1920, 5; "Quarantine Again Prevents Bible Classes and Sunday Schools," *Davidsonian,* 19 February 1920, 3.

43. Johnson, *David Played*; Davidson, 31.

44. Davidson Civic Club, Annual Report 1917, Civic League Records, DC025, Davidson Civic Club Records, DC Archives.

45. "Merchant of Venice Great Success," *Davidsonian,* 29 April 1914, 1. The revised version of the play used references to Davidson football and Henry Louis Smith's X-rays.

46. "Town News," *Davidsonian,* 29 April 1920, 7; Town of Davidson, Minutes, 30 March 1920, 29 April 1920, and 13 May 1920, DC Archives; Beaty, *History of Davidson College,* 171.

47. *Davidson College Magazine,* October 1913, 32.

48. "Town News," *Davidsonian,* 6 May 1914, 4; "Night School Organized," *Davidsonian,* 19 February 1915, 1; "Town News," *Davidsonian,* 24 March 1915, 1.

49. "Large Audience Hears Ex-Gov. Patterson," *Davidsonian,* 23 January 1918, 1; "Honorable W.J. Bryan Visits Davidson Campus: Forceful Address Made before SATC and Townspeople," *Davidsonian,* 23 October 1918, 1; "An Address Given on Woman Suffrage," *Davidsonian,* 6 December 1916, 2.

50. "Chautauqua to entertain Davidson's Citizens for First Time," *Davidsonian,* 17 September 1920, 7.

51. Town of Davidson, Minutes, 17 June 1920, DC074, DC Archives. "Dr Jno. W. MacConnell appeared before the board in behalf of the Community Supper to be served June 9th 1920 and it was moved and carried that the town donate ($25.00) twenty-five dollars to the expenses of the same."

52. "Citizen's Club Organized," *Davidsonian,* 24 January 1917, 3.

53. Don Moser, "At 75 the Boy Scouts still answer to the call of adventure," *Smithsonian,* July 1985, 33.

54. *Davidsonian,* 8 April 1914, 1; 18 November 1914, 1; "Local Boy Scouts," *Davidsonian,* 15 November 1916, 4.

55. "Many Civic Club Improvements," *Davidsonian,* 1 April 1914, 1; "The Davidson Civic League," *Davidsonian,* 6 May 1914; Civic Club of Davidson, Annual Reports 1913, 1914, 1917; Cornelia Shaw to Mrs. John W. Petty, 1 May 1918, DC025, Davidson Civic Club Records, DC Archives; "Entertainment Given by Civic League," *Davidsonian,* 2 February 1916, 2.

56. "Local Happenings During the Week," *Davidsonian,* 21 April 1915, 1; "Town News," *Davidsonian,* 24 November 1915, 3; 22 March 1916, 1; 25 October 1916, 1; 17 January 1917, 1; 20 January 1920, 6; "Mrs T.W. Lingle Active in Social Welfare Work," *Davidsonian,* 29 April 1920, 7.

57. Cornelia Shaw to Mrs. John W. Petty, 1 May 1918, DC025, Davidson Civic Club Records, DC Archives; "Red Cross News," *Davidsonian,* 24 April 1918, 5.

58. "Red Cross News," *Davidsonian,* 6 February 1918; "Excellent Program at Red Cross Concert," *Davidsonian,* 13 March 1918, 1; "Red Cross News," *Davidsonian,* 27 March 1918, 5.

59. Cornelia Shaw, *War Record Davidson College, 1917–1918* (Charlotte: Presbyterian Standard, 1923).

60. "Two Carloads of Coal Will Be Secured," *Davidsonian,* 23 January 1918, 3.

61. "President Woodrow Wilson Visits His First Alma Mater," *Davidsonian,* 1 June 1916, 1; "Address Next Tuesday," *Davidsonian,* 6 February 1918, 1.

Chapter 5. The Relatively Prosperous 1920s and the Depressed 1930s

1. Parker interview.

2. Town of Davidson, Minutes, 25 September 1933, DC074, DC Archives.

3. Town of Davidson, Minutes, 7 August 1933, 14 August 1933, 4 September 1933, and 12 September 1933, DC074, DC Archives. The first Fire Department consisted of E.N. Linker (Day Chief), J.F. Riley (Night Chief), F.D. Hobart (Assistant Chief), A.N. Adams (driver), and firemen W.A. Thompson, Frank Wilson, Oscar Gant, J.C. Washam, A.C. Knox, O.J. Thies, Jr., Dick Mauney, Rufus Reid, Lester Hannah, Legette Fidler, M.P. Henderson, A.F. Bolick, J. Lore, Howard Shelton, R.D. Mooney, and W.B. Evans. The fire limits were set as "from the alleyway on the south side of Mrs. M.A. Henderson's property on Main Street to the south side of the Civic League Hall on Main Street and on Depot Street from the Southern Depot to the intersection of Main."

4. "New Road Delayed by Lack of Material," *Davidsonian,* 19 October 1922, 5; "D.C. Highway Already Important Auto Road," *Davidsonian,* 15 November 1923, 1. The important towns were Charlotte and Statesville.

5. Town of Davidson, Minutes, 23 May 1940, DC074, DC Archives. Full statement, "BE IT RESOLVED: that the Town Commissioners having in mind the growing menace of the through traffic through Main Street of the town, and that the project now in operation on the part of the State Highway Authorities, involving the widening of Highway Number 21, which runs along the Town's Main street throughout its entire length, not only will fail to afford adequate relief from the existing serious condition, but will result in the destruction of valuable shade trees in town, damage to existing sidewalks and to valuable lots, do hereby heartily approve of the alternative proposal made by citizens of the town and advocated by Davidson College, viz. to construct a new link or by-pass west of the town."

6. "Davidson Suffering from Severest Drought in Years," *Davidsonian,* 5 October 1922; Town of Davidson, Minutes, 10 April 1922, 19 April 1922, 27 May 1922, 9 August 1922, and 11 October 1922, DC074, DC Archives.

7. "Bonds Give Davidson Municipal Waterworks," *The Davidson Observer,* 22 February 1923, 1; "Bonds Issue Provides Civic Improvements," *The Davidson Observer,* 29 March 1923, 1.

8. "Davidson Water System to Soon Be in Operation," *Davidsonian,* 20 December 1923, 6; Town of Davidson, Minutes, 10 June 1924, 27 June 1924, and 20 November 1936, DC074, DC Archives.

9. Town of Davidson, Minutes, 4 April 1932, DC074, DC Archives.

10. Town of Davidson, Minutes, 2 February 1925 and 2 August 1926, DC074, DC Archives.

11. Arbuckle had proven his interest in the town's sanitation even before coming to Davidson. The first time the college offered a teaching position to Arbuckle he refused because he thought the town's water system of wooden aboveground pipes was unhealthy for his family. He accepted a second offer after the pipes had been replaced. Logan interview.

12. Town of Davidson, Minutes, 7 May 1934, 9 July 1936, 20 February 1939, 1 May 1939, 3 May 1939, and 4 July 1939, DC074, DC Archives; "New Sewage Plant Attracts Interest: City Installs Experimental System," *Davidsonian,* 30 October 1935, 1.

13. Town of Davidson, Minutes, 17 December 1923, 4 February 1924, 30 May 1924, 5 April 1926, 5 July 1927, 6 December 1937, and 1 August 1938, DC074, DC Archives.

14. Town of Davidson, Minutes, 30 September 1922 and 29 March 1935, DC074, DC Archives.

15. Town of Davidson, Minutes, 5 October 1931, 6 December 1933, 2 April 1933, 10 November 1936, 5 April 1937, 27 March 1940, and 9 November 1936, DC074, DC Archives.

16. Town of Davidson, Minutes, 22 October 1923, 6 December 1933, 4 July 1938, and 7 November 1938, DC074, DC Archives.

17. Town of Davidson, Minutes, 20 November 1933, DC074, DC Archives.

18. "Louisiana Dormitory to Be Destroyed by CWA," *Davidsonian,* 10 January 1934, 3; "Louisiana, Historic Residence, Torn Down by CWA," *Davidsonian,* 31 January 1934; "Projects Carried Out by CWA in Davidson," *Davidsonian,* 31 January 1934, 1.

19. Town of Davidson, Minutes, 27 December 1933, 6 January 1933, 1 April 1935, and 2 December 1940, DC074, DC Archives.

20. "Survey and Research Report on the Davidson Colored School/Ada Jenkins Center," Charlotte-Mecklenburg Historic Landmarks Commission, www.cmhpf.org/surveys&rAdaJenkins.htm.

21. "'Y'Fund goes for Civic Hut," *Davidsonian,* 11 January 1940, 1; "Students Tell Colored Folks of Three Rs," *Davidsonian,* 24 October 1940, 3; "Davidson's Civic Club Helps Negro Center," *Davidsonian,* 30 January 1941, 3. "A meeting of the YMCA representatives in Negro work, the Civic Club representatives, and the colored Board of Control was held Monday afternoon. The purpose of the meeting was to determine future policies of the community center and generally plan for the coming season's activities. Application has been made to the WPA for two recreational workers to be supplied to this project."

22. Walter L. Lingle, Letter to C.E. McIntosh, 3 April 1837, RG 2/1.12, Presidents Office, Lingle, National Youth Administration, DC Archives.

23. Town of Davidson, Minutes, 4 May 1922, DC074, DC Archives; DC Trustees, Minutes, 30 May 1922 and 5 June 1923, RG 1/1, DC Archives. The sum of $750 was the equivalent of the taxable income of residences owned by the college.

24. Duke Endowment Year book No. 1: December 11, 1924 to and Including December 31, 1928, Charlotte, NC, Trustees of the Duke Endowment, 43.

25. Walter Lingle, President's Report to the Board of Trustees, 21 February 1934, RG 2/1.12, RG2/2, President, Annual Reports, DC Archives.

26. Walter Lingle, President's Report to the Board of Trustees, 2 June 1939, RG2/2, President, Annual Reports, DC Archives.

27. J.P. Munroe, Letter, 31 July 1923, DC0215s, Linden Manufacturing Company Papers, 1973–23, DC Archives.

28. "Survey and Research Report on The Davidson Cotton Mill," Charlotte Historic Landmark Commission, http:www.cmhpf.org/surveys/DavidsonCotton .htm; "Local Mill Now Being Sued," *Davidson Leader*, 12 December 1936, 1.

29. "County Is Quiet as Four Mills Keep Operating," *Charlotte Observer*, 11 September 1934, 2; "No Change in Textile Strike in This County," *Charlotte Observer*, 14 September 1934, 3; "County Strike Areas Quiet," *Charlotte Observer*, 15 September 1934, 1.

30. Town of Davidson, Minutes, 6 September 1934, DC074, DC Archives. The Minutes of 1 October show that "bills for feeding the special officers while on strike duty at the mills amounting to $38.50 were approved by the board and ordered paid."

31. "Factory to be Here," *Davidson Leader*, 22 October 1937, 1; "Lee Paper Firm to Build a Plant Here," *Davidsonian*, 20 October 1937, 3; "Fire at Lee Box Company," *Davidsonian*, 2 February 1938, 1.

32. "Conflagration Damages Johnson's Barber Shop," *Davidsonian*, 21 March 1934, 3.

33. "Norton's Barber Shop Prepared for Business," *Davidsonian*, 1 February 1933, 4.

34. "College and Town Improvements," *Davidsonian*, 2 September 1922, 2; Smiley's Advertisement, *Davidsonian*, 2 September 1922, 3.

35. "Maxwell Chambers Hotel Holds Informal Reception to Welcome Townspeople," *Davidsonian*, 25 September 1924, 1.

36. "Ford and Tractor Agency Established," *Davidsonian*, 22 February 1923; "Blue Establishes Chevrolet Agency," *Davidson Observer*, 22 March 1923; Henderson Filling Station advertisement, *Davidsonian*, 4 March 1926, 3; Town of Davidson, Minutes, 30 September 1922, 30 May 1924, and 10 December 1935, DC074, DC Archives.

37. "New Picture Show to Open Here Soon," *Davidsonian*, 11 March 1926, 1; "New Picture Opens Here Today," *Davidsonian*, 8 April 1926, 6; "Pictures Sponsored by 'Y' Discontinued," *Davidsonian*, 2 February 1928, 1; "Vitaphone Picture Shown in Davidson," *Davidsonian*, 2 May 1929, 1.

38. Johnson, *David Played*, 266.

39. "Tom Thumb Course To Be Opened Soon," *Davidsonian*, 18 September 1930, 3; "New Bowling Alleys Under Construction Near Davidson Bank," *Davidsonian*, 5 October 1938, 1; "Bowling Alley Changes Hands," *Davidsonian*, 8 February 1940, 1.

40. Town of Davidson, Minutes, 4 February 1935, DC074, DC Archives.

41. "Dr. Smith Speaks to Leaders of Town," *Davidson Observer*, 8 March 1923, 1.

42. "NRA Has Compliance Board at Davidson," *Davidsonian*, 27 September 1933, 6.

43. "Five Davidson Beauties Chosen ROTC Sponsors," *Davidsonian*, 13 October 1921, 1; "Armistice Day and Davidson Day Jointly Celebrated Last Friday," *Davidsonian*, 17 November 1921, 1. The explanation for the joint ceremony was that "the work of Davidson men during the recent war made it fitting that the founding of the college and the cessation of hostilities be jointly celebrated." "Mr. Hamilton Holt Speaks as Feature Event on Davidson-Armistice Day Bill," *Davidsonian*, 19 November 1922, 1.

44. "College Will Fittingly Observe Armistice Day," *Davidsonian*, 6 November 1924, 1; "Armistice Day is Locally Observed," *Davidsonian*, 13 November 1924, 1; "Automobile Races Feature Armistice Day In Charlotte," *Davidsonian*, 29 October 1925, 8.

45. "MacConnells Entertain Club," *Davidson Observer*, 8 February 1923, 8; "Town News," *Davidsonian*, 8 November 1923, 12; "Town News," *Davidsonian*, 10 April 1924, 8; "Davidson Students Plan to See European States," *Davidsonian*, 7 May 1925, 1; "Many Professors Spend Vacation in Travel and Study," *Davidsonian*, 15 September 1927, 8; "Dr. Lingle Sends Letter Citing Incidents of Trip," *Davidsonian*, 9 May 1929, 1.

46. Annie Mildred Lowery, "Growing up in Davidson: A Lifetime of Memories," Fall 2001, Davidson Reminiscence Project, http://www.davidson.edu/academic/psychology/MulthaupSite/DAVREMPRO/stories.htm.

47. "Martian Men Startle Audience in Radio Skit," *Davidsonian*, 2 November 1938, 5.

48. "Town News," *Davidsonian*, 19 October 1923, 8.

49. Town of Davidson, Minutes, 22 June 1931, 4 February 1935, and 4 October 1937, DC074, DC Archives.

50. "Junior Class Minstrel Is Progressing Rapidly" and "Aged Negro Speaks to Large Audience," *Davidsonian*, 9 December 1926, 7–8; "Aged Mammy Laid to Rest," *Davidsonian*, 23 October 1935, 3; "Reporter Collects Facts Concerning D.C. Janitors," *Davidsonian*, 8 April 1936, 3; "Colored Boys and Band Perform at Cambridge," *Davidsonian*, 24 November 1937, 3; "Students Welcomed by Negro's Usual Appeal," *Davidsonian*, 19 September 1934, 6; "Doc Charley Dies Following Quarter Century of Service," *Davidsonian*, 20 February 1935, 1.

51. "Excellent Progress Being Made at Colored Night School Conducted by Y," *Davidsonian*, 25 February 1921; "Street New Mill Pastor, " *Davidsonian*, 11 May 1938, 3; "Fall Program Is Begun for Negro Center," 10 October 1940; Women of the Church, Minutes, May 1925, DC023, DCPC Women of the Church Records, DC Archives; Civic Club, Minutes, 5 November 1940, DC025, Davidson Civic Club Records, DC Archives.

52. "YMCA Gift Fund Will Go to Unity Church this Year," *Davidsonian*, 6 December 1933, 1.

53. "Poor Housing Is Considered by Civic Club," *Davidsonian*, 2 November 1939, 6.

54. "YMCA Begins Civic Center," *Davidsonian*, 11 April 1940, 5; "Young Colored Folks Meet In McLean Hut," *Davidsonian*, 27 February 1941, 6.

55. In the Minutes for the women of the church, August 1921—the program was on "Dangerous Neighbors," including Christian Scientists, Romanists, and Mormons; October 1925—the program was on women of Africa "for so long in the hopeless darkness of cruel heathenism"; November 1925—after a discussion on Native Americans, a member "closed with a plea that we pay our debt to the red man by giving him Jesus Christ."

56. Women of the Church, Minutes, March 1922, DC023, DCPC Women of the Church Records, DC Archives; "Davidson College Church Approved by NC Synod," *Davidsonian*, 17 October 1929, 1.

57. "World's Greatest Evangelist Scorns Short Cut to Success," *Davidsonian*, 14 February 1924, 1.

58. "Men of Church Foster a Unique Organization," *Davidsonian*, 23 October 1924, 6; "Town News," *Davidsonian,* 27 October 1921, 5.

59. "YMCA Gift Fund Will Go to Unity Church this Year," *Davidsonian*, 6 December 1933, 1; "Oh Davidson," *Davidsonian,* 16 October 1930, 2; "Unity Church Sponsored Varied Program," *Davidsonian*, 15 March 1939, 5.

60. Town of Davidson, Minutes, 10 February 1922, DC074, DC Archives; Betty Schenck, Mary B. Erwin, and Elizabeth Cumming, Letter to Walter Lingle, 15 February 1939, RG 2/1.12, President's Office, Lingle, DC Archives.

61. "High School Building Erected During Summer," *Davidsonian,* 18 September 1924, 8; "Survey and Research Report on the Davidson Colored School/Ada Jenkins Center," Charlotte-Mecklenburg Historic Landmarks Commission, www.cmhpf.org/surveys&rAdaJenkins.htm.

62. "Town Tattle," *Davidsonian*, 23 October 1935, 3; "Negro School to Have Band," *Davidsonian*, 30 January 1941, 6.

63. "Around Town," *Davidsonian*, 17 April 1935, 3; Walter Lingle, Report to the Trustees, 11 November 1935 and 2 February 1939, RG 2/1.12, President's Office, Lingle, DC Archives.

64. "Around Town," *Davidsonian,* 2 May 1934, 3. We know more about the women's education because the Davidson College students paid attention to their comings and goings.

65. Scotia Womens College, *Annual Catalog*, 1920–39; "With the Alumni," *Ace Review*, 1938, 5.

66. "Red Cross to Start Drive November 6th," *Davidsonian,* 1 November 1933, 3.

Chapter 6. Moving Forward Slowly, 1941–60

1. "N.C. Drops to 45th Place in Per Capita Income in Nation," *Mecklenburg Gazette*, 27 August 1953, 6.

2. Puckett, *Olin, Oskeegum & Gizmo*, 304.

3. Johnson, *David Played*, 277–78; the quote is on page 278.

4. Merrell, *Soldiers and Sentinels*, 135. Cunningham told the student body shortly after the attack on Pearl Harbor: "Don't feel compelled to join the military [immediately]. Get all you can here."

5. See, for example, Cunningham to alumni, 2 April 1945, Box 10, Cunningham Papers, RG2/1.13, DC Archives.

6. C.K. Brown, "Memorandum on Faculty Salaries," 3 September 1945, 1, Box 13, Cunningham Papers, RG2/1.13, DC Archives.

7. David M. Kennedy, *Freedom from Fear: The American People in Depression and War, 1929–1945* (New York: Oxford University Press, 1999), 646.

8. Untitled financial statement, Davidson Cotton Mills, January 1945(?), Treasurer's Correspondence—General, 1940–48, Treasurer's Records, RG 4/3.2, DC Archives.

9. Examples of husbands/fathers who served include (among many others) Dr. John Woods and Charlie Parker. Blanche Parker recalled being upset that her husband chose to serve despite the fact that, with two small children, he was not required to. Parker interview. More detailed references to all interviews are in the Selected Bibliography.

10. "Town of Davidson Service Honor Roll," *Davidson News-Leader*, 30 October 1945, 5.

11. Merrell, *Soldiers and Sentinels*, 7.

12. Nationally, 16.4 million served and 407,000 died. See Michael Clodfelter, *Warfare and Armed Conflicts: A Statistical Reference to Casualty and Other Figures, 1500–2000*, 2nd ed. (Jefferson, NC: McFarland, 2002), 584.

13. "Thank You—," *Davidson College Bulletin* 41:9 (October 1942): 2.

14. *Post Exchange* 1:2 (April 1943[?]) and 1:9 (January 1944[?]).

15. Merrell, *Soldiers and Sentinels*, 146.

16. Blackwell interview.

17. Cashion interview.

18. Tish Kimbrough interview.

19. Untitled typewritten ms., April 1942(?), Box 31, Cunningham Papers, RG 2/.13, DC Archives.

20. Stough interview.

21. "Davidson Experiences Blackout on April 30," *Davidsonian*, 7 May 1942, 3.

22. Montgomery interview.

23. See, for example, Montgomery interview. As Montgomery notes, the Woodland/Lorimer area had several vegetable gardens.

24. Beaty, *History of Davidson College*, 321, note 5.

25. For discussions of keeping cows, see Martha Montgomery and Sandy Carnegie interviews; for evidence that Dr. Cunningham and Dr. Caleb Harding raised chickens, see J.R. Cunningham, Letter to R.E. Cashion, 23 August 1943; for comments on Dr. Cunningham's two horses, "Sarah Jane" and "Dan," see J.R. Cunningham, Letter to Mrs. Roy Willeford, 31 May 1945. Both letters are in Box 9, Cunningham Papers, RG 2/3.13, DC Archives.

26. *Post Exchange* 1:2 (February-March 1943).

27. *Post Exchange* 1:7 (January 1944).

28. John F. Cunningham, "For the Presbyterian News," Typewritten ms., 7 February 1944, Box 31, Cunningham Papers, RG 2/3.13, DC Archives.

29. Fund-raising letter from J.R. Cunningham, 19 December 1944, Box 31, Cunningham Papers, RG 2/3.13, DC Archives.

30. King interview.

31. Woods interview.

32. Federal Reserve Bank of Minneapolis, *What Is a Dollar Worth?* http://www.minneapolisfed.org/community_education/teacher/calc/hist1913.cfm. Accessed 15 July 2009. In 1945, $100 was worth approximately $1,200 in 2008 dollars.

33. Talmadge Connor, interviewed by Brian Campbell, 26 March 1999, Grundy Collection, Southern Historical Collection, UNC-Chapel Hill.

34. Tom Fesperson, "The Story of Davidson," *Charlotte News*, 25 September 1948. Reprinted in *Cornelius Davidson Gazette*, 7 October 1948.

35. "College Acquires New Housing Facilities," *Davidsonian*, 10 October 1947.

36. "Treasurer's Annual Report," Davidson College, 30 April 1947, 25; "Davidson College Budget Report, 1959–60," in Treasurer's Report; both in DC Archives.

37. John Cunningham, Letter to Aubrey Brown, 4 April 1950, Cunningham Papers, RG 2/3.13, DC Archives. A 1955 article in the *Davidsonian* about a janitor, Clint Torrence, noted sardonically that "Clint has carried on a life long experiment in the field of Social Economy, the title being 'How to raise eighteen children on thirty dollars a week.'" Andy Watson, "Ode to a Janitor," *Davidsonian*, 21 October 1955.

38. John Cunningham, Letter to Aubrey Brown, 4 April 1950, Cunningham Papers, RG 2/3.13, DC Archives.

39. Blackwell interview. In fairness to Cunningham, it is important to note that he wished that the college had had the funds to pay higher wages to hourly employees. As he wrote to Aubrey Brown in April 1950: "I do not feel comfortable as yet about their [hourly workers'] compensation as I do not feel comfortable about our faculty [compensation]."

40. James Howard, a young black man, helped to build Johnston Gym. He later worked as a lab assistant for the chemistry department. See Mel McKenzie, "James Howard Serves as the Stock Room Doc," *Davidsonian*, 29 April 1960. Howard's daughter, Brenda Tapia, worked at the college a generation later at the administrative level.

41. Cantrell interview.

42. "Davidson Cotton Mill Shuts Down," *Community*, 3 April 1947; Mrs. H.C. Broyles, "Idleness Forced Upon Workers," *Cornelius-Davidson Gazette*, 26 August 1948.

43. "Davidson Will Get New Fabric Plant," *Charlotte Observer*, 26 February 1955; "Machinery Being Installed in New Davidson Textile Plant; To Employ

100," *Gazette*, 28 April 1955; Bob Bradford, "Industries in Davidson Range From Cars to Cotton," *Davidsonian*, 27 February 1959.

44. "Carolina Asbestos Co. Completes $200,000 Addition to Plant," *Gazette*, 12 February 1953.

45. Meetze interview.

46. Brown interview; Blackwell and Fearington interview. Doodle Brown's given name was Smiley Walter Brown.

47. Stough interview.

48. Mary Fetter Stough, "The Fires of Davidson," Unpublished ms., 2006; "Southern Cotton Oil Name Being Dropped by Firm," *Gazette*, 15 August 1957; Bob Bradford, "Industries in Davidson Range from Cars to Cotton," *Davidsonian*, 27 February 1959.

49. Brown interview.

50. For a list of all the establishments—including three private residences—in the downtown in 1952, see "Plot Showing Numbering Plan for City of Davidson," revised 3 May 1952, Map collection, DC Archives.

51. Woods interview.

52. "Piedmont [Bank] and Trust Reports Gain," *Gazette*, 26 January 1950. Deposits nearly doubled to more than $2.1 million between 31 December 1948 and 31 December 1949, the *Gazette* reported.

53. "Closing Out Sale," Wrenn's Men's Shop, *Gazette*, 21 April 1950.

54. McArn interview. "Back then, hardly anybody owned, as far as I know," Elaine McArn commented.

55. Mabel Broyles, "Printing Firm History Tied to Mecklenburg Growth," *Mecklenburg Gazette*, 13 March 1967.

56. "Davidson Council Says Books Open to All Citizens," *Gazette*, 24 March 1955; "Statement of Publication," *Gazette*, 25 October 1956; "Is Southern Bell Telephone Company Discriminating Against North Mecklenburg?" *Gazette*, 24 January 1957; "Charlotte Phone Service to Be Offered to Cornelius and Davidson," *Gazette*, 20 June 1957.

57. Dick interview.

58. Fred Talbott, "Soda Shop a County Landmark," *Charlotte Observer*, 30 October 1976.

59. James Puckett described McKissick as "a kind man and the best leather worker I've ever met." Puckett, *Olin, Oskeegum & Gizmo,* 100. "Mr. McKissick always had time to talk to you," Elaine McArn recalls. McArn interview.

60. "Elvis' Influence is Fading in North Mecklenburg," *Mecklenburg Gazette*, 7 November 1957.

61. Puckett, *Olin, Oskeegum & Gizmo,* 90.

62. Thornburg interview.

63. Dick interview; Readling interview. The Western Auto Store, perhaps the town's first national chain store, opened in May 1950. "New Western Auto Associate Store to Open May 27 in Davidson," *Gazette*, 25 May 1950.

64. Al Mackay, "Whites Is New Center of Culture," *Davidsonian*, 28 September 1956.

65. McArn interview.

66. Malcolm Williamson, "Eye Witness Gives Account of Theater Fire Monday Night," *Davidsonian*, 17 February 1955. "I've never been in a burning building before," one fearless student commented as a reason for staying as long as possible.

67. Stough interview.

68. "Clean-Up Drive Is Launched by Davidson Students," *Gazette*, 6 April 1950.

69. Ratliff interview.

70. "Construction to Begin on St. Alban's Chapel," *Davidsonian*, 5 October 1956; "Davidson Baptist Mission Building New Church," *Mecklenburg Gazette*, 17 October 1957.

71. "Unity Church Dedicates Sunday School Building," *Gazette*, 15 December 1955.

72. "Many Improvements Made in North Meck Colored Schools," *Mecklenburg Gazette*, 28 November 1957. The story describes the addition as "four years old."

73. "New Davidson Post Office Among Finest in the U.S.; Open House Saturday Afternoon," *Mecklenburg Gazette*, 29 May 1958.

74. Puckett, *Olin, Oskeegum & Gizmo,* 106.

75. "New Development Is Accepted by Davidson Council," *Gazette*, 19 January 1956.

76. "Houses Bought for Improvement, Resale," *Gazette*, 16 November 1950.

77. "No Action Taken on Proposed Zoning Law for Davidson," *Gazette*, 9 May 1957; "Davidson Council Adopts Town Zoning Ordinance," *Gazette*, 18 July 1957.

78. J.R. Cunningham, Letter to W. Kerr Scott, 19 May 1952, Cunningham Papers, Box 34, RG 2/1.13, DC Archives.

79. M. Otis Poole, Letter to J.R. Cunningham, 18 September 1952; Scott, Letter to Cunningham, 2 December 1952; both in Cunningham Papers, Box 34, RG 2/1.13, DC Archives.

80. Quackenbush interview. Ralph Quackenbush moved to the area in 1959, and the rest of the family arrived in 1960.

81. J.R. Cunningham, Letter to D. Grier Martin, 28 February 1955, Cunningham Papers, Box 34, RG 2/1.13, DC Archives.

82. "Road to Connect Davidson to New Highway to Be Built," *Gazette*, 20 October 1955.

83. "Davidson Town Board Approves Highway Widening," *Mecklenburg Gazette*, 9 April 1959.

84. D. Grier Martin, Letter to Town of Davidson, 14 March 1959, Grier Martin Papers—Davidson (town), RG 2/1.14, DC Archives.

85. "Davidson Property Assessed at More than $3 Million," *Mecklenburg Gazette*, 19 December 1957.

86. Town of Davidson, Minutes, 17 July 1946 and 28 July 1960, DC074, DC Archives.

87. For a request to increase the college's "appropriation" to the town in lieu of real estate taxes, see E.A. Beaty, Letter to J.R. Cunningham, 5 December 1947 Papers; for the request for help in buying a new fire truck, see E.A. Beaty, Letter to J.R. Cunningham, 20 February 1951; both in Cunningham Papers, Box 10, RG 2/1.13, DC Archives; for the college's decision to loan the town $15,000 at no interest to help build the new town hall/fire station, see D. Grier Martin, Letter to F.J. Jackson, 6 September 1960, Martin Papers—Davidson (town), RG 2/1.14, DC Archives.

88. "7 Davidson Boys Brought Before Mayor's Court," *Mecklenburg Gazette*, 20 November 1958.

89. Thornburg interview.

90. For vandalism, see "Letter to Editor Tells of Vandalism at Bovaird Plant in Davidson," *Gazette*, 12 January 1956. For thefts, see "Supply of Narcotics Stolen from White's Drug Store," *Davidsonian*, 4 November 1949; "Burglars Enter Davidson Store," *Gazette*, 21 July 1949; "Negro Youth Caught Robbing Watts Dorm," *Davidsonian*, 9 February 1951; "Linker's Hunch Pays Off; Fields Awaits Jury Action," *Davidsonian*, 12 February 1954.

91. "Davidson Mayor Requests Residents to Keep Dogs Up," *Gazette*, 14 June 1951; "Mayor Says Dogs Must Be Curbed," *Mecklenburg Gazette*, 21 July 1960. All quotations are from the first article.

92. Readling interview.

93. Ibid.

94. "Davidson Maps War on Lawless Driving," *Charlotte Observer*, 18 September 1955.

95. "Local Safety Council Posts Traffic Signals," *Davidsonian*, 11 January 1957.

96. "Davidson Traffic Laws Should Be Enforced by Local Police Department," *Gazette*, 7 March 1957.

97. Ibid.

98. Porter Munn, "Davidson Approves First Zoning Plan," *Charlotte Observer*, 16 July 1957.

99. McArn interview.

100. "Negro House Collapses," *Cornelius Davidson Gazette*, 26 August 1948.

101. Kelton interview.

102. "Sabbath Blaze Levels Home; Clothes Requests Answered," *Davidsonian*, 24 February 1950; "Brady's Alley May Not Be Far From Your House," *Presbyterian Outlook*, 27 March 1950, 4–5. The reference to the eighty-seven people living in eleven houses is on page 4.

103. The members of the committee were F.W. Frederickson, J.F. Pinckney, Thomas Sadler, J.V. Lore, William Withers, and J.F. Harkness, "Town Meeting Forms Holding Company to Meet Local Problems," *Davidsonian*, 3 March 1950.

104. Town of Davidson, Minutes, 17 April 1950, DC074, DC Archives.

105. "$6,744 Contributed to Housing Fund," *Gazette*, 21 December 1950.

106. "Citizens Committee Makes Report; New Homes to Be Constructed," *Gazette*, 11 May 1950.

107. Ibid.

108. Ibid.

109. Henry Hansen, "Christian Ideals Brought to Life Through Gift Fund," *Davidsonian*, 3 December 1950.

110. "Seek $2,500 from Davidson Citizens for Negro Housing," *Gazette*, 14 December 1950.

111. "$6,744 Contributed to Housing Fund," *Gazette*, 21 December 1950.

112. For example, Professor Edwin F. Shewmake, in a letter to Pritchett on 6 January 1947, wrote that Pritchett's "position on the race question," as reflected in a recent sermon, was "dangerously extreme." Shewmake, Letter to Carl Pritchett, 6 January 1947, Cunningham Papers, Box 31, RG 2/1.13, DC Archives.

113. Parker interview.

114. Cantrell interview.

115. Ostwalt interview.

116. McArn interview.

117. The man quoted, George Hampton, lived on Walnut Street. Jane Schenck, "A Cantankerous Spirit," Unpublished ms., 2007.

118. Belle Banks, "Meanderin . . . ," *Mecklenburg Gazette*, 1 June 1961.

119. McClain interview.

120. See, for example, Bob Majors, "Tribute to a Janitor," *Davidsonian*, 13 January 1956.

121. Tish Kimbrough interview.

122. King interview.

123. Quoted in Mary Fetter Stough, "Davidson Memories," Unpublished ms., 2006.

124. Garfield Carr, interview by Jill E. Neumayer in 2001, Grundy Collection, Southern Historical Collection, UNC-Chapel Hill Library.

125. "Colored Activities," *Gazette*, 20 September 1956.

126. Montgomery interview.

127. Logan interview.

128. "Billy Graham to Speak; Overflow Crowd Expected," *Davidsonian*, 7 December 1956. In addition to this talk at the Davidson College Presbyterian Church, Graham spoke in Chambers Auditorium in October 1958.

129. Town of Davidson, Minutes, 19 September 1947, DC074, DC Archives.

130. "Davidson Presbyterian was the elite church," Roosevelt Wilson recalled. "It was the biggest church; it was the most popular church." Wilson interview.

131. Readling interview.

132. Park interview.

133. Quoted in Timberlake, "Trapped by Tradition," 40.

134. Ken Norton, interview by Brian Campbell, 23 March 1999, Grundy Collection, Southern Historical Collection, UNC-Chapel Hill Library.

135. "Lions to Celebrate Ladies' Night; Will be Gala Affair," *Gazette*, 9 February 1950; "Davidson Lions Club . . . Eleven Years of Community Service," *Gazette*, 29 March 1956.

136. "Dr. Guerrant Speaks to Davidson Lions," *Gazette*, 13 May 1954.

137. "Davidson Lions Club . . . Eleven Years of Community Service," *Gazette*, 29 March 1956.

138. "Broom Sale Report," *Gazette*, 28 September 1950.

139. "Davidson School Is On Accredited List," *Gazette*, 9 November 1950.

140. Advertisement for the Davidson P.T.A. Halloween Carnival, *Gazette*, 27 October 1949.

141. "Founder's Day Program Scheduled for Davidson P.T.A.," *Gazette*, 15 February 1951.

142. "North Mecklenburg Communities Are Ready for Mothers' March of Dimes," *Gazette*, 29 January 1953; "North Mecklenburg Tops Goal in United Appeal Drive," *Gazette*, 20 October 1955.

143. "316 Pints Donated in Drive; Workers Named," *Mecklenburg Gazette*, 5 May 1960.

144. A list of the 1954–55 hosts for "The Fat, Fair and Forty Square Dance Club," D. Grier Martin—Personal—Misc. Correspondence, 1952–57, D. Grier Martin Papers, RG 2/1.14, DC Archives.

145. Avis Johnson, "Colored Activities," *Gazette*, 1 November 1951.

146. "Colored Activities," *Gazette*, 27 November 1952.

147. "Christian Aid and Benevolent Society Dates to 1905," *Mecklenburg Gazette*, 19 July 1979.

148. Archie interview.

149. Garfield Carr interview, Grundy Collection, UNC-Chapel Hill.

150. "Many Improvements Made in North Mecklenburg Colored Schools," *Mecklenburg Gazette*, 28 November 1957.

151. Wilson interview.

152. Lawrence Kimbrough interview.

153. Blackwell interview.

154. "Two New Teachers at Davidson School," *Gazette*, 12 September 1957.

155. Montgomery interview.

156. Woods interview.

157. Dick interview.

158. Cumming interview.

159. Brown interview.

160. Blackwell interview.

161. Carnegie interview. "I had several white friends," Garfield Carr recalled. Garfield Carr interview, Grundy Collection, UNC-Chapel Hill.

162. Schenck interview.

163. Mary and Sterling Martin interview.

164. Garfield Carr interview, Grundy Collection, UNC-Chapel Hill.

165. Dick interview.

166. Brown interview.

167. Woods interview.

168. Franklin Bloodworth, "Negro Community Hut Is Almost Completed," *Davidsonian*, 19 October 1954.

169. "David McLean Center to be Dedicated Sunday," *Davidsonian*, 19 November 1954; Alice Reid, "Colored Activities," *Gazette*, 6 January 1955.

170. John Hobard, "On Erwin Lodge," *Community*, 15 May 1947.

171. A statistical breakdown of the use of the inside of the lodge is contained in Edward J. Erwin, Letter to J.C. Cunningham, 8 October 1951, Cunningham Papers, Box 13, RG 2/1.13, DC Archives.

172. Montgomery interview.

173. McArn interview.

174. "Davidson Lions Club Sponsors Annual Egg Hunt Saturday," *Mecklenburg Gazette*, 26 March 1959; "Scouts Join Service Frat," *Davidsonian*, 14 December 1951.

175. "Davidson Canteen Expected to Begin Operations in June," *Gazette*, 28 April 1955.

176. "Davidson Council Holds Regular Monthly Meeting," *Gazette*, 21 April 1955.

177. "Davidson Canteen to Open Saturday; Needs Furniture," *Gazette*, 16 June 1955.

178. "Rules Announced for Davidson's Teen-Canteen," *Gazette*, 20 September 1956.

179. "Davidson Canteen Providing Youth with Entertainment," *Gazette*, 3 October 1957.

180. "Teen Canteen at Davidson Answers Activity Problem," *Charlotte Observer*, 6 April 1960.

181. Ibid.

182. Ratliff interview.

183. McArn interview.

184. Stough interview.

185. Schenck interview.

186. Quackenbush interview.

187. Stough interview.

188. McArn interview.

189. Stough, "Davidson Memories."

190. Readling interview.

191. An exception was made for Ralph Johnson, who was allowed to sit in the projection booth to watch movies.

192. Town of Davidson, Minutes, 1 October 1945, DC074, DC Archives.

193. "Integration of Public Schools?" *Gazette*, 25 July 1957; "Readers Say Gazette Renders Valuable Service to Community," *Mecklenburg Gazette*, 19 September 1957.

194. On the general public passivity of blacks—including Davidson's black churches—during this era, see Timberlake, "Trapped by Tradition."

195. J.R. Cunningham, Letter to L. Maynard Catchings, 16 April 1954, Cunningham Papers, Box 19, RG 2/1.13, DC Archives.

196. "Local Officials Give Views on Supreme Court Segregation Ruling," *Gazette*, 20 May 1954.

197. J.R. Cunningham, Letter to J. Nat Hamrick, 31 August 1954, Cunningham Papers, Box 19, RG 2/1.13, DC Archives.

198. Brenda Tapia, telephone interview by Ralph Levering, 24 August 2010.

199. Spencer interview.

200. Ratliff interview.

201. Tapia telephone interview.

202. J.C. Cunningham, "Dear Friends and Neighbors," *Gazette*, 2 August 1956.

203. E.A. Beaty, C.A. Potts, T.E. Lothery, T.S. Sadler, E.T. McEver, and F.L. Jackson, Letter to J.R. Cunningham, 6 August 1956, Cunningham Papers, Box 10, RG 2/1.13, DC Archives.

204. J.R. Cunningham, Letter to Grier Martin and Sam Spencer, 5 December 1956; Malcolm C. McIver, Jr., Letter to J.R. Cunningham, 4 January 1957; both in Cunningham Papers, Box 10, RG 2/1.13, DC Archives.

205. J.R. Cunningham, Letter to B. Tartt Bell, 3 August 1956, Cunningham Papers, Box 10, RG 2/1.13, DC Archives.

206. "Segregation: Symposium of a Southern College," *Davidsonian*, 19 November 1954.

207. Jim Armistead, "Implications of Segregation Presentation Analyzed, Criticized," *Davidsonian*, 9 March 1956.

208. C.K. Brown, "The Southern Position with Respect to the Bi-Racial System; An Address Delivered to the Students of Davidson College, March 1, 1956," C.K. Brown Speeches, RG 3/1.1, DC Archives.

209. Maloney interview.

210. Frank E. Parker, Letter to Frederick W. Hengeveld, 16 April 1958, Martin Papers, Integration—Policy, etc., RG 2/1.14, DC Archives. The reference to Parker's class standing, "first in a class of 73," is in a letter from Grier Martin to J. McDowell Richards, 13 November 1958, Martin Papers, Integration—Policy, etc., RG 2/1.14, DC Archives.

211. Statement by Grier Martin, 6 October 1959, Martin Papers, Integration—Policy, etc., RG 2/1.14, DC Archives.

212. "Should Davidson Admit Negroes?" *Davidsonian*, 9 March 1959.

213. "Student Poll Reveals Views on Segregation," *Davidsonian*, 16 February 1960.

214. W.G. Workman, Letter to the Members of the Faculty, 8 December 1959, Martin Papers, Integration—Policy, etc., RG 2/1.14, DC Archives.

215. Statement signed by thirty-five Davidson College employees, mostly faculty, 8 January 1960, Martin Papers, Integration—Policy, etc., RG 2/1.14, DC Archives.

Chapter 7. The Times Were Changing, 1961–1984

1. "Residents Laud Town Committee," *Mecklenburg Gazette*, 13 June 1968.

2. To the surprise of many residents, Republicans came to power in county elections in 1966, partly as a reaction against racial integration and Lyndon Johnson's Great Society programs.

3. "Downtown Stores Renovate," *Davidsonian*, 3 February 1967.

4. "Mild Ordinance Gets Approval," *Mecklenburg Gazette*, 24 July 1974.

5. Tom Ratchford offered this insight in a conversation with Ralph Levering on 16 November 2009. He pointed out that the increased use of air conditioning may have led to a decline in neighborliness, because residents tended to stay inside on summer afternoons and evenings rather than sitting in their yards or on their porches where they could talk with neighbors.

6. For a photo and brief description of the ribbon-cutting ceremony that opened the final nine-mile stretch of I-77 in North Carolina, see "Interstate 77 Opening," *Mecklenburg Gazette*, 7 January 1976.

7. Karen Haywood, "Cable TV Winds Way toward Davidson, North Mecklenburg," *Mecklenburg Gazette*, 10 June 1982.

8. For annexation, see, for example, Francis Ghigo, "Davidson Town Board Takes in Three Tracts," *Mecklenburg Gazette*, 22 November 1979. For one of many Town Board discussions of perimeter zoning, see Town of Davidson, Minutes, 18 July 1977, DC074, DC Archives.

9. John Ruppenthal, "Greyhound to Discontinue Stop," *Davidsonian*, 25 March 1983.

10. General Time employed roughly 700 people in 1967, far more than the college. See "Davidson-Cornelius Economy Is on Up-Swing!" *Mecklenburg Gazette*, 23 November 1967.

11. The town's population figures for 1960 and 1980, cited here and in the following paragraph, are available in published U.S. census volumes available in the Davidson College library. Enrollment figures can be found in Davidson College catalogs for particular academic years, available in the college archives.

12. Betty Cumming, "The New Davidson," *Davidson College Bulletin* (June 1969): 2–10.

13. The letter, dated 5 February 1961, is located in "Martin—Integration—Policy, etc.," Grier Martin Papers, RG 2/1.14, DC Archives. "It would be a great tragedy for the Southern Presbyterian Church," the missionaries argued, "to propagate the gospel in Congo for seventy years and then see its message repudiated because of racial prejudices within the Church."

14. Richmond Blake, "The Long Haul: Integration of Davidson College," *Davidsonian*, 27 February 2008.

15. "Resolution Adopted by the Trustees of Davidson College, May 17, 1962," Grier Martin Papers, "Integration—Policy, etc.," RG 2/1.14, DC Archives.

16. "College to Accept American Negroes," *Mecklenburg Gazette*, 21 May 1964.

17. For Martin's awareness of the link between having black students and qualifying for a Ford Foundation grant, see F.W. Johnston to President Martin, 5 October 1961; Martin to James W. Armsey, 25 May 1964; and Martin to James W. Armsey, 21 September 1964; "Foundation Ford 1961–64," all in Martin Papers, RG 2/1.14, DC archives. We are grateful to Loretta Wertheimer for bringing these documents to our attention and pointing out their significance.

18. "Davidson Receives a Challenge Grant of $2,000,000 from Ford," *Mecklenburg Gazette*, 24 June 1965.

19. Ostwalt interview.

20. Bob Reid, "'Hasn't Exactly Been Easy,'" *Davidsonian*, 1 December 1967.

21. William Brown, talk in History 256 class at Davidson College, 15 October 2009.

22. Stough interview. Stough remembered hearing an older woman in town say "Thank goodness!" in response to King's death.

23. "Officials Urge Band to Drop 'Dixie,'" *Davidsonian*, 30 September 1966.

24. Nicholls interview.

25. Bob Reid, "Hasn't Been Exactly Easy," *Davidsonian*, 1 December 1967.

26. "Black Students Enrolling at Davidson, 1964–1977," in Spencer—Admissions—Minority Recruitment," Samuel Spencer Papers, RG 2/1.15, DC Archives. Working in the admissions department in the summer of 1969, Calvin Murphy helped to recruit the seven black students who enrolled in the fall of 1970; that number was equal to the total for the previous three years.

27. Ruby Houston, interviewed by Matt Richardson, 16 March 2007, in authors' possession.

28. Talmadge Connor, interviewed by Brian Campbell, 26 March 1999, Grundy Collection, Southern Historical Collection, UNC-Chapel Hill Library.

29. Ostwalt interview.

30. "Facts and Figures About North End Schools," *Mecklenburg Gazette*, 6 October 1966.

31. Archie interview.

32. Evelyn Carr interview.

33. Avinger interview.

34. "By Jim Banbury," *Mecklenburg Gazette*, 5 October 1967. Roberts also implicitly praised middle-class parents for making sure that every child in the school had "sufficient clothing and a hot lunch."

35. Ostwalt interview.

36. Shaw Smith interview, Grundy Collection, Southern Historical Collection, UNC-Chapel Hill Library; Woods interview.

37. Bill Strong interview, Grundy Collection, Southern Historical Collection, UNC-Chapel Hill Library. A cassette tape of the interview is in the DC Archives.

38. Brenda Tapia, interviewed by Jonetta Johnson, 2 February 2001, Grundy Collection, Southern Historical Collection, UNC-Chapel Hill Library.

39. Houston interview.

40. Garfield Carr, interview by Jill M. Neumayer, 28 April 2001, Gundy Collection, Southern Historical Collection, UNC-Chapel Hill Library.

41. Kelton interview.

42. Sailstad interview.

43. Ibid.

44. "Pre-School Ready to Open," *Mecklenburg Gazette*, 16 February 1967; Jim Cooley, "5-Year-Olds Enjoy Education," *Davidsonian*, 21 April 1967.

45. "$ for Land Is Start of Child Care Center," *Mecklenburg Gazette*, 9 May 1968; "Private Center Will be Pilot Project Say Sponsors; If $50,000 Total Can Be Raised," *Mecklenburg Gazette*, 16 May 1968; "Day Care Call Gets Good Response," *Mecklenburg Gazette*, 4 July 1968.

46. On fund-raising in the black community, led by Esther Johnson and others, see "Workers Progress Toward Day Care Center," *Mecklenburg Gazette*, 20 June 1968.

47. "Child Center Is Now Underway," *Mecklenburg Gazette*, 24 April 1969; "Day Care Center Sponsors Begin Building, Final Drive for Funds," *Mecklenburg Gazette*, 29 May 1969.

48. "Day Care Facility to Be Dedicated May 24," *Mecklenburg Gazette*, 21 May 1970. Some of Betty Cumming's reasons for supporting the day-care center are discussed in "Day Care Center Gives Aid to Area Children, Students," *Davidsonian*, 5 December 1969.

49. Avinger interview.

50. Minutes, Community Relations Committee, 25 October 1963, Grier Martin Papers, RG 2/1.14, DC Archives.

51. Bob Adams, "Group Guns at Core of Racial Prejudice," *Davidsonian*, 25 October 1963.

52. Calvin Zon, "DCRC Fosters Equality for Charlotte Marches," *Davidsonian*, 6 March 1964; "Zon Announces Two Projects for DCRC," *Davidsonian*, 2 October 1964.

53. Jay S. Federman, "Negroes Not Student Dates," *Davidsonian*, 28 February 1964.

54. One of the several newspaper sources for this paragraph is "Davidson Mayor Tells How Clean-Up, New Houses Began," *Mecklenburg Gazette*, 3 October 1968.

55. Ibid.

56. Earl Lawrimore, "Housing a Model for U.S.," *Charlotte Observer*, 21 February 1970.

57. "Davidson Mayor . . . ," *Mecklenburg Gazette*, 3 October 1968.

58. Rhodes interview.

59. Mildred Lowery, the first president of PADA, commented that Rhodes "would show you how to get more house for the money, how to manage. . . . he was very helpful." Lowery interview. James Raeford, who followed Lowery as president, noted that PADA "helped people with home planning and with other related things, such as financing." Quoted in Joe Smith, "Lakeside Park Project Eases Town Housing Needs," *Davidsonian*, 20 February 1970.

60. Tom Byrd, "Davidson Housing Development Is Model of What Can Be Done," *Mecklenburg Gazette*, 5 December 1968.

61. Polly Paddock, "Housing Proves Successful," *Charlotte Observer*, 17 February 1972.

62. Earl Lawrimore, "Housing a Model for U.S.," *Charlotte Observer*, 21 February 1970.

63. Joe Smith, "Lakeside Park Project Eases Town Housing Needs," *Davidsonian*, 20 February 1970.

64. Quackenbush interview.

65. Charles Ramberg, "Local Merchants Show Civil Rights Progress," *Davidsonian*, 27 September 1963.

66. "I remember the last thing he said before signing day," Sandy Carnegie recalled, "was, 'Yes, sir, Mr. Carnegie, I'm going to Davidson.'" Carnegie interview.

67. Belle Banks, "Random Glances," *Mecklenburg Gazette*, 5 May 1966.

68. Terry Holland, interviewed by J. Samuel Walker; information relayed to Ralph Levering by e-mail, 31 March 2008.

69. Belle Banks, "Random Glances," *Mecklenburg Gazette*, 5 May 1966.

70. Timberlake, "Trapped by Tradition," 24.

71. Abbott interview.

72. Johnson, *David Played a Harp*, 310.

73. According to Johnson, many local blacks believed that Johnson's family "thought ourselves their superiors." Ibid.

74. Ibid., 336.

75. According to a newspaper account, the vandalism included windows being shot out twice, a billiard ball being thrown through a window, and red paint smeared on the shop's outside walls. "Mayor Says Effort to Identify Vandal To Be Intensified," *Mecklenburg Gazette*, 8 September 1966.

76. Lowery's and Pyeatt's roles are discussed in Peter St. Onge, "Redress for Decades of Injustice in Davidson," a 2001 *Charlotte Observer article* located in the file "Davidson, Town of—Barber Shops," DC Archives. "To the Faculty and Administration of Davidson College," 3 April 1968, "Davidson, Town of—Barber Shops," DC Archives.

77. "Homer Faces Trial," *Davidsonian*, 12 April 1968.

78. "Furor About Haircuts Troubles Davidson," *Mecklenburg Gazette*, 11 April 1968.

79. Johnson, *David Played*, 397.

80. The issue of financial compensation is discussed in Dick Anderson, "Faculty Calls for End to Town's Racial Bars," *Davidsonian*, 19 April 1968. For the Methodist Church's efforts, see Ratliff interview.

81. Rhodes interview.

82. Maloney interview.

83. Polley interview.

84. Johnson, *David Played*, 421.

85. Dick Anderson, "Student Leaders Call Off Boycott," *Davidsonian*, 17 May 1968.

86. "Norton Opens Shop," *Davidsonian*, 11 October 1968.

87. "Davidson Barber Retires; 50 Yr. Vet.," *Mecklenburg Gazette*, 18 November 1971.

88. For faculty passage "by a large margin" of a resolution calling for the integration of "all public facilities in the town of Davidson," see Dick Anderson, "Faculty Calls for End to Town's Racial Bars," *Davidsonian*, 19 April 1968. Homer Sutton, a Davidson student at the time, believed that most students supported the boycott. Homer Sutton, informal interview, 14 November 2010. The judgment about the views of "town" whites comes from several oral interviews, including ones with Edith Anne Cashion, Aileen Cantrell, and Claude and Mary Jane McConnell. Blanche Parker, the wife of a coach at the college, also criticized the boycott. Transcripts of these interviews are available in the DC Archives.

89. Among the critics were a Davidson student at the time of the boycott who had become the college's president, Bobby Vagt, and another former Davidson student, James Puckett. Vagt offers criticisms of the boycott in the Peter St. Onge story cited in note 76. James Puckett wrote in his book on growing up in Davidson, published in 2002, that Johnson "was unjustly scapegoated for the sins of Jim Crow." Puckett, *Olin, Oskeegum & Gizmo*, 89.

90. Peter St. Onge story, cited in note 76. The student quoted is Bobby Vagt, identified in note 89.

91. Puckett, *Olin, Oskeegum & Gizmo*, 222.

92. John Wright, "Davidson Can't Believe It," *Charlotte News*, 19 December 1962.

93. Several "town" whites are quoted in the article by John Wright, cited in the previous footnote. Belle Banks, "Lefty's Trained 'Cats Break Loose—Claw Duke!" *Mecklenburg Gazette*, 20 December 1962.

94. "Eight Games Left for Third Ranked Wildcats," *Mecklenburg Gazette*, 30 January 1964.

95. Spencer interview.

96. Dreisell requested an increase to "a minimum of sixteen scholarships" in a memorandum to President Martin in July 1965. In his response Martin vaguely promised "some increase." Charles G. Dreisell to President Martin, 26 July 1965; Martin to Dreisell, 3 August 1965; both in Martin Papers—Athletics—Basketball, RG 2/1.14, DC Archives.

97. Martin interview.

98. Spencer interview.

99. Abbott interview.

100. Beaty, *History of Davidson College*, 395. "We are very proud of our basketball team," Martin wrote to John R. Howard in April 1968, "but we are also proud of some of the other progress which has been made in our academic program and in other areas of the college's life." Grier Martin to John R. Howard, 25 April 1968, Martin Papers—Athletics—basketball, RG 2/1.14, DC Archives.

101. Woods interview.

102. "Davidson Man Killed in Viet Nam Action," *Mecklenburg Gazette*, 21 October 1965; "Memorial Services Conducted Here," *Davidsonian*, 22 October 1965.

103. "Local Hero Alive in Viet Prison," *Mecklenburg Gazette*, 9 February 1967. A fine account of the experiences of Halyburton—information about his years as a POW and about his mother, wife, and daughter—is James S. Hirsch, *Two Souls Indivisible: The Friendship That Saved Two POWs in Vietnam* (Boston: Houghton Mifflin, 2004).

104. E.F. Patterson to Bertrand Russell, 13 February 1967; "Help Get Porter Home!" undated memo from Charles Lloyd; D. Grier Martin to Bishop James Shannon, 17 February 1967; all in Martin Papers—Katharine Halyburton, RG 2/1.14, DC Archives.

105. "Letters for Porter," *Mecklenburg Gazette*, 29 October 1970.

106. Taylor Blackwell, "War Prisoner's Home," *Mecklenburg Gazette*, 22 March 1973.

107. Bernie Petit, "Church Marks 100 Years," *Charlotte Observer*, 7 May 1996.

108. Kincaid interview.

109. Terry interview.

110. Memo from an unidentified administrative assistant to Grier Martin, 13 November 1967, Davidson College—Criticism, Grier Martin Papers, RG 2/1.14, DC Archives.

111. "Open Letter from Claude F. Ferbis, Davidson," *Mecklenburg Gazette*, 21 May 1970.

112. Kurt Geisinger, "Meager Faculty Turnout Did Not Slow Peace Vigil," *Davidsonian*, 15 May 1970.

113. "Anti-War Protestors Force Cancellation of ROTC Drill," *Davidsonian*, 8 May 1970. This story says that seventy students were involved in blocking the doorway to the offices, whereas President Spencer estimated that "40 to 50" were involved. Spencer to J. Marion Bryant, 16 July 1970, Spencer Papers—Davidson College—Criticisms/Complaints (1970), RG 2/1.15, DC Archives.

114. Spencer to J. Marion Bryant, 16 July 1970, Spencer Papers—Davidson College—Criticisms/Complaints (1970), RG 2/1.15, DC Archives.

115. Spencer mentions the "potentially explosive situation" in Spencer, Letter to Mayor Tom Sadler, 11 May 1970, Spencer Papers—Town of Davidson (1968–75), DC archives. A sentence in the Minutes of the meeting of the town commissioners on 15 June 1970 confirms Spencer's belief, stated in his letter to Sadler, that the po-

lice had acted in a "prompt and effective way": "The Police were commended for the wise handling of what could have developed into a serious demonstration and confrontation on the edge of the campus." Town of Davidson, Minutes, 15 June 1970, DC074, DC Archives.

116. Kurt Geisinger, "Meager Faculty Turnout Did Now Slow Peace Vigil," *Davidsonian*, 15 May 1970.

117. William Brown, talk in History 349 class, 13 April 2010.

118. For a response to one critical alumnus, see Spencer, Letter to William E. Robertson, 27 May 1971, Spencer—Davidson College—Criticisms/Complaints (1972–73), Spencer Papers, RG 2/1.14, DC Archives.

119. "Davidson Honors Grads, Naramore," *Mecklenburg Gazette*, 18 June 1970.

120. McClain's decision not to run for re-election in 1977 is mentioned in "Candidates File for November Election," *Mecklenburg Gazette*, 6 October 1977. For the first time in the town's history, two women, Nancy MacCormac and Patricia Stinson, were elected to the Town Board that year.

121. Norwood Poland, "Town Grocery Seeks Permit for ABC Sales; Action Brings Objection from Jackson, Council," *Davidsonian*, 22 November 1968. The town's resolution opposing the request may be read in Town of Davidson, Minutes, 11 November 1968, DC074, DC Archives.

122. "Davidson Goes Wet," *Mecklenburg Gazette*, 13 February 1969.

123. Ibid.

124. McConnell interview.

125. Dick interview.

126. For the 1995–96 academic year, the student body was roughly 51 percent male and 49 percent female. All of the percentages were provided by Davidson College librarian Sharon Byrd.

127. "College Applications Take Marked Jump," *Mecklenburg Gazette*, 26 December 1973; for the increase in the number of high-quality friendships between men and women on campus, see Abbott interview.

128. Joe Earle, "Exiled on Main Street: The Hub," *Davidsonian*, 21 December 1973.

129. For Chalmers Davidson's change of heart, expressed frequently to alumni groups, see Ava Spencer comments in Spencer interview.

130. "Substitute By-Law Provisions Approved by the Trustees—May 6, 1977," Spencer—Christian Commitment, Spencer Papers, RG 2/1.15, DC Archives.

131. John Van Dalen, "Students Continue Protests After Job Offer Revoked," *Mecklenburg Gazette*, 27 April 1977. The quotation by Linden also appeared in "College Withdraws Job Offer to a Jew, Touching Off Furor," *New York Times*, 1 May 1977. The fact that the Trustees had recently given tenure to an art professor, Herb Jackson, despite his honesty in stating that he had no ties to a church, may also have influenced the Trustees' decision. Jackson interview.

132. "Davidson's worldliness seems indistinguishable from any other secular college," an alumnus from the 1940s complained to President Spencer in 1982.

"The world seems to have secularized the college . . ." William W. Duke, Letter to Samuel R. Spencer, Jr., 3 May 1982, Spencer—DC—Criticisms/Compliments (1981–83), Spencer Papers, RG 2/1.15, DC Archives.

133. Larry Cain kindly obtained this information from the DCPC archives in November 2010. The twenty-two women ordained between 1974 and 1984—often leaders in the community as well as in the church—were Julia Maulden, Adeline Ostwalt, Betty Schenck, Annamarie Burts, Betty Cumming, Mildred Workman, Dot Kaylor, Anne White, Elizabeth "Pete" Barnes, Jean Jackson, Florence Cole, Paula Kelton, Ann Melton, Letitia Currie, Grace Lilly, Eleanor Northcott, Elizabeth Woods, Willi Messick, Mary Black, Annette Brawley, Ruth Coffey, and Van Lear Logan.

134. Scotty Nicholls, who lived on north Main Street, confirmed that the parties were often loud. Nicholls interview. For the reference to "wild" parties, see Wood interview. See Will Terry interview for references to the frequent use of illegal drugs by students. Earl Edmondson, a history professor at the time, recalled "walking into a residence hall and almost being bowled over by the smell of marijuana smoke." Earl Edmondson, e-mail to Ralph Levering, 6 October 2004.

135. Moreland Hogan, "The Village Green," *Mecklenburg Gazette*, 7 September 1978.

136. On the practice of "open marriage," i.e., spouse-swapping, see the Carnegie, Klein, and Wood interviews.

137. E-mail communication from Laura Grosch to Ralph Levering, 9 December 2010.

138. For the "leadership" of Brandon, Carr, Howard, and Johnson, see "United Appeal Will Help West Canteen," *Mecklenburg Gazette*, 28 February 1963. Some of the whites who helped the canteen succeed in its early years included John Kelton, Jim Martin, Gene McKeever, Max Polley, and Pat Sailstad. See "West Davidson Teen-Canteen to Hold July Jamboree Saturday," *Mecklenburg Gazette*, 28 June 1962.

139. Nancy MacCormac interview. "Sam Maloney loves to tell that story," MacCormac noted.

140. "Mrs. MacCormac Enters Race," *Mecklenburg Gazette*, 10 April 1973.

141. Abbott interview.

142. MacCormac was the unanimous choice for mayor at a meeting of the town board on 3 November 1978; Town of Davidson, Minutes, 3 November 1978, DC074, DC Archives.

143. For Stone's inspiration and persistence, see King interview. For the Y's history, see "YMCA: 'A People Business,'" *Mecklenburg Gazette*, 15 January 1981.

144. "We'd all go down to the games at McEver Field and sit with the black parents," Tony Abbott recalled. Abbott interview.

145. "Clean-Up Leaders Make Plans," *Mecklenburg Gazette*, 26 March 1970.

146. "Clean-Up Drive Starts Monday," *Mecklenburg Gazette*, 16 April 1970.

147. "Mayor Proclaims Town Day," *Mecklenburg Gazette*, 15 April 1971.

148. Nancy MacCormac interview.

149. "Town Day Approaches; Work, Fun Is Offered," *Mecklenburg Gazette*, 6 May 1971.

150. Nicholls interview.

151. Quackenbush interview.

152. Town of Davidson, Minutes, 15 April 1974, DC074, DC Archives.

153. "Either Foot or Pedal Power for This Year's Town Day," *Mecklenburg Gazette*, 27 April 1978.

154. "Davidson Gives Itself a Day-Long Party," *Mecklenburg Gazette*, 11 May 1978.

155. The quotation is from Evelyn Carr in Carr interview. Carr's words are positive in the sense that blacks felt ownership of Town Day in the early years—a view also expressed by Mildred Lowery in Lowery interview.

156. "Citizens to Hear Facts on 'Open House' Here on Oct. 19th," *Mecklenburg Gazette*, 18 October 1973.

157. Richard Romeyn, "Citizens Uproar Forces Drug Center Removal," *Davidsonian*, 26 October 1973.

158. For an example of specific proposals, see "Town Manager Is Proposed," *Mecklenburg Gazette*, 29 March 1973. The group that presented these ideas called itself the Davidson Citizens Betterment Association.

159. "Ada Jenkins School Proposed to House Community Center," *Mecklenburg Gazette*, 5 December 1973.

160. The new name was Davidson Area Development Association. For Bright's ideas about the center, see "Davidson Eyes Abandoned School," *Charlotte Observer*, 19 December 1973.

161. Power issues arose among whites, of course, as well as between whites and blacks. After programs at the center began in September 1974, Nancy MacCormac once offered Sauni Wood more advice about how to do her job than Sauni wanted to hear. "Who has what job here, Nancy?" Sauni inquired, and "to her credit" Nancy "backed off and apologized." "She's a really outstanding woman—bright and able," Wood noted. "But she did have this [controlling] temperament." Wood interview.

162. Mark Scandling, "Active Ada Jenkins Offers Variety," *Davidsonian*, 30 April 1976.

163. Harold Warren, "Lunch for Elderly," *Charlotte Observer*, 24 October 1974.

164. M.A. Farrell, "Director Says Community Center Is For All Mecklenburg Residents," *Mecklenburg Gazette*, 12 March 1975. This article noted that "approximately 525 people participate in the center's various programs and activities."

165. Ibid.

166. Klein interview; Avinger interview.

167. John Krotchko, "Welsh's Schoolhouse Provides Culture for the Young," *Davidsonian*, 19 September 1980; Grosch interview.

168. "Service Program for Senior Citizens to Start in Davidson," *Mecklenburg Gazette*, 24 August 1977.

169. In December 1977 the Senior Citizens Club had forty-seven members; see "Depot Opens to Senior Citizens," *Mecklenburg Gazette*, 1 December 1977. Pat Sailstad recalled that three blacks—Louis Connor, Esther Johnson, and Roosevelt Wilson—attended regularly, with other blacks coming for a special program in February to celebrate black contributions to the community. Sailstad interview.

170. Francis Ghigo, "The Fourth Proves Glorious in Davidson," *Mecklenburg Gazette*, 7 July 1976.

171. "Editor Has Last Word, Too," *Mecklenburg Gazette*, 24 May 1973.

172. The quotation from Woods is in Earl Lawrimore, "Town Honors Jim Woods, M.D. Saturday," *Mecklenburg Gazette*, 17 May 1973; the $5.00 charge per visit is from Carnegie interview.

173. "Editor Has Last Word, Too," *Mecklenburg Gazette*, 24 May 1973.

174. Phil Duncan, "Davidson Celebrates Centennial," *Charlotte Observer*, 6 May 1979.

175. Sterling Martin and Taine Alison, "Happy Centennial Birthday, Davidson," *Davidsonian*, 4 May 1979.

176. Wister Jackson, "Mayor Sadler Sees End to Poor Housing; Census Report Shows 51 Houses as Substandard," *Mecklenburg Gazette*, 9 October 1974.

177. "Better Public Housing Object of HUD Letter," *Mecklenburg Gazette*, 12 March 1975.

178. Sadler is cited in ibid. For the views of Ratliff and Raeford, see Charlie Ratliff to Robert A. Currie, 27 November 1976; and Daisy Raeford, statement to Davidson Planning Committee, n.d. (April 1978?); both in Spencer Papers, Town of Davidson—1976–83, RG 2/1.15, DC Archives.

179. On the $40,000 guarantee, see Robert Currie to Dr. Spencer, 28 June 1977 Papers; and Robert Currie to Paul Leonard, 5 July 1977; both in Spencer Papers, Town of Davidson, 1976–83, DC Archives.

180. Sam Spencer to Nancy MacCormac, 4 December 1978, Spencer Papers—Town of Davidson, 1976–83, RG 2/1.15, DC Archives.

181. "New Development Requires Special Use Permit from Town," *Mecklenburg Gazette*, 23 March 1978.

182. Town of Davidson, Minutes, Addendum, 24 April 1978, DC074, DC Archives.

183. Moreland Hogan, "Citizens Jam Hall on Apartments Issue," *Mecklenburg Gazette*, 27 April 1978.

184. Quoted in Al Connette and Carole Loptson, "Town and College: A Curious and Changing Partnership," *Davidsonian*, 2 May 1980.

185. "Open House at Lakeside," *Mecklenburg Gazette*, 24 May 1979.

186. Julia Maulden, "Lakeside: 'Community Is Here in Embryo, Lord. Help Me to Nurture It,'" *Charlotte Observer*, 27 June 1979.

187. Town of Davidson. Minutes, 23 May 1979, DC074, DC Archives.

188. An early expression of black anger occurred at a Town Council meeting in November 1974. See "Griffith Street Dwellers Uneasy About Rezoning," *Mecklenburg Gazette*, 20 November 1974.

189. Ratliff interview.

190. Mark Wilensky, "Davidson Blacks Blast College, Town," *Davidsonian*, 13 February 1976.

191. Town Board, Minutes, 18 December 1978, DC074, DC Archives; "Construction of Local Shopping Center to Begin Soon," *Davidsonian*, 11 May 1979; Carolyn Sanford, "Davidson Gets a Shopping Center," *Charlotte Observer*, 8 January 1980.

192. Ross Holt, "Alumni Group Seeks to Buy Griffith Street Land," *Davidsonian*, 3 February 1984.

193. Manley Heidt, "Residents Question Use of HUD Funds in West Davidson Neighborhood," *Mecklenburg Gazette*, 27 August 1981.

194. Jeri Fischer, "Davidson Blacks Unhappy about Housing," *Charlotte Observer*, 18 August 1981.

195. Francis Ghigo," Davidson Town Commission Cites 'Philosophical Differences,'" *Mecklenburg Gazette*, 19 July 1979.

196. Burl Naramore, "An Open Letter to the Citizens of Davidson," *Mecklenburg Gazette*, 26 July 1979.

197. Town of Davidson, Minutes, 10 March 1980, DC074, DC Archives; "Davidson Merchants Reactivate Association, Plan Special Promotions," *Mecklenburg Gazette*, 27 March 1980.

198. Glen Kellum, "New Post Office May Spur Town Plans," *Davidsonian*, 19 September 1980.

199. Meg Kello, "Official Says 'Contract in the Mail' on Davidson Post Office Deal," *Mecklenburg Gazette*, 27 May 1982.

200. On the negotiations with the Postal Service in 1981, see, for example, Thomas A. Williams, "Post Office Land Purchase Near in Davidson," *Mecklenburg Gazette*, 3 September 1981. On the negotiations in 1982, see, for example, "Howie: Post Office Contract Signed, Sealed, Delivered," *Mecklenburg Gazette*, 1 July 1982.

201. Town of Davidson, Minutes, 11 September 1984, DC074, DC Archives.

202. Town of Davidson, Minutes,, 13 December 1983, DC074, DC Archives.

203. David McGee, "Resident Plans to Open Bed-and-Breakfast Inn," *Davidsonian*, 20 January 1984.

204. Kincaid interview.

205. Nancy MacCormac interview; Town of Davidson, Minutes, 14 March 1984, DC074, DC Archives.

206. Carnegie interview. After condemnation procedures had begun, Clark tried to pressure local officials by mailing a letter to town residents arguing that he had been treated unfairly and urging them to ask board members to support his project. This letter exacerbated the already strained relations between Clark and

Russell Knox, the town's new mayor. See David Van Pelt, "Inn Plans Run Afoul of Zoning," *Davidsonian*, 28 September 1984.

207. Leland Park, "Will Davidson Be the Same?" *Davidsonian*, 19 December 1980.

208. Leland Park, Letter to the Editor, *Mecklenburg Gazette*, 9 October 1980.

209. "An Opportunity," *Mecklenburg Gazette*, 9 October 1980.

210. Cassandra Lawton, "Special-Use Permit Granted to Lake Norman Development," *Charlotte News*, 19 January 1983.

211. Ibid.

212. For the unanimous decision to transfer the town's sewer system, see Town Board, Minutes, 30 January 1984, DC074, DC Archives. At a public meeting on 24 April 1984 attended by about fifty town residents, Commissioners Randy Kincaid, Russell Knox, and Bill Ward spoke in favor of the proposed sale of the water system, and Commissioners Sandy Carnegie and Rutledge Withers spoke against it. Mayor MacCormac did not take a position. See Donna Clark, "Davidson Citizens Discuss Water System Sale," *Mecklenburg Gazette*, 26 April 1984.

213. See, for example, Kathleen Galligher, "Charlotte Administrators Taking a Firm Stance on Sewer System Takeover," *Charlotte Observer*, 5 May 1982.

214. "Merger Completed December 31," *Mecklenburg Gazette*, 5 January 1984.

215. "College Improves Radio Station," *Mecklenburg Gazette*, 5 January 1978. For opposition by students, see George Berkin, "Parties Fuming Over Radio Station," *Charlotte Weekly South*, 2 October 1978, and the resolution opposing the change that the student senate passed unanimously on 26 September 1978. These and other sources on the controversy are in the Sam Spencer Papers, "Radio Station WDAV—Controversy," DC Archives. Another helpful source is "Entire Staff of WDAV Resigns," *Davidsonian*, 20 October 1978.

216. Spencer interview.

217. Kuykendall interview.

218. Beaty, *History of Davidson College*, 404.

Epilogue: Growing Smartly and Compassionately, 1985–2011

1. Scott Burns, "St. Alban's Is Centerpiece of Newest Lake Norman Neighborhood," *Lake Norman Times*, 24 October 2001.

2. "About Us," St. Alban's Episcopal Church website, www.saintalbans-davidson .org, accessed 9 February 2011.

3. "Is Bigger Better?" *Charlotte Observer*, 8 June 1998.

4. Ibid.

5. "Deal May Open Up Rural Corner of Mecklenburg to Growth," *Charlotte Observer*, 16 April 1989. The number of lots and acres is contained in M.S. Van Hecke, "Virginia Woman Guides Progress of River Run," *Charlotte Observer*, 23 April 1990.

6. "Mayor's Musings," *Town Message*, Winter 2007.

7. Quoted in Bill Giduz, "Know Thy Neighbor; Preserving What Matters in Davidson," *Davidson Journal*, Fall 2008.

8. "Grassroots Group Wants to Keep Davidson Just the Way It Is," *North Meck Leader*, 14 May 1999.

9. M.E. Pellin, "From Land-Grab to Land Rush?" *North Meck Leader*, 25 May 2001.

10. "Committee Makes Short Work of Davidson Land-Plan Compromise," *North Meck Leader*, 8 June 2001.

11. Tiffany R. Leonard, "Coalition to Town: Talk with Us More," *Charlotte Observer*, 13 January 2008.

12. According to U.S. census data, African-Americans were 8.1 percent of the town's 7,139 residents in 2000 and 6.4 percent of the town's 10,944 residents in 2010.

13. Luann Laubscher, "Davidson's Black Community Voices Concerns, Mistrust," *Lake Norman Times*, 4 April 2006.

14. Kincaid interview.

15. Nicholls interview. Others interviewees who expressed regrets about changes in the town included Nancy Blackwell, Malcolm Lester, Mary Martin, Louise Nelson, and Mary Ferrer Stough.

16. "West Davidson Stakeholder Committee Report, July 2007" (draft), in Local—Davidson, Town of—Commissioners, Davidsoniana File, DC Archives.

17. These figures are from American FactFinder, http://factfinder.census.gov.

18. The figures for 2000 and 2009 are in ibid. For 2007, see "Davidson Quick Facts," Charlotte.com, 23 July 2007.

19. "Survey: We Think Davidson Is Great," *DavidsonNews.net*, 14 November 2007; Tiffany R. Leonard, "Sense of Community Tops Poll," *Charlotte Observer*, 25 November 2007.

20. Rosie Molinary, "Careful Planning Helped Shape This College Town," *Charlotte Observer*, 3 May 2009.

21. The Davidson Housing Coalition grew out of the town's Affordable Housing Committee, chaired by Randy Kincaid. For details about the DHC's work, see Marguerite [Margo] Williams, "Affordable Housing; Davidson, North Carolina," in *What's Right about Our Region: Authentic Urbanism in the Carolinas,* ed. Deborah E. Ryan (vol. 1: 2008).

22. Pat Border Gubbins, "Who Rules Davidson's Gateway?" *Charlotte Observer*, 3 June 1990.

23. Figures provided by an administrative assistant serving in town government, 15 February 2011.

24. "HOOT Gets Loan for Housing," *Campus Chronicle* (Davidson College), 16 December 1987.

25. "Building Community by Building Homes," *Charlotte Observer*, 4 September 1988.

26. "Davidson Habitat for Humanity Issues Annual Report," 20 February 1989, Davidson, Town of—Habitat for Humanity, Davidsoniana File, DC Archives.

27. "Davidson Habitat for Humanity—1992 Annual Report," Davidson, Town of—Habitat for Humanity, Davidsoniana File, DC Archives.

28. See the annual reports for 1990 and 1992, Davidson, Town of—Habitat for Humanity, Davidsoniana File, DC Archives.

29. Pat Borden Gubbins, "Habitat Merger to Boost Housing," *Charlotte Observer*, 4 December 1994.

30. E-mail from Terry Laney to Jan Blodgett and others, "100th House Dedication," Davidson, Town of—Habitat for Humanity, Davidsoniana File, DC Archives.

31. Pat Borden Gubbins, "5-Year Lease for Ada Jenkins Center?" *Mecklenburg Gazette*, 17 September 1995; Diane Johnson, "They're Building Community Bridges," *Mecklenburg Gazette*, 28 May 1997.

32. Quoted in *Community Connection; News from the Ada Jenkins Center*, Fall 2001.

33. Ada Jenkins Center, *Annual Report, July 1, 2002–June 30, 2003*, Local, Davidson, Town of—Ada Jenkins Center, Davidsoniana File, DC Archives.

34. Ada Jenkins Center, *Annual Report, July 1, 2006–June 30, 2007*, Local, Davidson, Town of—Ada Jenkins Center, Davidsoniana File, DC Archives.

35. "Parish Nurse Program Just What the Doctor Ordered," *North Meck Leader*, 30 April 1999.

36. Ada Jenkins Center, *Annual Report, July 1, 2006–June 30, 2007*, Local, Davidson, Town of—Ada Jenkins Center, Davidsoniana File, DC Archives.

37. Ibid.

38. Barbara Barnett, "Davidson College Rally to Precede Klan Event," *Charlotte Observer*, 26 April 1986; Harold Warren, "Celebration a Response to Klan," *Charlotte Observer*, 27 April 1986.

39. Warren, "Celebration a Response to Klan."

40. Ibid. According to Police Chief Hank McKiernan, the thirty-seven included "women and children" who, McKiernan implied, probably were not Klan members.

41. Gail Dewort, "'Solidarity Day' Gets Positive Response," *Mecklenburg Gazette*, 1 May 1986.

42. "On Campus: Shredded Trees and Unified Cleanup," *Charlotte Observer*, 21 September 2009.

43. Ted Mellnik, "Davidson to Fight for Library," *Charlotte Observer*, 31 August 1989.

44. Ibid.

45. "Mayor's Musings," *Town Message* [Town of Davidson], Fall 2005.

46. Diane Whitacre, "Davidson Library Campaign Raises $100,000 Over Goal," *Charlotte Observer*, 21 January 1996.

47. Nancy Vendley, "Aid for Katrina Victims Comes in Many Forms," *Charlotte.com*, 18 September 2005.

48. "Remarks by Mayor Randall Kincaid," G. Jackson Burney Community Service Award, 23 November 2005, Local, Davidson, Town of—Burney Award, Davidsoniana File, DC Archives.

Selected Bibliography

I. Sources Available in the Davidson College Archives

A. Personal Papers and Other Materials

Burwell, Dandridge Reminiscences, 1918, DC0168s.
Carson, William Waller Carson Reminisences, 1918, DC0166s.
Chambers, Henry Reminiscences, 1918, DC0141s.
Chambers, Pinckney B. Letter, 1837, DC0111s.
Davidson Civic Club, DC025.
Davidson Music Club, DC0221s.
Davidson, NC. Newspaper Collection, 1883–1958, DC091.
Fries, Henry E. Papers, 1874–77.
Greenlee, James Logan Letters, 1859–62, DC0115s.
Hamilton, Thomas H. Letters, 1835–39, DC0116s.
Helper and Sloan, Collection, 1852–1916, DC063.
Knights of Pythias, Papers. DC0189s.
Lacy Family Papers, 1851–60, DC0147s.
Lynch, Rebecca Neal Reminiscences, 1920, DC0161s.
Morrow, James Letters, 1840–53, DC0122s.
Petrie, George Laurens, Speech, 1856, DC0072s.
Sampson, Anne E. Reminiscences, 1920, DC0156s.
Scofield Family Collection, 1883–1962, DC0190s.
Smith, William A. Reminiscences, 1920, DC0154s.
Thompson, Joseph Papers, 1859–61, DC0090s.
Town Commission. Davidson, NC, Minutes, 1879–present, DC074.

RG 1/1. Davidson College. Board of Trustee Minutes.

RG 2/3.2 Davidson College. President's Office. Faculty Minutes.

RG 3/3.2 Registrar. Catalogs, 1842–present.

RG 6/13. YMCA Records, 1928–91.

RG 6/14.02 Philanthropic Society, Records, 1837–2004.

RG 10/2.16 Student Publications. *Davidson Monthly/Davidson College Magazine.*

RG 10/2.12. Student Publications. *Quips and Cranks.*

B. Interviews Conducted by Authors in Davidson and Vicinity

Tony and Susan Abbott, interviewed by Ralph Levering (hereinafter cited as RL), August 1, 2006.

Ada Jenkins group, interviewed by Jan Blodgett (hereinafter cited as JB), August 17, 2002.

Mary Archie, interviewed by JB, February 27, 2007.

Bob and Jane Avinger, interviewed by RL, August 9, 2006.

Carol Barber, interviewed by RL, July 18, 2006.

Nancy Blackwell and Mabel Fearington, interviewed by RL, July 25, 2006.

Taylor Blackwell, interviewed by RL, July 25, 2006.

Bill Brannon, interviewed by RL, June 12, 2007.

Smiley "Doodle" Brown, interviewed by RL, June 27, 2007.

Jane Leighton Burts, interviewed by RL, August 1, 2006.

Aileen Cantrell, interviewed by JB, January 8, 2001.

Sandy Carnegie, interviewed by RL, January 19, 2009.

Evelyn Carr, interviewed by JB, September 4, 2002.

Edith Anne Cashion, interviewed by RL, July 24, 2006.

Don Coffey, interviewed by RL, May 26, 2006.

Common Ground meeting, conducted and recorded by JB, April 15, 2000.

Bob Cumming, interviewed by RL and Patricia Massey, July 19, 2006.

Bob Davidson, interviewed by Ralph Levering, July 6, 2006.

Lacy Woods Dick, interviewed by RL, July 26, 2006.

Hansford Epes, interviewed by RL, October 29, 2008.

Dave Fagg, interviewed by RL, August 4, 2006.

Ralph and Wendell Gable, interviewed by RL, August 10, 2007.

Dave Grant, interviewed by RL, September 18, 2006.

Laura Grosch, interviewed by RL, June 15, 2007.

Ann Haley, interviewed by RL, August 2, 2007.

Ruby Houston, interviewed by Matt Richardson, March 15, 2007.

Herb Jackson, interviewed by RL and Patricia Massey, July 20, 2006.

David and Dot Kaylor, interviewed by RL and Patricia Massey, July 18, 2006.

John and Paula Kelton, interviewed by RL, July 7, 2006.

Lawrence Kimbrough, interviewed by RL and Patricia Massey, July 19, 2006.

Tish Kimbrough, interviewed by RL and Patricia Massey, July 19, 2006.

Richie and Patty King, interviewed by RL and Patricia Massey, July 20, 2006.

June Kimmel, interviewed by RL, August 4, 2006.

Rosemary Klein, interviewed by RL, August 8, 2007.

Randy Kincaid, interviewed by RL, August 20, 2007.

John Kuykendall, interviewed by RL, August 8, 2006.

Malcolm Lester, interviewed by RL, December 7, 2007.

Van Lear Logan, interviewed by JB, September 5, 2000.

Annie Mildred Lowery, interviewed by JB, September 16, 2003.

Susie Lowrey, interviewed by JB, May 22, 2000.

Earl MacCormac, interviewed by RL, May 3, 2008.

Nancy MacCormac, interviewed by RL, May 3, 2008.

Sam Maloney, interviewed by RL, August 9, 2006.

Claude and Mary Jane McConnell, interviewed by RL, August 8, 2007.

Jim Martin, interviewed by RL, August 7, 2007.

Mary and Sterling Martin, interviewed by RL, August 7, 2007.

Bill and Chris Mayhew, interviewed by RL, June 14, 2007.

Elaine and Jerry McArn, interviewed by RL, June 28, 2007.

Erving McClain, interviewed by JB, March 30, 2001.

Grover Meetze, interviewed by RL, July 31, 2006.

Martha Montgomery, interviewed by RL and Patricia Massey, July 17, 2006.

Louise Nelson, interviewed by RL, August 2, 2006.

Scotty Nicholls, interviewed by RL and Patricia Massey, July 26, 2006.

Adeline Ostwalt, interviewed by RL, July 24, 2006.

Leland Park, interviewed by RL, June 15, 2007.

Blanche Parker, interviewed by RL, July 26, 2006.

Jackie and Max Polley, interviewed by RL, August 3, 2006.

Anna Pritchett, interviewed by RL, June 4, 2007.

Carol and Ralph Quackenbush, interviewed by RL, July 24, 2006.

James Raeford, interviewed by JB, January 2, 2001.

Charlie Ratliff, interviewed by RL, July 2, 2006.

Clark and Carolyn Readling, interviewed by RL, June 18, 2007.

Ethel Rhodes, interviewed by RL, July 3, 2006.

Lucy Roddy and Ada Jenkins group, interviewed by JB, April 10, 2002.

Patricia Sailstad, interviewed by JB, September 20, 2001.

Charlie and Jane Power Schenck, interviewed by RL, June 27, 2007.

Nancy Smith, interviewed by RL, August 1, 2006.

Ava and Sam Spencer, interviewed by RL and Patricia Massey, July 17, 2006.

Mary Fetter Stough, interviewed by RL and Patricia Massey, July 20, 2006.

Wayne Stowe, interviewed by RL, August 14, 2007.

Will Terry, interviewed by RL, August 9, 2006.

Margaret Thornburg, interviewed by RL, November 8, 2007.

Bill Ward, interviewed by RL, May 26, 2006.

Roosevelt Wilson, interviewed by JB, September 20, 2002.

Ken and Sauni Wood, interviewed by RL, June 26, 2007.

Priscilla and Scott Woodmansee, interviewed by RL, August 8, 2006.

John Woods, interviewed by RL, December 7, 2007.

Price Zimmermann, interviewed by RL, May 9, 2006.

C. Other Materials in the Archives

Brown, C.K. "The Southern Position with Respect to the Bi-Racial System; An Address Delivered to the Students of Davidson College, March 1, 1956." In C.K. Brown speeches file.

Brown, Mrs. J. W. "Calvary Presbyterian Church, Davidson, North Carolina History," Unpublished ms. Calvary Presbyterian Church Davidsoniana File. Davidson College Archives, Davidson, NC.

Cumming, Betty. "The New Davidson," *Davidson College Bulletin* (June 1969): 2–10.

Hopewell Baptist Church, 1879–1979: A Centennial History. Privately printed for Hopewell Baptist Church, 1979. Hopewell Baptist Church Davidsoniana File.

McIver, George Willcox. *Memoirs of George Willcox McIver, A Native of North Carolina.* Typescript in Davidson College Archives. Original in possession of family members.

"A Need, An Opportunity, A Privilege" Flyer. 8 February 1953. Calvary Presbyterian Church Davidsoniana File. Davidson College Archives, Davidson, NC.

Timberlake, Grey. "Trapped by Tradition: Davidson's African-American Community from 1930 to 1970." History Honors Thesis at Davidson College, 1993.

2. Materials in Other Archives

David E. Gordon to Thomas Britton, 6 March 1851 #29–USC.

R.G. Dun & Co. Collection, Baker Library Historical Collections, Harvard Business School.

Catherine McGeachy Buie Papers, 1819–99, Special Collections, Perkins Library, Duke University, Durham.

Hector H. McNeill Collection. Special Collections, Perkins Library, Duke University, Durham.

Alexander McIver to Cornelia Phillips Spencer, Southern Historical Collection, Wilson Library, UNC-Chapel Hill.

Pamela Grundy Collection of Oral History Interviews, Southern Historical Collection, Wilson Library, UNC-Chapel Hill.

3. More Widely Available Books and Articles

"The Ball in Motion," *Charlotte Journal*, 21 March 1845, p. 2.

Beaty, Mary D. *Davidson: A History of the Town from 1835 until 1937.* Davidson: Briarpatch Press, 1979.

———. *A History of Davidson College.* Davidson: Briarpatch Press, 1988.

———. *History of the Davidson College Presbyterian Church.* Davidson: Davidson College Presbyterian Church, 1987.

Blythe, LeGette and Charles Raven Brockman. *Hornet's Nest: The Story of Charlotte and Mecklenburg County*. Charlotte: McNally, 1961.

"Brady's Alley May Not Be Far from Your House," *Presbyterian Outlook*, 27 March 1950, pp. 4–5.

Bureau of the Census. 1850 Census. Washington, DC: GPO, 1850.

Burtchaell, James Tunstead. *The Dying of the Light; The Disengagement of Colleges and Universities from Their Christian Churches*. Grand Rapids: Eerdmans, 1998.

Davidson, Chalmers G. *Piedmont Partisan; The Life and Times of General William Lee Davidson*. Davidson: Davidson College, 1951.

———. *The Plantation World around Davidson*, rev. and enl. ed. Davidson: Briarpatch Press, 1982.

"Davidson College O.K.," *Iredell Express*, 2 November 1860.

Davidson Reminiscence Project; an online collection of thirty-three "life stories" of residents of Davidson put together between 2001 and 2009 by students in Davidson Professor Kristi Multhaup's Psychology 377 class; click on "List of Life Stories" at http://www.davidson.edu/academic/psychology/MulthaupSite/DAVREMPRO/davrempro.htm.

Drake, William. *Higher Education in North Carolina before 1860*. New York: Carleton Press, 1964.

"Dr. Morrison's Colored Family." Typescript. Lincoln County Historical Society.

Goodman, Paul. "The Manual Labor Movement and the Origins of Abolitionism," *Journal of the Early Republic* 13 (Fall 1993): 363.

Hanchett, Thomas W., *Sorting Out the New South City: Race, Class and Urban Development in Charlotte, 1875–1975*. Chapel Hill: University of North Carolina, 1998.

Harper, J. W. F., "Davidson 'Befo' de War," *Davidson College Magazine*, May 1912.

Lafferty, Robert, *The North Carolina Medical College: Davidson and Charlotte, North Carolina*. Charlotte, 1946.

Lefler, Hugh and Albert Newsome, *North Carolina: The History of a Southern State*. Chapel Hill: University of North Carolina Press, 1973.

Herran, Kathy. *They Married Confederate Officers*. Davidson, N.C. : Warren Publishing, c1997.

Hirsch, James S. *Two Souls Indivisible; The Friendship That Saved Two POWs in Vietnam*. Boston: Houghton Mifflin, 2004.

Hunter, Margaret, "Rev. W.P. Williams, Davidson's First Mayor" *Mecklenburg Gazette*, 21 August 1980.

Johnson, Ralph W. *David Played a Harp; An Autobiography*. Davidson: Blackwell Ink, 2000.

Lingle, Walter L. *Memories of Davidson College*. Richmond: John Knox Press, 1947.

———. *Presbyterians; Their History and Beliefs*. Richmond: John Knox Press, 1944.

"Manual Labor School of the Concord Presbytery," *Western Carolinian*, 30 May 1835.

Lemmon, Sarah McCulloh, "The Decline of the Church, 1776–1816," in *The Episcopal Church in North Carolina, 1701–19*, eds. Lawrence London and Sarah McCulloh Lemmon. Raleigh: Episcopal Diocese of North Carolina, 1987.

McGeachy, Neill R. *Confronted by Challenge: A History of the Presbytery of Concord, 1795–1973*. Charlotte: Delmar, 1985.

Merrell, Matthew B., ed., *Soldiers and Sentinels; Davidson's World War II Veterans Speak*. Davidson: Davidson College, 2002.

Morrill, Dan, "Jim Crow Comes to Mecklenburg County," http://www.cmhpf .org/educationjimcrow.htm.

Orr, Jr. and Alfred W. Stuart, ed., *The North Carolina Atlas: Portrait for a New Century*. Chapel Hill: University of North Carolina Press, 2000.

Powell, William S., *North Carolina Through Four Centuries*. Chapel Hill: University of North Carolina Press, 1989.

Puckett, James B. *Olin, Oskeegum & Gizmo: Growing Up in a Small Southern College Town 1950–1970*. Davidson: Blackwell Ink, 2003.

Russell, Lucy Phillips, *A Rare Pattern*. Chapel Hill: University of North Carolina Press, 1957.

Satchwell, S. S. "Obstacles to Medical Progress: Annual Address Delivered Before the Medical Society of the State of North Carolina, Edenton, NC." April 1857.

Shaw, Cornelia. *Davidson College*. New York: Fleming H. Revell Press, 1923.

———. *War Record Davidson College, 1917–1918*. Charlotte: Presbyterian Standard, 1923.

Stringfellow, J. J., "Memories of the 50s," *Davidson College Magazine* (May 1912), 295.

"Survey and Research Report on the Davidson Colored School/Ada Jenkins Center," Charlotte-Mecklenburg Historic Landmarks Commission. www .cmhpf.org/surveys&rAdaJenkins.htm.

"Temperance Society of Davidson College, NC." *Charlotte Journal*, 12 January 1838.

Tompkins, D. A., *History of Mecklenburg County and the City of Charlotte from 1740 to 1903*. Charlotte: Observer Printing House, 1903.

Williams, Marguerite [Margo], "Affordable Housing; Davidson, North Carolina," in Deborah E. Ryan, ed., *What's Right about Our Region; Authentic Urbanism in the Carolinas* (vol. 1: 2008).

Winn, Paul, "Davidson from 1867 to 1869," *Davidson College Magazine* (May 1912), 299.

Woloch, Nancy. *Women and the American Experience*. New York: Knopf, 1984.

Index

White, Anne, 207, 276n133
White, Suel, 65
White supremacy, 47–49
White's Drug Store, 110, 156
Whittle, Heath, 150
Wildcat minstrels, 142
Wiley, Calvin, 25
Williams, T.J., 61
Williams, Tom, 221
Williams, William P., 50, 55, 59, 60
Williamson, Gertrude, 83
Williamson, Jane, 11
Williamson, John, 24
Williamson, Samuel, 11, 24, 241n47
Wilson, Emory, 128–29
Wilson, Frank, 255n3
Wilson, George, 49
Wilson, Luther (Reverend), 68
Wilson, Ronald, 178
Wilson, Samuel, 11
Wilson, Roosevelt, 162, 170, 265n130, 278n169
Wilson, Woodrow, 42, 87, 113, 124
Winkler, Ellen, 208
Winston-Salem, 87
Withers, J. Rutledge, 221, 280n212
Withers, Mamie, 250–51n65
Withers, William (Doctor), 43, 44, 46, 51, 264–65n103
Withers Electric, 156

Women, 20, 21, 204
    as missionaries, 74
    role of in civic fundraising, 169–70
    role in public life in 1970s, 205–7
    in the workforce, 44, 99, 126–27, 140, 252n18
Women of the Church, 136
Women's Committee on National Defense, 112
Women's Missionary Society, 104, 135
Wood, Ken, 230
Wood, Sauni, 210, 277n161
Woods, Dan, 198
Woods, Elizabeth, 198, 276n133
Woods, James (Doctor), 148, 150, 177, 199–200, *212; see also* Dr. James B. Woods Jr. Day
Woods, Jimmy (son of James), 198
Woods, John, 171, 172, 186, 225, 226, 260n9
Wooten (Doctor), 68, 94
Workman, Mildred, 276n133
World War I, 87, 112–13, 141
World War II, 144, 145–50

Young Men's Christian Association (YMCA), 97, 110, 123, 137, 176, 256n21
    adult education classes of, 135
    committee for "Colored Work," 135
    and the "Y Hut," 172